Discover Bats!

A Bat Conservation International Publication
by Merlin D. Tuttle

Editor
Janet Tyburec

Project Manager
Steve Walker

Illustrator
David Chapman

Associate Editor
Sara McCabe

Copyeditors
Connie Giles
Arnold Phifer
Sara Schroeder

Design and Layout
Joan Ivy

Production Associate
Jeannette Ivy

Financial Manager
Linda Moore

Project Sponsors

The Geraldine R. Dodge Foundation
Survival Anglia, LTD
The Bass Foundation
The Captain Planet Foundation
The Columbus Zoo
The Gold Institute
The Harris and Eliza Kempner Foundation
The Northwest Mining Association
The Turner Foundation
The W. Alton Jones Foundation
Jeff and Helen Acopian
Chuck Pease and Cynthia Vann
Dr. Sue Ellen Young

Acknowledgements

Discover Bats! could not have been completed without the creative ideas, review, and constructive criticism of teachers and environmental educators throughout North America, especially: Bunny Marechal, Jackson Middle School, San Antonio TX; Gayle Marechal, Bradley Middle School, San Antonio TX; Cindy Phillips, Eanes Elementary School, Austin TX; Gail Tatum and Jan Wendland, Smith Elementary School, Corpus Christi TX.

The following individuals provided thorough reviews and suggestions: Christi Baldino, Great Basin National Park, Great Basin NV; Laura Busby, Greenacres Foundation, Cincinnati OH; Diane Crowe, Gullett Elementary School, Austin TX; Steve Crowell, United Methodist Church, Barree PA; Rosemarie Curcio, New York City PS-134M, New York NY; Sharon Ely, Gullett Elementary School, Austin TX; Kim Hoskins, San Antonio Zoo, San Antonio TX; Angela Knight, Frankfort Middle School, Frankfort IN; Irma Flores Manges, City of Austin Public Library, Austin TX; Linda McAtee, Austin Independent School District Curriculum Support, Austin TX; Richard Penn, Lago Vista High School, Lago Vista TX; Anita Rizley, City of Austin Public Library: Youth Services Division, Austin TX; Nona Sansom, Zilker Elementary School, Austin TX; Mary Kay Sexton, Hillcrest Elementary School, Del Valle TX; Lynne Shoemaker, Southern Regional High School, Barnegat NJ; and Diana Simons, Indepedent Education Consultant and Seasonal U.S. Forest Service Biologist, Pasadena CA.

We thank the Dodge Earthwatch Teachers from New Jersey who tested and commented on early lesson ideas: Silvia Acosta, Henreitta Hawes, Ridgewood; Bess Adams, Beach Haven School, Beach Haven; Irene Bognar, West Windsor-Plainsboro Upper, Plainsboro; Laura Borgess; Susan Cole, Wayside School, Wayside; Judy Czarnecki, Fisher School, Trenton; Deobrah Dobrow, Macopin Middle School, West Milford; Patricia Flores, Lalor, Sunnybrae, Wilson and Yardville, Trenton; Paula Giblin, Forest Avenue School, Verona; Danita Guarino, Ethel McKnight School, East Windsor; Marcia Haller, South River High School, South River; Jeffrey Keith, Mount Lakes Public School, Mount Lakes; Kenneth Kopperl, Stanhope Elementary, Stanhope; Robert Laura, Highland Elementary School, Midland Park; Phil Levy, Lacey Township High School, Lanoka Harbor; Cynthia MacGonagle, Roosevelt Intermediate School, Westfield; Teresa Maltz, CCIS Unit, Monmouth Medical Center, Longbranch; David Mazsa, Rutgers Preparatory School, Somerset; Kerrinne Menezes-Yezuita, Hamburg School, Hamburg; Stephen Michaelchuck, West Depford High School, Westville; Frances Mirabelli, Midtown Community School, Bayonne; Michelle Mongey, West Morris Central High School, Chester; Susan Needleman, Ridge Ranch, Paramus; Deborah Orzechowski, Lakeview School, Denville; Kathy Prout, Frank Antonides School, West Long Branch; Judith Rogin, Frelinghuysen Middle School, Morristown; Monica Shah, West Orange High School, West Orange; Martin Stickle, Summit High School, Summit; Julie Stine, Heritage Middle School, Livingston; John Streko, West Morris Central High School, Chester; Suzanne Werner, Kreas Middle School, East Windsor; and Robert Zimmerman, Southern Regional High School, Manahawkin.

Many Bat Conservation International staff contributed greatly to proofing, fact-checking and field-testing lessons, particularly: Mahala Archer, Bob Benson, Angela England, Barbara French, Brian Keeley, Jim Kennedy, Mark Kiser, Phyllis Meckel, and Arnold Phifer. We also thank Jane F. G. Jennings and Patricia Platt for assistance with early project coordination and development and Judith Walther for creative consultation and concept development.

TABLE OF CONTENTS

Introduction

> Though the lessons are labeled as beginner, intermediate, or advanced, all can be adapted for any grade level by increasing or decreasing the amount of group discovery involved.

Lessons

Introductory Activities

Identification and Behavior

Habitats and Ecosystems

Research and Conservation

Appendices and Additional Resources

Introduction

Discover Bats!

Preface

Discover Bats! is inspired by the countless inquisitive children and enthusiastic educators who have shared their questions and ideas with me over the past 30 years. Bats lived long ago with dinosaurs, yet today they still can be seen in almost any town. Many are colorful and cute. Others are incredibly weird. Some are tiny, and a few are giants. But wherever they live, bats play essential roles in the balance of nature. No other group of mammals is more diverse or better suited for captivating young minds to learn about the world around us.

Discover Bats! combines my personal experiences from a lifetime of research with the creative suggestions of experienced educators from many backgrounds. It is based on broad collaboration and is designed to stimulate students in grades 4-8 to have fun learning valuable concepts in the academic disciplines of science, language arts, social studies, mathematics, and much more. Some lessons are more advanced than others, but all are flexible and can be adapted for varied grade levels and uses.

This is a dynamic resource, not limited to formal educational institutions or traditions. It is designed to encourage creativity among students and instructors alike. As you will also see, lessons from the world of bats provide compelling models for ensuring that education is fun. We encourage your comments and suggestions.

Merlin D. Tuttle

Founder and Executive Director
Bat Conservation International

What Discover Bats! Offers

The *Discover Bats!* Handbook comprises the backbone of this kit. It contains 21 integrated lessons, library references, background information, a detailed glossary, and a comprehensive bibliography of supporting resources. The lessons are divided into three difficulty levels: beginner, intermediate, and advanced. Each lesson is supported by one or more video segments and contains detailed "extension" activities designed for learning assessment, independent study, or extracurricular assignments. Lessons are divided into "Instructor Pages," identified by the "Instructor Icon" and "Student Pages," identified by the "Student Icon."

Instructor Icon

Student Icon

Each lesson includes the following elements:

Student Background Information:
- Read About Bats — An introduction to the subject matter of each lesson. This information covers 2 to 4 pages (600-1,600 words) at the beginning of each lesson and is designed to be read by the students.
- "Read More About" References — Bibliographic references relevant to the lesson. These references help students learn more about the lesson subject and spark interest in further reading and research.
- "Discover" References on the Internet — Relevant articles and information available electronically from BCI's quarterly magazine, *BATS*. This service provides students an opportunity to do on-line computer research.

Teacher Instruction Pages:
- Overview — A summary of each lesson's primary learning objectives.
- Skills — A list of the skills developed in the lesson.
- Video Connection — The segment of the *Discover Bats!* video which best supports the lesson. Most lessons, except for numbers 1, 6, and 18, can easily be completed without the video.
- Presentation Time — The estimated time required, including field trips, and/or homework assignments (assuming class periods of 45 minutes). The amount of classroom time can be adjusted by assigning some tasks (reading assignments and certain student activity pages) as homework.
- Activity Steps — A detailed, step-by-step "recipe" for presenting the lesson. "Teacher Notes" provide helpful tips for presenting and/or preparing for a lesson.
- Materials List — A list of all classroom resources needed to present the lesson.
- Extension — Additional activities, used at instructor's discretion, to assess student learning, to challenge students to investigate beyond the scope of the lesson, or to provide opportunities for independent study, extra credit, or science fair projects.

Student Activity Pages:
Activity pages are located after the instruction pages and identified by the "Student Icon." They are designed for photocopying. Activity pages labeled: "Investigate This!" require short-answer solutions to problems. Those labeled: "Calculate This!" require basic math skills, graphing, or data collection, and "Discuss This!" pages require longer written or oral answers to questions. Additional activity pages and figures are used as reference guides and are simply identified with the lesson number and an appropriate title. Answers and completed illustrations, charts, and graphs (where applicable) are found in Appendix A, Teacher's Answers.

(more)

The *Discover Bats!* Video is a 48-minute film about the natural history and conservation of bats. Young narrators introduce each segment and appear throughout, along with amazing footage of bats in action taken from the BCI and Survival Anglia award-winning *Secret World of Bats* documentary. The video is divided into four segments that can stand alone or be presented together. Each lesson in the *Discover Bats!* Handbook is supported by at least one segment of the video. The video also can be viewed in its entirety apart from the lessons. It contains the following segments:

Discover Bats! How They Live (running time: 11:12) — Dispels myths and misinformation about bats while introducing viewers to the diversity and wonder of bats around the world. Shows bats rearing young, catching insects, fishing, picking fruits, pollinating flowers, and flying in spectacular columns. Also shows Vampire Bats feeding and discusses bat navigation and anatomy.

Discover Bats! Where They Live And What They Do (running time: 13:34) — Introduces the wide variety of bat lifestyles, habitats, and ecological roles. Bats are seen living in cut-leaf tents, tree foliage, hollow trees, and in caves for both hibernation and rearing young. The value of bats as insect-eaters, pollinators, and seed dispersers is clearly shown in footage from deserts and savannah to rain forests.

Discover Bats! How They Can Be Helped (running time: 13:14) — Provides role models and approaches for pursuing a career in science. Also emphasizes conservation needs and negotiating skills that minimize conflict while solving problems. Real-life accounts illustrate important conservation needs and positive approaches. Actual case-studies include how the once feared bats of Austin's famous Congress Avenue Bridge became a much valued tourist attraction, how a major hibernation cave in Tennessee was saved, how a Buddhist monastery in Thailand protects its bats, and how teaching Latin American ranchers about vampire bats is saving beneficial bat species.

Discover Bats! Valuable Neighbors (running time: 10:00) — Follows BCI founder Merlin Tuttle on a brief walk through a small town looking for possible bat roosts. The narrators join Tuttle in discussing the need for artificial roosts for bats that are losing their traditional homes. The segment includes instruction on building and mounting a backyard bat house.

How to Use Discover Bats!

Planning for Discovery

Instructors should prepare for each lesson by reading all student background information in the "Read About Bats" section. Carefully review activity steps and obtain the needed materials. Then prepare handouts and copy the activity pages for student use. Lessons are designed to encourage students to be inquisitive, as if they were scientists or field biologists conducting research on bats and their habitats. You can encourage this curiosity by asking questions posed in each activity and by promoting student participation in discussions. Before leading discussions, become familiar with the questions and answers on the teacher instruction pages and student activity pages.

Although the lessons are labeled as beginner, intermediate, or advanced in the Table of Contents, instructors can use any lessons for any grade level by increasing or decreasing the amount of group discovery involved. Lessons can also be assigned as independent-study or extra-credit projects for advanced students. The activity pages following each lesson are designed to help instructors assess students' mastery of the skills presented in the lessons. Extensions following each activity provide additional opportunities for independent research. You can incorporate extensions into the lesson or assign them as needed to stimulate independent thought and research.

Some lessons encourage students to keep a "Field Journal" of wildlife observations, especially those related to bats and their habitats. Students should be reminded to include notes on the time, day, month, year, and location of their observations in all entries. Their observations can include narratives answering: Who?, What?, When?, Where?, and How? Emphasize the importance of documenting complete information, for example stating how tall instead of just saying "tall." Creative students can include sketches or drawings in their journals.

Most lessons include vocabulary words printed in boldface type. Instructors can provide the simplified glossary definitions from Appendix E in the handbook or encourage students to look up the words in their own dictionaries. Students should be encouraged to use the glossary words in their class discussions.

How to Check Facts

Instructors should be aware that all facts and figures presented in the *Discover Bats!* handbook and video are as accurate as possible at the time of publication. However, scientists continually make progress through new discoveries that change the "facts," sometimes even the names of bats. Many books and other publications students may use as references will contain outdated information based on old research or simple misinformation. Even some back-issues of BCI's own *BATS* magazine may be outdated by new discoveries. You can challenge students to find the latest information and the most reliable sources. Teach them to assess reference information based on publication date, the training and experience of authors, corroborating publications, and their own knowledge. In some cases, they may wish to conduct research on an author. If you find an apparent error in *Discover Bats!*, please let us know so we can explain or correct it in a future revision.

World Bat Diversity — There are at least 1,105 species of bats in the world. Scientists never fully agree on how many there are, and new species are discovered each year. Four new species recently have been recognized in North America, which were previously thought to be subspecies. Taxonomists are continually refining relationships between and among species of bats and other mammals. Just as new species are often found and described, other formerly unique species are sometimes combined into a single species. Recent advances in molecular biology and genetic typing will continue to refine taxonomist abilities to distinguish species. For the purposes of the *Discover Bats!* kit, 1,105 species of bats, from 18 families are recognized, but because new species are routinely described, this number is clearly low. For instructional convenience, vampire bats (*Desmodus rotundus*, *Diaemus youngi*, and *Diphylla ecaudata*) are treated as belonging to a separate family, even though taxonomists classify them as a subfamily of the Phyllostomidae family (New World Leaf-nosed Bats). There is a single family containing 185 species in the Megachiropteran suborder of bats (flying foxes), and there are 17 families containing 920 species in the Microchiropteran suborder of bats (microbats).

Common Names of Bats — There is no worldwide standard for common names of bats (as there is for birds), and some bats don't even have common names. The common names included in this kit are those accepted by BCI in our official style guide. For ease of reference, all common names of bats are printed in "Initial Capitals" in the text of the handbook, though common names of other animals and common names for groups of bats (e.g., "fruit bats") are printed in all lowercase. Common names of bats can vary regionally and therefore may differ among references. When researching bats, students should be encouraged to use the Latin "scientific names" of bats, printed in italics in this kit. A complete list of bat species from Canada and the United States is included in Appendix C of the *Discover Bats!* handbook. There are also several common synonyms for bats which do not include the word "bat." Many of these common names are based on the family or generic name of a group of bats. These include:

Flying Fox — all bats belonging to the family Pteropodidae.
Myotis — all bats belonging to the genus *Myotis* and family Vespertilionidae.
Noctule — all bats belonging to the genus *Nyctalus* and family Vespertilionidae.
Rousette — all bats belonging to the genus *Rousettus* and family Pteropodidae.
Serotine — all Old World bats belonging to the genus *Eptesicus* and family Vespertilionidae.

How to Find More Information

Materials on BCI's website include an automated database containing more than 25 years of articles from *BATS* magazine, a full range of reference materials and reading lists, bat house and public health information, regional species lists, and much more. This resource is continually updated and provides links to other bat-related sites. We suggest making "bookmarks" for the following web addresses for easy access:

BCI Home Page
www.batcon.org

The *Discover Bats!* appendices provide a wide range of additional information and bibliographic resources, as follows:

Appendix-A: Teacher's Answers — Solutions to problems and answers to questions from the Student Activity Pages for each lesson.

Appendix-B: Bibliography — An annotated reference list of bat-related texts, plus regional references for further study of local bats or bats worldwide.

Appendix C: Bats of the United States and Canada — A complete list of bat species from the United States and Canada, their common name(s), and distributions.

Appendix-D: Bats and Public Health — Many people are misinformed about the role of bats in public health issues. Because instructors may be called upon to defend the use of bat houses, or students may have opportunities to write letters about bats to newspaper editors or health officials, we have included information facts about rabies and other public health concerns. For further details and updated facts, go to BCI's website: www.batcon.org.

Appendix-E: Glossary — A complete list of boldfaced glossary words from the "Read About Bats" selection and the student activity pages. The glossary gives simple definitions and phonetic pronounciations with accented syllables printed in ALL CAPS.

How to Contact Bat Conservation International

Write to us at: Bat Conservation International
Education Department
P.O. Box 162603
Austin, Texas 78716
www.batcon.org

Lessons

Discover Bats!

1 Thinking About Our Bat Attitudes

READ ABOUT BATS

You are not alone if you have ever been afraid of bats. It's easy to fear mysterious animals that fly at night. So many bad things have been said about bats that people who don't understand them often think they are blind, spooky creatures that will chase you, bite you, get caught in your hair, or suck your blood—especially on Halloween. Some think that bats live in haunted houses and can become monsters like Dracula. You have probably even heard negative expressions about bats, such as: "blind as a bat," "going batty," and having "bats in your belfry."

None of these fears or **superstitions** (SOO-per-STISH-ins) is true. The truth is that bats are among the most gentle, helpful, and misunderstood mammals. Bats can see well. They can **navigate** in the dark. They don't get caught in people's hair. They do not attack people.

"We fear most what we understand least," —Dr. Merlin Tuttle

Nevertheless, you should never attempt to handle a bat. It might become frightened and bite in self-defense. Any bat that can be caught may be sick, and a bite from any animal may require vaccination against **rabies** as a safety measure. You do not need to fear even a sick bat if you simply leave it alone.

As you do the activities in this book and watch the *Discover Bats!* video, you will learn how interesting and important bats are to the balance of nature. While bats fly through the night skies, they catch huge numbers of insects, **pollinate** flowers, and help spread the seeds of many plants. We need to protect bats, not fear them. But because many people fear bats, they have purposely tried to harm them. A main cause of bat decline is humans who kill them out of fear.

WHAT ARE SOME GOOD BAT ATTITUDES?
The Chinese view bats as symbols of good luck and happiness. A popular symbol in Asian art is the "Wu-Fu," which is made of five bats

touching wings surrounding the symbol of longevity. The bats represent health, long life, wealth, virtue, and natural death. Bat Conservation International uses the Wu-Fu symbol in its logo.

DID NATIVE AMERICANS HAVE BAT MYTHS?

Some early Americans in Central America thought bats were winged gods who made sure the cycles of nature ran smoothly. Native Americans liked bats and told stories about them saving people and being clever. Navajo Indians believed that bats, as creatures of the night, were a link between gods and people and could offer people helpful guidance.

WHAT ABOUT "BATMAN?"

Not all modern stories about bats are bad. One of America's most popular superheroes is Batman. He has a mask with pointed bat ears and a cape that looks like bat wings, and he helps people. His popularity has helped kids appreciate bats.

As you learn more about bats, you can help improve people's bat attitudes and turn their ideas around! By doing this, you can play an important part in bat conservation.

Read More About Bat Attitudes!

Strohm, Bob. 1982. "Most 'Facts' about Bats are Myths." *National Wildlife*. 20(5): 35-39.

Tuttle, Merlin D. 1997. *America's Neighborhood Bats*. (Rev. Ed.) University of Texas Press, Austin, 98 pages.

Discover Bat Attitudes on the Internet!
www.batcon.org "BATS *Magazine Archive*."

McCracken, Gary F. 1992. "Bats and Human Hair." *BATS*. 10(2): 15-16.

McCracken, Gary F. 1992. "Bats in Magic, Potions and Medicinal Preparations." *BATS*. 10(3): 14-16.

McCracken, Gary F. 1993. "Folklore and the Origin of Bats." *BATS*. 11(4): 11-13.

Visit BCI's website and search through 25 years of BATS magazines.

Overview

Students learn how "bat attitudes" change with knowledge, by graphing opinions, comparing results of a short True/False test, and holding group discussions both before and after viewing Part One of the *Discover Bats!* video.

Skills

Comparing and interpreting data, making a chart, graphing, making predictions, and understanding fears and prejudices

Video Connection

Part One: *Discover Bats!* How They Live, 12 minutes

Time

One activity period

Activity

1

Teacher tells the class that they are going to take a poll to discover class attitudes about bats. Students are asked to respond to the question "How do you feel about bats?" by answering "Like" "Don't Like" or "Don't Know." Students will mark their answers on the top of 1-A: Investigate This! Then students take the True/False test marking their answers in the BEFORE column on the bottom of 1-A: Investigate This! (The test is not corrected at this point; students will be taking the test again after viewing the video.)

2

Teacher asks all the students who marked "Like" to raise their hands. Students who marked "Don't Like" or "Don't Know" are also polled in this manner. Teacher hands out 1-B: Calculate This! All the votes are counted and graphed on the top of 1-B Calculate This! in the BEFORE column.

3

Class holds a brief discussion about the "How Do We Feel About Bats?" graph and the True/False test. Topics for discussion might include:

✓ Conclusions about the results of the poll
✓ Reasons for students' opinions
✓ Ways in which our opinions are influenced by movies, stories, etc.

Materials

1

1-A: Investigate This!
(one copy for each student)

2

1-B: Calculate This!
(one copy for each student)

4

Students make a group list: "Why People Do or Do Not Like Bats"
   Examples might include:
✓ Bats are a scary part of Halloween and haunted houses.
✓ Bats are vampires like Dracula.
✓ Bats attack people/bite you/get stuck in your hair.
✓ Bats fly at night/can see in the dark and dart around.
✓ Bats live in spooky, weird places.
✓ Bats are the subject of many negative expressions, such as:
   dingbat, going bats, blind as a bat.

5

Teacher hands out "Read About Bats" background information. Students will
find some answers to the True/False test in the selection, but most answers will
come from the video.

5

"Read About
Bats" background
information
*(one copy for each
student)*

6

Class views Part One of the *Discover Bats!* video. Students will find answers to
the True/False test in the video.

6

Video, Part One

7

Students complete the AFTER section of the "How Do I Feel About Bats?" poll
on 1-A: Investigate This! again.

7

1-A: Investigate
This!
(from step 1)

8

Students next take the True/False test on 1-A: Investigate This! again, marking
their answers in the AFTER columns.

9

Students exchange papers and grade both True/False tests. (See Appendix A for
answers.) Teacher hands out 1-C: Calculate This! and surveys the class,
recording the True/False test scores in the BEFORE and AFTER columns for
each of the three "Like," "Don't Like," and "Don't Know" poll groups. Average
the scores for each of the six categories, and enter the results in the chart.

9

Appendix A for
answers to 1-A:
Investigate This!

1-C: Calculate
This!
*(one copy for each
student)*

10

Class discusses the chart, drawing conclusions, and making predictions, while
responding to questions at the bottom of 1-B: Calculate This! including:

✓ How many more voted "Like" bats after learning about them?
✓ How many who voted "Don't Like" bats like them now?
✓ How many who voted "Don't Know" like bats now?
✓ Did your classmates change their opinions about bats after viewing video?

11

Teacher uses questions at the bottom of 1-C: Calculate This! to discuss the True/False test including:

✓ Did the scores on the True/False test change after the class watched the video?

✓ What were the changes?

✓ How did learning about bats change student opinions?

✓ What were some of the things students learned that helped to change their opinions about bats?

✓ Did the people who liked bats from the beginning have higher scores on the first True/False test? What does this result show you?

✓ Predict the results if friends, brothers and sisters, or parents took this test.

11

Completed copies of 1-C: Calculate This!

(from step 9)

12

Class makes a list of the things everyone learned about bats that helped to change their opinions.

Teacher leads a discussion about bat attitudes which might include:
"We fear most what we understand least," is a saying often used by Merlin Tuttle when he introduces bats to a new group of people.

✓ How does this apply to bats?

✓ How does it apply to other subjects or situations?

✓ Has there been a time when you didn't like something (or someone) before you learned about it (or them), and then changed your mind?

E

Extension

Challenge students to design a survey form to test attitudes about bats. The survey can be given to friends or family to determine if age, sex, or profession affects attitudes. The results of the survey can be incorporated in written reports or "science fair" projects and can include graphs, pie charts, statistics, etc.

E

Student "Field Journals"

How I Feel About Bats

Circle your choices before and after watching the video.

BEFORE   **AFTER**

LIKE   LIKE

DON'T LIKE   DON'T LIKE

DON'T KNOW   DON'T KNOW

What I Know About Bats

TRUE AND FALSE TEST

BEFORE   AFTER

BEFORE			AFTER	
T	F	1. Bats are blind.	T	F
T	F	2. Bats are birds.	T	F
T	F	3. Some bats are vampires and drink only blood.	T	F
T	F	4. Bats get caught in people's hair.	T	F
T	F	5. There are fewer than ten different kinds of bats.	T	F
T	F	6. Some bats catch fish.	T	F
T	F	7. Some bats eat fruit.	T	F
T	F	8. Lots of bats have rabies.	T	F
T	F	9. Some bats can catch 1,000 insects in an hour.	T	F
T	F	10. Mother bats nurse their babies.	T	F

My Score
Before
Watching:
/10

My Score
After
Watching:
/10

How Do We Feel About Bats?

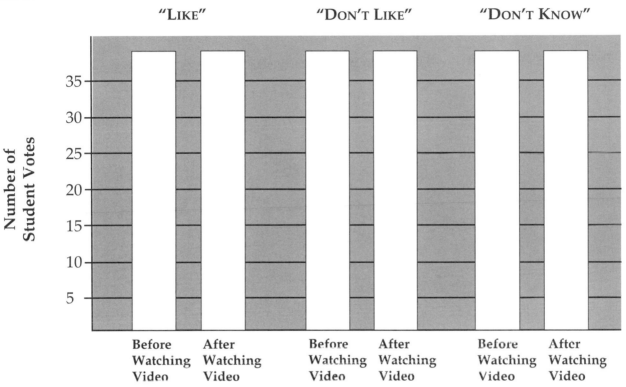

"LIKE"   "DON'T LIKE"   "DON'T KNOW"

Number of Student Votes

35
30
25
20
15
10
5

Before Watching Video   After Watching Video   Before Watching Video   After Watching Video   Before Watching Video   After Watching Video

Interpreting the Graph

1. How many more voted "Like" bats after learning about them?

2. How many who voted "Don't Like" bats like them now?

3. How many who voted "Don't Know" like bats now?

4. Did your classmates change their opinions about bats after viewing the video?

True/False Test: Class Results

	"LIKE"	"DON'T LIKE"	"DON'T KNOW"
Before Video: Average # Correct			
After Video: Average # Correct			

Interpreting the True/False Test

1. Did the scores on the True/False test change after the class watched the video?

2. What were the changes?

3. How do you think learning about bats changed student opinions?

4. What were some of the things you learned that helped to change your opinions about bats?

5. Did the people who liked bats from the beginning have higher scores on the first True/False test?

6. What does this result show you?

7. Predict the results you would expect if your friends, brothers and sisters, or parents took this test.

2 Understanding Bats

READ ABOUT BATS

Just as you go to sleep at the end of the day, bats are waking up and beginning to fly out for the night. They are nature's night shift workers, as comfortable getting around in the dark as we are during the day. There are more than 1,100 different kinds, or **species**, of bats. They live everywhere in the world except Antarctica. Most bats live in the **tropics** where there are lots of insects, plants, and fruit to eat and the weather is warm all year long. Bats come in an amazing **diversity** of sizes, shapes, and colors.

WHAT MAKES A BAT A MAMMAL?

One thing that all bats have in common is that bats are **mammals**. What does that mean? There are about 4,000 different kinds of mammals on our planet, nearly a quarter of which are bats. Mammals are animals that have at least some hair or fur and typically give birth to live young (except **echidnas** (eh-KID-nas) and **platypuses**, which lay eggs). Mammals nurse their young

There are about 4,000 different kinds of mammals on our planet, nearly a quarter of which are bats.

with milk, and are able to maintain a constant body temperature. Birds, frogs, and insects are animals, but can you see why they are not mammals?

A bat's soft fur helps to protect its body from hot and cold weather. Many bats are brown or black, but they can also be bright orange, yellow, silver, white, or gray, and some have spots and stripes.

Bats give birth to live young that sometimes live for more than 40 years. Most bats have only one baby, called a **pup**, each year. Pups are born in spring while their mothers hang from a **roost**. Bat pups are big. They weigh more than one-fourth of their mother's weight! This is similar to a 100-pound (45 kg) human mother having a 25-pound (11.25 kg) baby. Most mother bats leave their babies in **nursery colonies** while they go out to hunt. There the pups are kept warm by sharing body heat with many other pups. When the mothers return, each recognizes its own baby, even when there are millions in the colony.

Bat mothers nurse their babies. Bat pups drink milk from their mothers until they are old enough to hunt on their

Bats are the only mammals that can truly fly. So-called "flying" squirrels merely glide. Bats have true wings that they flap to fly. A bat skeleton is very lightweight. It is shaped much like a human skeleton, and the bat's wing is similar to a human hand, except with much longer finger bones. For this reason, bats are classified scientifically as *Chiroptera* (k'eye-ROP-ter-ah), a Greek word that means "hand wing."

ARE BATS THE SAME ALL OVER THE WORLD?

Scientists divide bats into two main groups: **"megabats"** and **"microbats."** *Mega-* means large, and these bats live up to their name—some megabats have six-foot (1.8 m) wingspans! People call them **flying foxes** because of their fox- or dog-like faces. There are about 185 kinds of Megabats, and they live in **tropica**l areas of Asia, Africa, Australia, and South Pacific islands.

Flying foxes live out in the open in trees. Scientists call a place where a group of flying foxes live a "**camp**." They look like large fruit as they hang upside-down from branches with their wings wrapped around their bodies. All flying foxes eat fruit or **nectar** from plants.

All of the other bat species (about 920 of them) are called microbats. *Micro-* means small. The smallest microbat, the Bumblebee Bat of Thailand, weighs less than a penny and has a wingspan of only six inches (15.25 cm). Most microbats have wingspans of about 10 to 16 inches (25.5-40.5 cm), but one **carnivorous** species from **Latin America** has wings that are nearly three feet (0.9 m) long!

There are many kinds of microbats. Some of them eat fruit and nectar like

own. Mothers give them lots of attention, keeping them warm as they grow, and feeding them several times a day. Mothers teach them which food is good to eat and where to find it.

Bats are **homeothermic** (ho-MEE-oh-THUR-mick). This means they make and maintain their own body heat. But unlike people and many other mammals, a bat can adjust its body temperature. While resting during the day, bats often save energy by lowering their **metabolism** and body temperatures. This is called **torpor**. They lower their metabolism and body temperature even more in winter when they **hibernate**. In hibernation, they can live on stored fat for six to eight months without eating!

megabats. Most, however, eat insects, and a few eat fish and small animals like frogs and lizards. Also, in Latin America, there are three species of microbats that are grouped together under the name "Vampire Bats" because they drink the blood of other animals.

WHY DO BATS HANG UPSIDE DOWN?

Bats eat, sleep, and groom themselves while hanging upside down. This would bother us, but it is comfortable for them because of their specially **adapted** skeletal, muscular, and circulatory systems. Being the only mammals that hang upside down makes it easier for bats to find safe homes. Not many animals can live on the roof of a cave or at the top of a tree hollow. Hanging upside down also makes it easier to fly. They just drop and spread their wings to take off in a hurry.

HOW SMART ARE BATS?

Bats are exceptionally smart. Scientists are able to train them, as they do porpoises, and the bats learn as quickly as most dogs. Many of the bats in the *Discover Bats!* video were trained so they could be filmed more easily. The Vampire Bat was as tame as a hamster, and others quickly learned to come when called.

Read More About Bats!

Rink, Deane and Linda C. Wood. 1989. *Zoobooks: Bats*. Wildlife Education Ltd., San Diego, 17 pages.

Wilson, Don E. 1997. *Bats in Question: The Smithsonian Answer Book*. Smithsonian Institution Press, Washington D.C., 168 pages.

Discover Bats on the Internet!
www.batcon.org "BATS *Magazine Archive.*"

Anon. 1990. "A Year of Filming Bats Around the World." *BATS*. 8(2): 3-4.

Anon. 1995. "The Tale of the Flying Fox Midwife." *BATS*. 13(2): 16-17.

French, Barbara. 1997. "False Vampires and Other Carnivores." *BATS*. 15(2): 11-14.

Visit BCI's website and search through
25 years of BATS *magazines.*

Overview

Students are introduced to bats as they read a summary of bat characteristics and behavior. They learn why bats are mammals and how they are unique. After identifying unusual bat characteristics, students fill out an anatomy diagram and relate bat parts to those of humans.

Skills
Reading, vocabulary, observation, anatomy

Video Connection
Part One: *Discover Bats!* How They Live, 12 minutes

Time
One activity period

Activity

1 Teacher hands out "Read About Bats" background information for students to read aloud or independently.

2 Class discusses the unique and unusual characteristics of bats that they learned through reading. Teacher makes a list on the blackboard or tells students to do so on paper themselves. The list should have two columns. The first column might be titled "How Bats Are Unique." The second column is left blank for step 3, below.

3 Class discusses how the unique characteristics of bats are advantageous, then adds these notes to the list, under the second column, which might be titled simply "Advantages." Students should make educated guesses about the advantages if they don't know exact answers. They should then try to find the answers to any unanswered questions as they view the *Discover Bats!* video.

4 Class views Part One of the *Discover Bats!* video. After viewing, class adds anything new they learned to the list from steps 2 and 3 including:
"How Bats Are Unique"
✓ Bats are the only mammals that can fly.
✓ Bats are the only mammals that hang upside down when they rest.
✓ Bats, whales, and dolphins are the only mammals with sophisticated echolocation.
✓ Bats live far longer than other small mammals.
✓ Compared to their mothers, bat pups are born larger than other mammals.

Materials

1 "Read About Bats" background information *(one copy for each student)*

2 a blackboard or paper for each student

4 Video, Part One

"Advantages of Being a Bat"

✓ Flight helps bats to hunt flying insects, escape predators, and travel long distances to hunt food or to migrate.

✓ Hanging upside down enables bats to live in large colonies on cave ceilings where no other mammals or birds can live. This ability also allows bats to escape most predators and to trap shared body heat that keeps babies warm and helps them grow.

✓ "Seeing" with echolocation enables bats to catch and eat the huge numbers of insects that fly at night with very little competition from birds. It also enables them to live in protected caves where many other animals cannot see to enter.

✓ Long lifespans enable animals to learn more about their environment and to pass more information on from generation to generation. This knowledge may include migratory routes, special feeding places, roosting sites, and how to avoid predators.

✓ Being born very large makes it easier to stay warm and survive.

5

Teacher hands out 2-A: Investigate This! (two pages) and explains to the students that they will be reading about and identifying the anatomical parts of a bat. The class fills in the answers on the bat diagram and discusses the special body parts that make bats so unique. (See Appendix A for answers.) Teacher can lead a discussion of bat characteristics.

5

2-A: Investigate This! (two pages) *(one copy for each student)*

Appendix A for answers to 2-A: Investigate This!

E

Extension

Challenge students to research the different orders of mammals to investigate relative diversity in each. Mammals are a class of animals comprising more than 4,000 species. The Mammalian Class is subdivided into two sub-classes, the Prototheria (egg-laying mammals) and the Theria (live-bearing mammals). Theria are further divided into *infra-* classes: Metatheria (marsupials) and Eutheria (placental mammals). The Chiroptera (Bats) represent just one of the 21 different orders of eutherian mammals. But bats are arguably the most diverse mammalian order.

Ask students to record the number of families, genera, and species found in each order they are investigating.

✓ What are the distributions, diets, behaviors, and ranges in physical chacteristics for members of other mammalian orders?

✓ How do bats compare?

✓ How many orders of mammals are found in the local area?

✓ Have students summarize their findings in a report or poster display.

E

An encyclopedia to world mammals

(For example, Nowak, Ronald M. (Ed.) 1991. *Walker's Mammals of the World*, 5th edition. Johns Hopkins University press, 1,629 pages.)

Instructions: Read the descriptions of bat body parts and their uses listed below and on the following page, and label each part of the bat drawing with the corresponding number. Some parts will be familiar and easy to find, but some are unique to bats, the world's only flying mammals.

HEAD

1. EAR: Bats hear well, and their ears come in many different shapes. Large ears have extra-sensitive hearing. Some bats with very large ears can hear even the faint sounds of a cricket walking on sand. To demonstrate the effectiveness of large ears, use your hands to make "ear cups" and listen to whispers. You should notice improved hearing.

2. TRAGUS: A small, sword-shaped piece of flesh inside the front of the ear. It is believed to be used in **echolocation**. Scientists are still studying its use.

3. NOSE LEAF: Some bats have fleshy triangles on top of their noses. They are present only on bats that send out echolocation signals through their noses. They appear to be used to direct echolocation sounds towards particular targets.

4. EYE: Bat eyes are sometimes small, but all bats can see well; none are blind.

BODY

5. FUR: Bats' fur comes in many colors and patterns: black, brown, silver, orange, spotted, or striped. Their fur can be short and dense, or long and fluffy. Some bats have hair on their **tail membranes** and wrap themselves up to stay warm.

6. TAIL: Bat tails can be long or short. Some bats don't have tails at all. The tail helps a bat to shape its tail membrane for slowing down or turning in flight.

7. TAIL MEMBRANE: The tail membrane is the skin between the legs and it can be wide or narrow. It is used like a rudder or brakes to steer or slow the bat as it flies. Bats that don't chase insects sometimes have no tail membranes at all.

8. CALCAR: A small spur of bone or **cartilage** that sticks out from the ankle. It is used to control the tail membrane while flying.

9. LEG: Bat legs are thin and have weak muscles because bats don't need to walk much.

10. KNEE: Bat knees point backwards (compared to ours) so that they can grip the surface where they are roosting.

11. TOES: Bat toes have sharp, curved claws that grip even when bats sleep. As a bat hangs upside down, the weight of its body pulls its knees straight and its claws tight so they automatically hook onto the roost. This way, a bat can hang on without getting tired. This is similar to a horse's legs locking as it sleeps standing up.

HAND WINGS

Bat bones (especially their upper arm, **forearm**, and elbow) are much lighter than ours but look similar. Bats have a thumb and four fingers that are like human fingers but much longer and narrower. They use their thumbs to grab roost surfaces or to grab tree branches with flowers or fruit. The fingers help to change the shape of the wing so bats can change their direction of flight or even grab a flying insect.

12. ARMS: Bats have large, strong arm muscles that are used to move their wings.

13. ELBOW: Bat elbows work very much like our own.

14. THUMB: A bat thumb points forward and has a claw.

15. SECOND FINGER: The long bone on the outside edge of the wing.

16. THIRD FINGER: The long bone extending to the tip of the wing.

17. FOURTH FINGER: The long bone extending along the width of the wing.

18. FIFTH FINGER: The long bone extending parallel to the body.

19. WING MEMBRANE: A tough, elastic, double skin between a bat's body, tail, arm, and fingers which makes up the wing.

3 Finding Bats

READ ABOUT BATS

There are 46 **species** of bats in the United States, and almost all of them (42 species) eat insects. Three species live in the Southwest and feed on flower **nectar** or fruit of **desert** plants such as **agave** and **cactus**. Only one tropical fruit bat, the Jamaican Fruit-eating Bat, can be found in the United States. It lives in the Florida Keys.

WHAT KINDS OF BATS LIVE IN NORTH AMERICA?

The Big Brown Bat is one of the most widespread species in North America. Big Brown Bats are actually small, weighing less than a sparrow. One of the most likely bats to live in cities, they are often found in buildings. But they also live in forests and in farmlands, where they are very helpful to farmers because they catch large numbers of crop pests, such as cucumber beetles. In one summer, 150 Big Brown Bats can eat 600,000 cucumber beetles. If these beetles were allowed to lay eggs, they could produce 33 million rootworms, which cost U.S. farmers close to a billion dollars each summer.

Even though bats live in all parts of North America, most are active only in warm weather. To survive cold winter weather, most bats either **migrate** south or **hibernate**. In general, you can find bats out and about after the last freeze in spring and before the first freeze in fall.

WHERE DO BATS ROOST?

Bats in North America live in many different kinds of **roosts**. Sometimes small groups of bats live in hollow trees, in woodpecker holes, or behind loose bark on dead trees. Others live in narrow rock crevices, 1/2- to 1-inch (1.25-2.5 cm) wide on cliff faces or in similar places beneath highway bridges. In buildings, they most often enter attics through small openings under the eaves or live in narrow spaces behind window shutters or chimneys. Bat researchers are also discovering that bats will move into specially constructed **bat houses**. Hundreds or even thousands of bats can easily live in one bat house.

Some large **colonies** of bats live in caves; or when they can't find caves, they live in old, abandoned mines. There are thousands of empty mines across North America that people have abandoned after digging out all the minerals they could find. These mine tunnels often make

Even though bats live in all parts of North America, most are active only in warm weather.

ideal bat **habitat**. Bat conservationists are working to protect old mines, making them safe for both bats and people. Bats need these new homes more and more as their natural homes are destroyed by the growth of cities.

There are many species of bats which do not enter caves. Red Bats, Yellow Bats, Seminole Bats, and Hoary Bats roost in trees, right among the leaves. These bats hang from just one foot, often resembling dead leaves.

What Should You Do if You Find a Bat?

Sometimes bats enter homes or yards. *No one except a bat scientist or animal rescue professional should ever handle a bat. The bat might become frightened and bite in self-defense.* Any bat that can be caught may be sick, and its bite could be dangerous. You do not need to fear a sick bat if you simply leave it alone and keep dogs and cats away. If you discover roosting bats, be very careful not to frighten them or tell anyone who would. You might want to quietly observe the bats as they leave at sundown to feed.

What About Rabies?

One of the most damaging misconceptions about bats is that most of them have **rabies**. Bats, just as any **mammal**, can get rabies, but people are not likely to get rabies from bats if they simply do not attempt to handle them. In fact, many more people die from dog *attacks* than from rabies from bats. But, rabies is a good reason why you should not pick up or handle bats.

The best time to go bat watching is in the summer, when bats are most plentiful in North America. Bats are not easy to watch, but you can catch glimpses of them if you know where to look. Sometimes you can see bats hunting for food and water. (Learn how to tell a flying bat from a bird in *Lesson 7: Experimenting with Flight*.) Because almost all of the bats in North America eat insects, you can look for bats in buggy areas. A common place to see bats is around lights that attract insects in parks and outside buildings. Since there are a lot of insects near ponds, lakes, and rivers, these are also likely places to see bats. If there is a cave near your town, or a known place where large colonies of bats roost, you might go there just at dusk to quietly watch the bats **emerge**. It is very important not to disturb bats near roosts, so never try to go into these places.

Read More About Finding Bats!

Tuttle, Merlin D. 1997. *America's Neighborhood Bats.* (Rev. Ed.) University of Texas Press, Austin, 98 pages.

Discover Finding Bats on the Internet!
www.batcon.org

Fenton, M. Brock. 1991. "Tuning in with a Bat Detector." *BATS.* 9(2): 12.

Murphy, Mari. 1991. "Bats: A Farmer's Best Friend." *BATS.* 11(1): 21-23.

Visit BCI's website and search through 25 years of BATS magazines.

Overview

Students learn about the bats that live in North America and identify likely bat feeding and roosting areas. Students investigate observations and experiences that people they know have had with bats and share them with the class.

Skills

Observation, habitat analysis, investigative reporting, verbal communication

Video Connection

Part Two: *Discover Bats!* Where They Live and What They Do, 14 minutes

Time

One activity period plus homework

Activity

1 Class views Part Two of the *Discover Bats!* video.

2 Teacher hands out "Read About Bats" background information for students to read aloud or independently.

3 Teacher hands out 3-A: Investigate This! Students follow instructions, completing the activity individually or in groups. (See Appendix A for answers.)

4 **Homework**
Students take a "bat walk," either in their neighborhood or around the school, to identify possible places where bats could roost or feed and record their observations in a "Field Journal." With help from parents, students may also find feeding bats by looking over lakes, ponds, or rivers in the first hour and a half after sundown, using a bright light.

Materials

1 Video, Part Two

2 "Read About Bats" background information *(one copy for each student)*

3 3-A: Investigate This! *(one copy for each student)*

Appendix A for answers to 3-A: Investigate This!

4 Student "Field Journals"

5

Students ask their family, neighbors, friends, etc., for stories about bats in their area. Students share the stories with the class. Topics for discussion might include:

✓ Identification of places where bats might live.
✓ Discussion of some public health concerns about bats.
✓ Analysis of ways that people understand or misunderstand bats.
✓ Plans to educate community members. (See *Lesson 21: Planning a Bat Conservation Project*.)

5

Student "Field Journals"

E

Extension

Challenge students to use 13-A: Range Maps for Common North American Bat Species from *Lesson 13: Studying Neighborhood Bats*, to determine which areas of North America have the greatest numbers of bat species. Have students answer the following questions: (See Appendix A for answers.)

✓What do you know about how many kinds of habitats there are in these areas?

✓Why do you suppose some areas of the country have more species of bats than others?

✓Which of the common North American bat species can be found in your area?

✓Using the information you've learned about habitat selection, predict where different species would occur locally.

✓Are there local needs for bat conservation?

Findings can be sumarized in a poster or report.

E

13-A: Range Maps for Common North American Bat Species
(two pages)

Appendix A for answers

Instructions: If you were a bat arriving in this town, you would have to find food, water, and a place to roost. As you fly around town, identify where you would go to meet your needs:

■ Draw the letter *R* over possible roosts. Try to find eight or more different kinds of roosts.

■ Draw the letter *F* over places where you can find insects to eat. See if you can find at least three or four different locations where insects would be especially abundant.

■ Draw the letter *W* over two different drinking sources.

4 Identifying Bats

Ears, wings, legs, teeth, noses, and tails... all of these characteristics are important to notice when identifying unfamiliar bats.

READ ABOUT BATS

Imagine you are a bat scientist, and you spot some bats **emerging** from a cave. You have never seen these types of bats before, so you are curious to figure out what kind they are. Because you are a trained researcher, you catch one bat and carefully hold it with your gloved hand. Taking a good look at it, you see it's about three inches long, has thick golden fur, and a face full of folds and crinkles. You can barely see its little eyes and nose. Is this enough information to tell what **species** it is?

WHAT ARE IDENTIFICATION KEYS?

Scientists use a written tool called an identification key to identify animals and plants. With a key, a scientist can sort bats by their characteristics, such as the size and shape of their ears, wings, legs, teeth, noses, or tails.

EARS?

Many bats have small mouse-like ears. Other bats have very large ears, almost as long as their bodies. Bat ears can be pointed, rounded, covered with hair, joined over the forehead, or separate. **Microbats** (smaller bats) have an additional projection in each ear called a **tragus** (TRAY-gus). The tragus comes in many sizes and shapes, too. It can be short and rounded, club-shaped, or long and sharply pointed.

WINGS?

Bat wings come in all shapes and sizes, and even in many colors. The Yellow-winged Bat of Africa has bright orange-yellow wings, and the Spotted Bat of North America has see-through pink wings. Some wings are long and narrow; others are short and stubby. Some bats have fur or color patterns on the underside of their wings which are very distinctive.

The finger bones in a bat's wings are also important in identification. The length of a bat's thumb can help you decide which species it is. Sometimes thumbs have large fleshy pads or round disks, and sometimes the second finger has a claw.

LEGS AND FEET?

All bats have legs, but few can use them to walk upright. Some bats, such as the Vampire Bat and the Pallid Bat, have more sturdy legs with larger muscles.

All bats have knees that bend

backward. This helps them to hang upside down. Bats have feet with five toes, just like humans, and each toe has a sharp claw for clinging to a surface, such as a cave wall. Some bats' feet are very hairy; you can sometimes identify a bat species by how hairy its feet are.

TEETH?

The standard number of teeth found in **mammals** is 44. The most teeth found in a bat is 38. Many bat species have different numbers of teeth, different sizes, and also different arrangements. These differences mean that teeth are another way that scientists can identify bats. For example, Common Vampire Bats have only 20 teeth, the smallest number of any bat.

NOSES?

Most bats have plain noses. Some bats have a piece of flesh above the nose that is shaped like a triangle. This is called a "**nose leaf**," and it can come in many shapes and sizes.

Other bats have U-shaped flaps below the nose as well. Sometimes the folds around a bat's nose are so unique that they can be used to determine which species a bat is. A few bats also have flaps and wrinkles around the lips, above the eyes, or on the sides of the face and muzzle. All of these characteristics are important to notice when identifying unfamiliar bats.

TAILS?

Not all bats have tails. Very few of the **flying foxes** (the largest bats) do, and a few microbats have no tails or very short tails. Most bats have tails that are completely enclosed in the **tail membrane**, but sometimes the tip or much more will stick out beyond the membrane. Sometimes the tail actually projects out from the top of the membrane. Most bats have tail membranes that are bare, others have very hairy tail

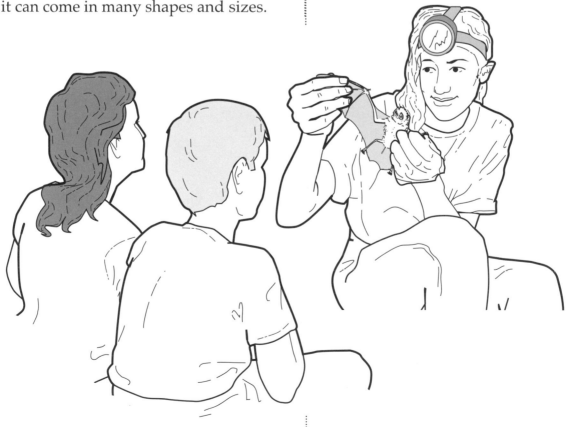

membranes, and still others have only a small fringe of hairs along the edge.

HOW ARE BATS DIVIDED INTO GROUPS?

All forms of life known to science are classified and given a scientific name. These names are in Latin, used so scientists all over the world can understand each other. Many organisms also have common names, and these names may change from region to region. Our scientific name is *Homo sapiens* and our common name is "human." To classify or divide organisms into groups, scientists use a system showing how a single species of animal is related to all other kinds. Bats with similar characteristics belong to the same groups. There are large groups which are divided into smaller groups. This dividing goes on until you have identified the species. This system makes it possible to understand and compare a lot of information about different organisms.

Read More About Bat Identification!
Graham, G.L. 1994. *Bats of the World: A Golden Guide.* Golden Press, N.Y., 160 pages.

Discover Bat Identification on the Internet!
www.batcon.org
"Species Lists: The U.S. and Europe"

Visit BCI's website and search through 25 years of BATS magazines.

The relationship of bats to all other members of the animal kingdom and all members of the mammalian class is diagramed below:

Kingdom = Animalia (animals)
  Phylum = Chordata (chordates — animals with a spinal chord)
    Subphylum = Vertebrata (have back bones made of vertebrae)
      Class = Mammalia (mammals; e.g., whales, opossums, **platypuses**, humans)
        Subclass = Theria (live-bearing mammals; e.g., whales, opossums, humans, and bats)
          Infra-class = Eutheria (placental mammals; e.g., whales, humans, and bats)
            Order = **Chiroptera** (bats)
              Suborder = **Megachiroptera** (flying foxes)
                Family = Pteropodidae (with about 185 species)
              Suborder = **Microchiroptera** (microbats)
                17* Distinct Families with about 920 species
            20 Additional Orders of Mammals
          Infra-class = Metaheria (marsupials; e.g., opposums and kangaroos)
        Subclass = Protheria (egg-laying mammals; e.g., platypuses and **echidnas**)

Overview

Students will learn how to identify the seven* bat families featured in the *Discover Bats!* video by using a simplified, dichotomous identification key that presents generalized characteristics of each family.

* For the purposes of this lesson, the Vampire Bats are considered a separate family, even though they are actually classified as a sub-family. There is debate among bat scientists whether to include them with the Leaf-nosed family or to split them off separately.

Skills

Classification, observation, comparison, grouping, cooperative research, animal identification

Video Connection

Part One: *Discover Bats!* How They Live, 12 minutes

Time

Two activity periods

Activity 1

1

Class discusses the characteristics of different bats and the groupings of animals after reading the "Read About Bats" background information—either as homework or during class time. Topics for discussion might include:
✓ What is an Identification Key?
✓ Draw or describe two different ways a bat's ear might look.
✓ Draw or describe two different ways a bat's nose might look.
✓ Do all bats have tails?
✓ Why do scientists classify organisms?
✓ What are some of the names of different groups of organisms?
✓ Why do scientists use "scientific names?"

2

Class views Part One of the *Discover Bats!* video observing different bat characteristics (e.g., nose-leaves, tails, ears, etc.). Afterwards, teacher should list students' descriptions of bat characteristics on the board.

3

Class discusses what kind of family groups they would use to classify bats, given what they've learned about the similarities and differences between species of bats.

4

Teacher displays copies of Bat Picture Cards using transparency copies and an overhead projector. Students examine the pictures, asking themselves: "What makes this bat different?" Students then list the characteristics, such as long tail, big feet or big ears, that they might use to classify these bats.

Materials

1

"Read About Bats" background information
(one copy for each student)

2

Video, Part One

4

Bat Picture Cards
(one copy of each)

Overhead projector

Activity 2

Materials

1

Teacher (or student) writes the names of the seven featured bat families on the board, leaving room for the Bat Picture Cards.

2

Teacher proposes to the class that they are mammalogists who have just found a bat. How would they figure out what kind of bat it is? Suggest observing its characteristics: body shape, size, ears, teeth, wings, etc.

3

Class goes through the key for one of the Bat Picture Cards on an overhead projector.
Note: Teacher can use a transparency copy of 2-A: Investigate This! to review bat anatomy before continuing this lesson.

3
Overhead projector and transparency copy of 2-A: Investigate This!

4

Teacher divides the class into six groups, giving each group one of the remaining Bat Picture Cards, a copy of 4-A: Investigate This!, and a copy of 4-B: Bat Identification Key.

Note: There are seven Bat Picture Cards. They are numbered, but not identified by name, so students will be able to complete the key process before discovering which Bat Picture Card represents each family. Laminate each card for strength. The correct identification for the cards is as follows:

1. Flying Foxes (Pteropodidae)
2. Fishing Bats (Noctilionidae)
3. Free-tailed Bats (Molossidae)
4. Ghost-faced Bats (Mormoopidae)
5. Leaf-nosed Bats (Phyllostomidae)
6. Plain-nosed Bats (Vespertilionidae)
7. Vampire Bats (Desmodontidae)

4
4-A: Investigate This!
(one copy for each group)

4-B: Bat Identification Key
(one copy for each group)

Copies of Bat Picture Cards
(cut cards, laminating them for durability, and distribute a different card to each group)

5

Each group follows the instructions on 4-A: Investigate This! and identifies its bat using the key. Once each group has identified the bat family in which its picture belongs, a representative from the group should signal the teacher by raising his or her hand. If correct, the teacher should give them the appropriate Bat Family Information Card which has the bat family's description. If incorrect, the teacher should encourage the group to look through the key again.

5
Globe or world map

Bat Family Information Cards
(One for each group. Cut cards, laminating them for durability, and distribute the appropriate card to each group of students after they have correctly identified their Bat Picture Card.)

6

Once each group has correctly identified its bat family members decide upon a format for presenting the bat family information to the entire class. presentations should include:

✓ Which family the bat is from, and what unique features identified the bat?

✓ Where in the world does the bat family live?

✓ What are the most interesting facts about the bat family?

7

Once the group presentations are finished, group representatives place the Bat Picture and Information Card under each family name. (Teacher or student volunteer should present the bat family used as the example on the overhead projector from step #3.)

E1

Extension One

Challenge students to draw their own imaginary bats. By combining various characteristics, each student creates a bat that would "live" in a habitat and eat the food of the students' choice. Students share their drawings with the class, describing what kind of bat was drawn, where it would live, and what it would eat. Each explains why he or she selected the characteristics such as size, color, wing style, size of ears, and teeth, etc., and how the bat's characteristics adapt it to the imaginary situation.

E1

Drawing paper, markers, pens, and pencils

E2

Extension Two

Challenge students to research the bat families and species living in their area and use local references to make their own dichotomous keys. (See Appendix B for bibliography.)

E2

Appendix B for bibliography of regional reference resources

There are eighteen bat families living in the entire world. This identification key is for the seven bat families featured in the *Discover Bats!* video. Four of these families live in the United States. Each family has developed different characteristics that help it survive in its **habitats**. To identify each bat, you will have to carefully observe the characteristics on the Bat Picture Cards.

Instructions:

■ To identify the family in which each pictured bat belongs, begin with question 1. Have a group member first read aloud both 1a. and 1b. ***Only one of the statements can be true about the bat on the card you are trying to identify***. Discuss and decide whether 1a. or 1b. is true, and follow the dots for your instructions.

■ If the dots lead you to a bat family name, you are finished identifying your bat family.

■ If the dots lead you to another number, go to that number and read both parts of that question. Decide which one is correct, and follow the dots for more instructions.

■ If the dots keep leading you to more numbers, keep going. You will finally come to your bat family name.

Once your group finds the name of your bat family, someone should raise a hand, and your teacher will give you the Bat Family Information Card, which gives you more details about the family.

Choose a representative from your group to prepare a presentation about your bat family for the class. Be sure to include information that completes the following statements:

1. Our bat family has the scientific name: _____

　　　　　　and the common name: _____

　　Unique features that identify bats in this family include: _____

　　_____

2. Our bat family lives on the following continents: _____

3. Some additional interesting facts about our bat family include: _____

_____

_____

_____

1

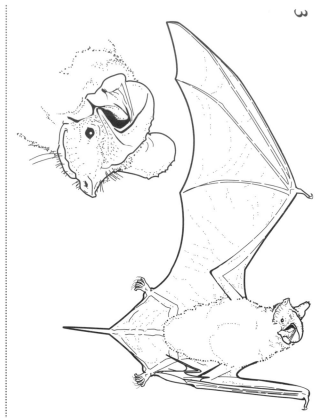

3

2

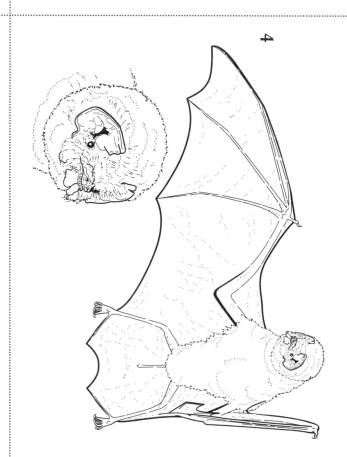

4

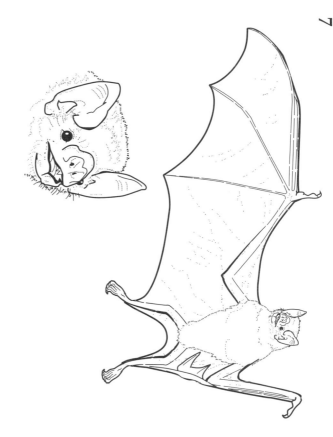

7

5

Bat Picture Cards

6

Bat Family Information Cards

1. My family lives in **tropical** areas of Africa, Asia, and Australia. We live in large **colonies,** hanging in trees. Our eyes are large, and we see very well. We have a keen sense of smell, which helps us find our food—ripe fruit and **nectar** in flowers. Our strong jaws and flat teeth are perfect for crushing fruit to get juice. Our faces look like dogs or foxes, hence our name. Most of us never use **echolocation.** Our enemies include large hawks and eagles, pythons, and humans. Sometimes we eat fruit crops, but mostly we help by **pollinating** flowers and spreading seeds of valuable plants. Several of our family are **endangered** or **extinct,** because some people who don't understand our importance kill us.

2. My small family lives in Central and South America near rivers, streams, or ocean bays. We roost in caves, hollow trees, or buildings. We fly close to water and have water-repellent fur. Our feet are huge, with sharp claws for spearing fish. We carry fish in our cheek pouches, catching several small fish each night. We use echolocation to search for ripples or fins. If we have to, we eat insects. Our short tails hold the tail-membrane up while our legs reach into water to catch minnows. Our enemies include snakes and owls, but our biggest problems are roost destruction and polluted streams where we fish.

3. My family lives all over the world. Sometimes millions of us live in huge **colonies** in caves, tunnels, or dark places in buildings and bridges where we are safe and warm. We use **echolocation** to find food. We eat millions of insects each night; in fact there is one colony in Texas that can eat over 400,000 pounds of insects in one night. We fly fast and straight with long, narrow wings. We catch insects as we fly. Our long tails stick out past our tail membrane. Our enemies include hawks, owls, snakes, and raccoons. Some people disturb our caves or poison us because they fear us. But the truth is we help farmers by eating large numbers of insects that are crop pests.

4. My small family lives in the southwestern U.S. and Central and South America. We **echolocate** using special flaps of skin around our mouths. These flaps help amplify our sound when our mouths are open. Our bristly mouth hairs look like a moustache. We eat insects near the ground. Our long narrow wings help us fly fast as we hunt. Our strange ears help us **navigate.** We live in caves, tunnels, or old mines, often near water, in **colonies** that contain hundreds or thousands of individuals. We can live in **rain forests** or **deserts.** We fear snakes and owls, but our biggest problems are caused by people who disturb our **roosts** in caves.

Bat Family Information Cards

5. Mine is a large family; we include many different sizes and shapes. We live in the southern U.S. and Central and South America. We eat many foods, including insects, fruit, small animals, **pollen**, and **nectar**. We **echolocate** through our nostrils, using a nose leaf, which is a fleshy triangle shape on our snout. We have many different sizes of tails, and some of us don't even have tails. Our hair is brown, gray, reddish, white, or striped, sometimes for **camouflage** in trees. We live in caves, tunnels, buildings, road culverts, and hollow trees and logs. We also live under large leaves that we cut to make tents. Our enemies are mostly owls and snakes. Also, some people mistakenly kill us, thinking we are Vampire Bats.

6. Mine is the largest bat family. We live in North America and throughout the world. We live in more places than any other bat family. We have no nose leaf; we **echolocate** through our mouths. We have short jaws and sometimes large ears. We eat insects and occasionally fish. We live in caves, tunnels, mines, cliffs, tree holes, tree leaves, and buildings. We often form groups that include hundreds or even tens of thousands of individuals. Our natural enemies are mostly owls and snakes, but house cats kill us by the thousands. Careless people often cause us to starve to death by waking us up when we are **hibernating** in caves. Some of us are **endangered** because of so much disturbance to our cave **roosts**.

7. My family lives in Mexico, Central, and South America in small colonies. We are affectionate. We groom and help each other, and we adopt orphaned babies. We eat blood, mostly from mammals, using a grooved tongue for lapping. We have only a few sharp teeth, because blood needs no chewing. We find our food by smell, by listening for breathing, and by using special heat sensors on our face to find blood near the skin's surface. Our bite doesn't awaken the prey, and our saliva keeps the blood flowing. Because we sometimes feed on livestock, such as horses and cattle, people find us to be a costly problem.

1a. Second finger and thumb both have claws.............................. Flying Fox Bat Family
(Pteropodidae)
TARE-ah-POH-did-day

1b. Second finger never has a claw.. 2

2a. Bat has a nose leaf (a fleshy "triangle shape" above nose) ..... New World Leaf-nosed Bat Family
(Phyllostomidae)
FYE-low-STOW-mid-day

2b. Bat does not have a nose leaf... 3

3a. Bat does not have a tail. .... Vampire Bat Family
(Desmodontidae)
DEZ-mow-DON-tid-day

3b. Bat has a tail.. 4

4a. Feet are very large, more than twice as long as the bat's thumbs. .... Fishing Bat Family
(Noctilionidae)
NOCK-til-lee-ON-nid-day

4b. Feet are small, never more than slightly longer than the thumbs. 5*

5a. Face has leaf-like flaps around the mouth. Short tail extends only halfway to the edge of the tail
membrane. .... Ghost-faced Bat Family
(Mormoopidae)
more-MOO-pid-day

5b. Face does not have leaf-like flaps around the mouth. Tail is long, reaching the edge or extending
beyond the edge of the tail membrane 6

6a. Tail does not extend beyond the tail membrane. Ears are widely separated.................
.... Plain-nosed Bat Family
(Vespertilionidae)
VESS-per-til-lee-ON-nid-day

6b. At least one-third of the tail extends beyond the tail membrane. Ears are joined or nearly joined on
the forehead.. Free-tailed Bat Family
(Molossidae)
mow-LOS-sid-day

Except for select species in the Vespertilionidae family that fish and live in tropical areas.

5 Reporting on Bats

READ ABOUT BATS

Deep in the heart of a Venezuelan **rain forest**, research scientists sit quietly in the dark, listening for the soft sounds of a bat striking a long, finely threaded net they have set across a stream. This light-weight net is called a **mist-net**, and it is the main tool that scientists use to catch bats. The bats are easily caught over the stream because they use it like a highway at night, flying over the water where there are few trees in their way.

In the past hour, the group has already caught 15 **species** of bats, including ones that eat fruit, **nectar**, insects, frogs, and even fish. Then, a soft swooshing sound announces yet another arrival. The scientists turn on their headlamps, and, with gloved hands, one of them carefully removes a Vampire Bat, being sure not to injure its delicate wings.

WHAT KINDS OF BATS DO SCIENTISTS CATCH?

Viewing bats in a rain forest is always exciting because there are so many kinds. The research team has already caught bats with tiny ears, huge ears, long white fur, and short red fur; with faces as strange as dinosaurs and as cute as puppies. Up to a hundred species of bats could be caught in this one rain forest. Worldwide, there are more than 1,100 kinds of bats. Most bats live in **tropical** areas, where up to half of all **mammal** species are bats. There are many wonderful discoveries to make, because most of these bats have never been studied, and new species are occasionally found.

The Vampire Bat the scientists have just caught is easily identified, because it is the only species here that has neither a tail nor a **nose leaf** (a triangle-shaped piece of **cartilage** above the nose). With luck they might even catch a **carnivorous** (meat-eating) bat with an almost three-foot (0.9 m) wingspan. If they were netting bats in Southeast Asia, they might catch a **flying fox** with a six-foot (1.8 m) wingspan or a Bumblebee Bat weighing less than a penny.

In the United States, there are 46 species of bats. These include some of the world's most beautiful bats, such as the Spotted Bat, the Silver-haired Bat, and the brilliant, silky-

There are many wonderful discoveries to make because most bats have never been studied and new species are occasionally discovered.

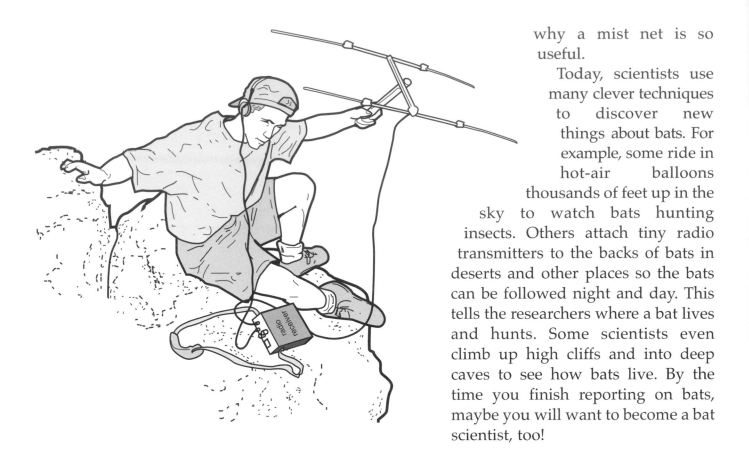

why a mist net is so useful.

Today, scientists use many clever techniques to discover new things about bats. For example, some ride in hot-air balloons thousands of feet up in the sky to watch bats hunting insects. Others attach tiny radio transmitters to the backs of bats in deserts and other places so the bats can be followed night and day. This tells the researchers where a bat lives and hunts. Some scientists even climb up high cliffs and into deep caves to see how bats live. By the time you finish reporting on bats, maybe you will want to become a bat scientist, too!

furred Red Bat. In fact, the Red Bat is one of the bats you are most likely to see in your own backyard.

ARE THERE OTHER METHODS FOR STUDYING BATS?

Using a special piece of equipment called a night-vision scope, researchers can watch bats in the dark as they feed, court, and care for their young. They can also listen to bat **echolocation** (ECK-coh-low-CAY-shun) sounds with an instrument called a **bat detector**. These instruments tell scientists if bats are just traveling through an area or if they are actively hunting for insects. Sometimes scientists can even identify bats in flight by recording and analyzing **high-frequency** bat calls with sophisticated electronic equipment. However, most bats must be caught and looked at close-up to be positively identified. That is

Read More About Bat Research!

Halton, Cheryl M. 1991. *Those Amazing Bats.* Dillon Press, Inc., Minneapolis, 96 pages.

Tuttle, Merlin D. 1982. "The Amazing Frog-Eating Bat." *National Geographic.* 161(1): 78-91.

Discover Bat Research on the Internet!
www.batcon.org "BATS Magazine Archive."

Fleming, Theodore H. 1989. "Climb Every Cactus." *BATS.* 7(3): 3-6.

Murphy, Mari. 1994. "On the Track of Forest Bats." *BATS.* 12(2): 4-9.

Perlmeter, Stuart and Pat Greenlee. 1993. "Bats 101: High School Students and Field Research." *BATS.* 11(4): 4.

Visit BCI's website and search through 25 years of BATS *magazines.*

Overview

Students select a topic for a report on bats and are encouraged to collect their own information, using books, magazines, and articles or Bat Conservation International's website. The completed reports are presented to the class and may be shared with the school.

Skills

Library and computer research, reporting, written, verbal, visual communication

Video Connection

Parts One, Two, and Three: *Discover Bats!*, 39 minutes

Time

One activity period plus homework

Activity

1 Students make their own lists of at least three things they would like to learn about bats. This is an opportunity for students to identify their individual interests. They may wish to study a group or species of bats, or specific topics such as behavior, echolocation, hibernation, conservation, etc. The topics should reflect the student's curiosity. Students may use 5-A and 5-B: Investigate This! to assist them in studying a specific bat family.

Note: Common names given to bats can vary regionally. Encourage students to use scientific names when researching their bat species and families.

2 Class views parts One, Two, and Three of the *Discover Bats!* video.

3 Teacher hands out "Read About Bats" background information for students to read aloud or independently.

4 Teachers can work with students to develop topic outlines. Creative approaches should be encouraged. Topics for creative report formats might include:
✓ A report written from the bat's point of view about a problem it faces
✓ An investigation of why bats and other animals or plants need each other
✓ A "newspaper article" about an issue, topic, or species
✓ A song containing bat information
✓ A picture book about the activities of a bat species

Materials

1 5-A: Investigate This!

5-B: Investigate This!
(copies as needed for students who wish to report on a bat family)

2 Video, Parts One, Two, and Three

3 "Read About Bats" background information
(one copy for each student)

5

Students are encouraged to use the following resources for their research:

—**Library:** A list of reference materials in the back of the *Discover Bats!* book includes books and magazine articles. (See Appendix B for references.)

—**BCI website (www.batcon.org):** The BCI website has information on a wide variety of bat-related topics and species.

—*Discover Bats!* **book:** Students will be able to collect information as they complete the activity pages in this book. Students should collect their completed Activity Pages in a special folder.

—*Discover Bats!* **video**: Students may view relevant parts of any of the four video sections on their own.

5

Appendix B for bibliography of reference resources

6

Students write their reports or make a poster, picture book, or song about their subject. Encourage students to be creative by using drawings, pictures, and interesting graphics.

E

Extension
Challenge students to share their knowledge with others. The class may want to make oral reports, display creative art in the hall, or hold a schoolwide exhibition about bats. Some projects may interest local news media, especially around Halloween.

E

display materials as needed

Bats belong to a very ancient order of **mammals** that have been on our planet since the days of the dinosaurs. The many kinds of bats are broken up into 18 different families.* All family members in a particular order of mammals have similar characteristics. For example, the order "Carnivora," the **carnivores**, is made up of families that include dogs, cats, bears, raccoons, weasels, and hyenas. Just as it is easy to distinguish between species of these families, it can also be easy to distinguish between species of different bat families. Below is a list of some of the different bat families and some of the species included in each:

Pteropodidae (TARE-ah-POH-did-day) = Flying Fox Family
  Eidolon (EYE-doh-lyn) *helvum* (HEL-vum), African Straw-colored Flying Fox
  Rousettus (ROE-zet-us) *aegypticaus* (AY-gypp-tick-us), Egyptian Rousette
  Pteropus (TER-rope-us) *poliocephalus* (POE-lee-oh-CEF-ah-lus), Grey-headed
       Flying Fox
Rhinolophidae (RYE-nah-LOW-fid-day) = Horseshoe Bat Family
  Rhinolophus (RYE-nah-LOW-fus) *ferrumiquinum* (FARE-ah-mah-QUINE-um), Greater
       Horseshoe Bat
Noctilionidae = Fishing or Bulldog Bat Family
  Noctilio (NOCK-til-ee-oh) *leporinus* (LEP-oh-RINE-us), Fishing Bat
Phyllostomidae = New World Leaf-nosed Bat Family
  Artibeus (AR-tib-ee-us) *jamaicensis* (JAM-eye-CEN-sus), Jamaican Fruit-eating Bat
  Leptonycteris (LEP-toe-NICK-ter-us) *curasoae* (CUR-ah-SOE-ay), Lesser Long-nosed Bat
Desmodontidae = Vampire Bat Family*
  Desmodus (DES-moe-dus) *rotundus* (roe-TUN-dus), Common Vampire Bat
Vespertilionidae = Vesper or Plain-nosed Bat Family
  Eptesicus (ep-TES-ah-cus) *fuscus* (FUS-cus), Big Brown Bat
  Myotis (MY-oh-tis) *lucifugus* (loo-CIF-you-gus), Little Brown Myotis
Molossidae = Free-tailed Bat Family
  Tadarida (tah-DARE-id-dah) *brasiliensis* (brah-SIL-ee-EN-sis), Mexican Free-tailed Bat

Learn more about the different bat family characteristics by researching one or more species in one of these families.

Note: Common names given to bats can vary regionally, therefore, the scientific (Latin names given in italics) should be used when researching bat species and families.

THE FOLLOWING TEXTS CAN BE USED FOR RESEARCH:

Graham, G.L. 1994. *Bats of the World: A Golden Guide*, Golden Press, New York. 160 pages.
Nowak, R.M. 1994. *Walker's Bats of the World*, Johns Hopkins University Press, Baltimore, 287 pages.
Wilson, D.E., 1997. *Bats in Question: The Smithsonian Answer Book*. Smithsonian Institution Press, Washington D.C., 168 pages.

* *For the purposes of this curriculum, Vampire Bats are considered as a separate family, though they typically are referred to as a subfamily, Desmondontinae, in the family Phyllostomidae.*

Instructions: Choose a bat family to research from the list on 5-A: Investigate This! Report on the bats in that family by answering the questions below. Decide how you will present your answers and findings.

1. Family common name:_____

2. Family scientific name:_____

_____

3. Representative species — common and scientific names:_____

_____

4. Describe how this bat family looks. What are its unique features? _____

_____

5. What do bats in this family eat? _____

_____

6. In what part(s) of the world does this bat family live? What are its habitats?_____

_____

7. Describe this bat family's role in **ecosystems**. _____

_____

8. Are members of this family threatened or **endangered**? What can be done to help them survive?

_____

_____

9. What are the five most interesting facts you learned about this bat family?

_____

_____

6 Investigating Bat Adaptations

Adaptations increase a bat's chance of finding food and surviving in a particular habitat.

READ ABOUT BATS

Did you ever stop to think what the world would be like if all the animals suddenly tried to eat just one kind of food? What if they all decided to eat just grass? The answer is simple. They soon would run out of grass and starve to death. Because animals eat a wide variety of foods, they compete less and help keep each other's numbers in balance. That way, far more different kinds of animals can live in the same **habitat** and keep **ecosystems** healthy.

WHAT DO BATS EAT?

Most of the world's bats eat insects, and in areas with cold winters, that is all they eat. Many **tropical** bats eat fruit and nectar, and a few are **carnivores** that eat other animals, including rats and mice, small birds, frogs, lizards, or even fish. Only three out of nearly a thousand species of bats are vampires that drink blood.

Each kind of bat is **adapted** for the food it eats. Some bats specialize in eating just one or a few kinds of food, but others are generalists that eat a wide variety of foods. Long-nosed bats have noses of varied lengths and widths that match the sizes and shapes of the flowers from which they drink **nectar**. *Carollia* (kah-ROLL-ee-ah) fruit bats are adapted to feed almost entirely on small **piper** fruits, but some **flying foxes** are generalists that eat many sizes and kinds of fruit as well as nectar.

HOW HAVE INSECT-EATING BATS ADAPTED?

Some bats that catch insects have unique adaptations for hunting certain kinds of **prey** or for capturing them in certain kinds of places. Free-tailed bats are like little jet airplanes, using their long, narrow wings and far-reaching **echolocation** for chasing moths high up in the sky. California Leaf-nosed Bats are more like helicopters, relying on short, broad wings to snatch crickets and other insects from plants or the ground. They can use their extra large eyes and ears to find insects without even using echolocation. Big Brown Bats have especially strong jaws and teeth for chewing hard beetles. Canyon Bats have tiny teeth for eating gnats and mosquitoes, and Gray Myotis have large feet for catching mayflies as they hatch from a pond's surface.

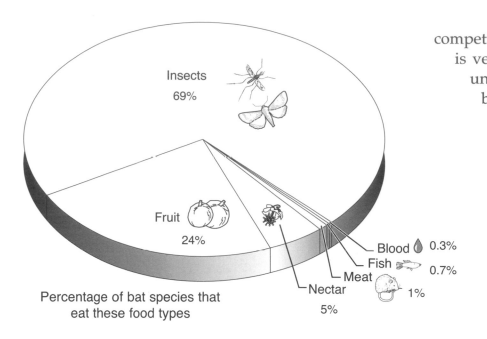

Insects
69%

Fruit
24%

Blood 0.3%

Fish 0.7%

Meat 1%

Nectar
5%

Percentage of bat species that
eat these food types

CAN I TELL WHAT A BAT EATS BY LOOKING AT
ITS ADAPTATIONS?

Most experienced bat scientists can guess
what a bat eats by looking closely at its
adaptations. Long, narrow wings or large
tail membranes are usually adaptations for
catching insects, but if the bat also has huge
feet and claws, it probably eats fish. Just
having large, but not overly large, feet would
indicate a bat that catches insects from pond
surfaces. If a bat is large, has strong jaws,
long **canine** teeth, and a large tail membrane,
it is probably a **carnivore**, adapted both to
eat meat and to turn quickly while chasing
prey. If it has strong jaws and long canine
teeth, but has only a very small tail
membrane, it is a fruit bat that does not need
to chase prey, but is adapted for biting into
tough-skinned fruit to squeeze the juice out.
Both insect-eating and meat-eating bats
always have long tails or tail membranes,
but meat-eaters are the largest and have the
strongest jaws.

WHY DO SOME BATS SPECIALIZE WHILE
OTHERS EAT A VARIETY OF FOODS?

Special adaptations allow bats to find and
eat certain kinds of food with little or no

competition from other species. This
is very successful as long as their
unique food type is abundant,
but such specialization is risky,
because the kinds of prey,
fruit, or flowers a bat eats
might die out, leaving the
bat to starve. Animals
that eat a variety of
foods can switch types
if one disappears, but
they cannot compete
well with specialized
animals for any one
food. Most specialists,
such as the huge-footed
fishing bats or long-nosed
nectar bats, live only in tropical areas where
climates and food sources are the most
predictable. Bats that live in northern
climates, where changes are frequent and
unpredictable, are all insect-eaters that
seldom specialize on any one insect type. In
these places, it is rare to find a bat with
highly specialized wings, feet, or ears.

Read More About Bat Adaptations!

Tuttle, Merlin D. 1982. "The Amazing Frog-
eating Bat." *National Geographic*. 161(1): 78-91.

Wilson, Don E. 1997. *Bats in Question: The
Smithsonian Answer Book*, Smithsonian
Institution Press, Washington D.C., 165 pages.

Discover Bat Adaptations on the Internet!
www.batcon.org "*BATS Magazine Archive*."

Belwood, Jacqueline J. 1988. "Sounds of
Silence." *BATS*. 6(2): 4-9.

Lee, David S. and Mary K. Clark. 1993.
"Arizona's Night Visitors." *BATS*. 11(2): 3-5.

Sahley, Catherine. 1995. "Peru's Bat-Cactus
Connection." *BATS*. 13(3): 6-11.

*Visit BCI's website and search through
25 years of BATS magazines.*

Overview

Students watch the *Discover Bats!* video and read background information to learn about how bats have adapted to eat a wide variety of foods, then answer questions about unique adaptations for different foraging strategies.

Skills

Observation, comparison, cooperative hypothesizing, understanding relationships between anatomical adaptations and behavior, habitat use

Video Connection

Part One: *Discover Bats!* How They Live, 12 minutes

Time

Two activity periods

Activity 1

1 Teacher hands out "Read About Bats" background information for students to read aloud or independently, telling them to pay special attention to the different feeding habits of bats.

2 Teacher explains that the students are going to watch the *Discover Bats!* video to see how bats are adapted to eating certain kinds of food. Teacher then hands out 6-A: Investigate This! and tells students to observe different eating habits and how the bats' shapes and behaviors help each kind of bat to feed. Students should read, but not answer, the questions on 6-A: Investigate This! prior to viewing the video.

3 Class views Part One of the *Discover Bats!* video. Students have 15 minutes to complete the questions on 6-A: Investigate This! after they watch the video.

4 Teacher leads a class discussion of student answers. (See Appendix A for answers.)

Materials

1 "Read About Bats" background information *(one copy for each student)*

2 6-A: Investigate This! *(one copy for each student)*

3 Video, Part One

4 Appendix A for answers to 6-A: Investigate This!

1

Teacher divides class into groups of six or more students each.

2

Teacher makes enough copies of the "Bats Adapt for Food" cards to distribute one complete set of cards to each group. Cards may be laminated for durability. Each group divides the fact cards among its members so that every student gets to become an expert on one of the bat eating habits. (Two students can share a single card in groups with more than six students.)

2

"Bats Adapt for Food" Cards
(one set of six cards for each group)

3

Teacher asks students to take out a piece of paper and number it from one to twelve down the left-hand side. Teacher asks questions by reading the "Bat Food Clues" to the class one at a time.

3

Bat Food Clues at the end of the lesson

Paper for students to write answers

4

Each group has a minute or two to discuss each given clue, and decide what feeding habit (for example, insects, fruit, fish, nectar, blood, or meat) the bat has.

5

After all Bat Food Clues are given and answers have been written down, teacher goes back through the "Bat Food Clues" and leads the class in discussing the correct answers. Bonus questions after each Bat Food Clue can be used to stimulate additional discussion. Each group's expert on each feeding type can be called upon to help lead discussions.

E

Extension
Challenge students to investigate other animals that have similar food habits as bats. For example, some birds snatch insects out of the air, others pick them from foliage. How do the habits and habitats of these birds and bats compare and contrast? What about fruit-eating birds? Nectar-eating birds? Fish-eating birds? Are there any other animals that eat blood? Students can present their results in poster or report format.

E

Animal encyclopedias, natural history magazines, etc.

1. Who am I?
Clue: My toes and claws are exceptionally long, and the sides of my toes and claws are flat.

I am a fish-eating bat.

> Bonus Questions:
> * What is the advantage of having long toes and claws?

* Can reach into water without submerging body

> * What is the advantage of having flattened toes and claws?

* To glide easily through water

2. Who am I?
Clue: My legs are extra strong and my kidneys work quickly so I can eliminate water as fast as I eat.

I am a blood-eating bat.

> Bonus Questions:
> * How do fast-working kidneys help a blood-eating bat?

* To get rid of the water, so the bat won't be too heavy to fly

> * What is the advantage of extra strong legs?

* To walk on the ground while stalking large prey or to jump away quickly if the prey wakes

3. Who am I?
Clue: I am a large, strong bat with large ears and broad wings.

I am a meat-eating bat

> Bonus Questions:
> * Why does a carnivorous bat need big ears?
> * What is the advantage of having broad wings?

* To listen to and find prey
* To better lift heavy prey

4. Who am I?
Clue: I fly fast over quiet water, searching for tiny moving objects. My fur is oily.

I am a fish-eating bat.

> Bonus Questions:
> * What is the advantage of flying over calm water?

* To easily detect tiny fin tips using echolocation

> * What is the advantage of oily fur?

* To shed water, keep bat fur dry, and avoid getting cold

5. Who am I?
Clue: My short, broad wings and my large tail membrane allow me to dart in and out of branches.

I am an insect-eating bat that catches prey on the ground or on plants.

> Bonus Questions:
> * What is the advantage of being able to dart in and out of branches?

* To avoid obstacles and catch prey

> * What is the advantage of being able to catch insects on the ground or in bushes?

* To avoid competing for food with other bats that feed in the open

6. Who am I?
Clue: I have sharp teeth and strong jaws that can cut or crush big meals. I also have a big tail membrane.

I am a meat-eater.

> Bonus Questions:
> * What is the advantage of having sharp teeth and strong jaws?

* To quickly kill and cut up large prey and break bones

> * What is the advantage of a big tail membrane?

* To maneuver better when chasing prey

7. Who am I?
Clue: My teeth are small, except for my front teeth, which are sharp and can cut like a razor. My nose can detect heat.

Bonus Questions:
- *Why are razor-sharp teeth important?*
- *What is the advantage of a heat-sensitive nose?*

I am a blood-eating bat.

- *To make quick, painless cuts*
- *To find areas on prey that are rich in blood*

8. Who am I?
Clue: I have sophisticated echolocation abilities; long, narrow wings; and small ears.

Bonus Questions:
- *Why do bats have echolocation as well as good eyesight?*

- *What advantages do long, narrow wings have?*

I am an insect-eating bat that catches prey in the air.

- *To pursue prey on the darkest nights and to roost in deep, dark caves where they are safe from predators*
- *To chase fast-flying insects and travel far*

9. Who am I?
Clue: I can smell my food from a long way off and I don't have to echolocate.

Bonus Questions:
- *Why do many of these bats not need to echolocate?*

- *Why is a good sense of smell important?*

I am a fruit-eating bat.

- *They don't live in caves and echolocation isn't necessary for finding fruit.*
- *To smell ripe fruits, because color can't be seen in the dark*

10. Who am I?
Clue: My tongue is long and my wings allow me to hover.

Bonus Questions:
- *Why does this bat need to be able to hover in flight?*

- *What is the value of a long tongue?*

I am a nectar-eating bat.

- *To visit flowers rapidly without landing, therefore staying safe from predators*
- *To reach deep into flowers and lap up nectar*

11. Who am I?
Clue: My teeth are flat and my jaws are strong so I can squeeze juice from my food.

Bonus Questions:
- *Why does this bat discard as much pulp as possible?*

- *What is the advantage of having flat teeth?*

I am fruit-eating bat.

- *To get the most nutritious part of the fruit without carrying extra weight*
- *To squeeze out juice without cutting up the pulp*

12. Who am I?
Clue: My nose is long and narrow and my teeth are very small.

Bonus Questions:
- *What is the advantage of small teeth?*

- *What is the advantage of a long, narrow nose?*

I am a nectar-eating bat.

- *Nectar doesn't need to be chewed, so heavy teeth aren't needed.*
- *To reach deep into long, narrow flowers*

Instructions: As you watch the *Discover Bats!* video, use this space to write down all the different eating habits you see:

After viewing, answer the following questions:

1. What was the most interesting eating habit you saw? Why?

2. Why do small fruit- and nectar-eating bats have to hover or snatch food quickly and leave, while large flying foxes land and eat while perched?

3. List the adaptations you saw that help bats catch or find their food more effectively and explain the value of each adaptation?

4. What are the advantages of different species eating different foods?

5. What are the advantages and disadvantages of becoming adapted to feed on one or only a few kinds of food?

Bats Adapt for Food

1. Meat-eating Bat — Carnivore (CAR-nih-VORE)
Body: Large size for capturing and carrying off other animals
Head: Strong jaws for killing prey; large ears help identify and locate a mouse's footsteps or the call of a frog
Wings: Broad, with up to three-foot wingspan; large tail membrane for maneuvering rapidly
Teeth: Sharp molars and long canines for chopping flesh and crushing bone

Bats Adapt for Food

2. Fish-eating Bat — Piscivore (PISK-kah-vore)
Body: Larger than average size; long legs and enormous feet; long, sharp, hooked claws; toes flat for knifing through water; oily fur that sheds water to keep dry
Head: Strong jaws for killing and chewing fish; special echolocation ability to detect ripples or fins on water surface
Wings: Narrow and long for flying fast over water
Teeth: Sharp teeth (similar to insectivores), for chopping and grinding fish

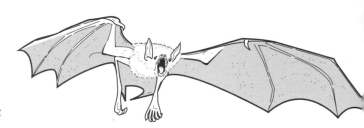

Bats Adapt for Food

3. Blood-eating Bat — Sanguivore (SAN-gua-VORE)
Body: Strong legs for walking on ground or climbing on prey and for jumping into flight when full of blood
Head: Heat-sensitive nose helps find blood vessels closest to prey's skin surface; short pug muzzle makes biting easier
Wings: Broad and short; strong enough to carry heavy food loads with a full stomach
Teeth: Tiny molars; incisors forming large, razor-sharp blades for puncturing prey's skin; grooved tongue for lapping blood; special saliva keeps blood from clotting so bat can keep drinking.
Special: Kidneys allow bat to urinate as fast as it eats to lighten the load before flying home.

Bats Adapt for Food

4. Insect-eating Bat — Insectivore
(in-SECK-tih-vore)
Body: Many body shapes, all small
Head: Many kinds of faces and ears
designed to aid echolocation and hearing
while hunting for insects
Wings: Insectivores that catch insects on the
ground or on plants (**gleaning insectivores**)
have broad, short wings and large tail membranes for darting in and out of branches or
hovering close to the ground.
Insectivores that chase insects in the air while flying (**aerial insectivores**) have longer,
narrower wings and often have smaller ears for speed; some use their tail membrane to help
catch prey.
Teeth: Sharp teeth for grinding and chopping tough insect bodies

Bats Adapt for Food

5. Fruit-eating Bat — Frugivore (FROO-gah-VORE)
Body: Often large with bright colors; most have no
tail and little or no tail membrane
Head: Medium to short snouts; keen nose for
smelling ripe fruit; strong jaws for biting fruit; large
eyes with excellent vision, many don't echolocate
Wings: Wide and short for carrying heavy fruits;
small tail membrane
Teeth: Wide, flat grinding teeth and strong jaws for
crushing fruit—separates juice and spits out pulp;
some have grooved teeth to more easily collect juice

Bats Adapt for Food

6. Nectar-eating Bat — Nectarivore
(NECT-ter-ah-VORE)
Body: Small body
Head: Long, slender snout fits perfectly into
flowers; long, delicate jaw; grooved lower lip and
rough, scaly tongue to catch nectar; excellent vision
and sense of smell
Wings: Short, wide wings with long wingtips for
hovering above flowers
Teeth: Small teeth; not used much for chewing due
to liquid diet

7 Experimenting with Flight

READ ABOUT BATS

Bats are the only **mammals** that fly. Flying squirrels are mammals, but they don't actually fly; they glide. The only other animals that truly fly are birds and insects.

WHY FLY?

Flying is the most efficient and safe way for bats to travel because it allows them hunt more safely. Insect-eating bats catch their **prey** "on the wing" or swoop down to pick insects off plants or the ground, typically without having to touch down. Most fruit-eating bats (all but the largest ones) fly from tree to tree, grabbing ripe fruits and flying off to eat in a safe place, beyond a **predator's** reach. Flying is efficient for bats because it allows them to travel long distances each night. Some fly up to 100 miles (161 km) in a night just to find food.

By flying, bats can get to safe **roosts** other animals can't reach. Finding cracks in a steep cliff or living on a cave ceiling keeps many bats safe from predators. Also, in winter they can fly deep into caves where they **hibernate**, or they can **migrate** long distances to warmer climates.

IS IT A WING OR A HAND—OR BOTH?

The bat wing is an amazing design. In fact, early scientists were so impressed with unique bat wings that they classified bats under the name *Chiroptera* (k'eye-ROP-ter-ah), which means "hand-wing" in Latin. The wing has the same arm and hand bones as humans, but the proportions are different: The arms are similar to ours, while the fingers are much longer.

Bat wings are made of a thin but tough **membrane** that is actually two layers of skin. This membrane surrounds the arm, hand, legs, and tail. Most bats have a thumb that sticks out beyond the membrane so they can hold on to food or roosts.

HAVE YOU EVER SEEN AN ACRO-BAT?

Bats can fold their wing tips like a hand to grab an insect while flying. Sometimes they use their wings like tennis rackets to knock an insect toward their mouth. They also can use their **tail membranes** like nets to scoop up insects. When landing in their roosts, bats flip around in the air to land upside down. When taking off, they simply

Bats move their wings in the same motion that people use to swim the butterfly stroke, cutting through the air the way a person's arms cut through the water.

Animal Wings

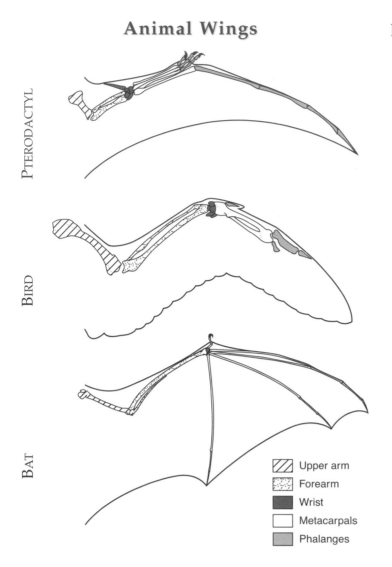

PTERODACTYL

BIRD

BAT

	Upper arm
	Forearm
	Wrist
	Metacarpals
	Phalanges

have to handle lots of air pressure during flight, bats' wings and shoulder muscles are very strong. Their wing membranes also have to resist tearing and puncture by sharp objects, such as thorns and twigs. When they do tear, they heal quickly.

WHAT GOOD ARE WINGS WHEN BATS AREN'T FLYING?

Bat wings have other uses, too. When wrapped around a bat, the wings help keep it warm. The membranes also function as cooling devices when a bat is too hot—extra blood flows into the wings and is cooled by the surrounding air. In cold weather, bats' blood flow to the wings is reduced, conserving heat. Colorful wings also serve as **camouflage** for bats roosting in trees or other exposed places.

IS IT A BAT OR A BIRD?

How can you tell if a flying animal is a bird or a bat? Here are some clues: Birds frequently glide between flaps. Bats rarely glide; they flap their wings constantly. (Little Brown Myotis flap their wings twelve times each second!) While some birds fly, they bring their wings in close to their body. Bats need to keep their wings almost completely extended while they fly, except when they are catching insects.

Most birds are going home as bats are coming out for the night. At dusk, it might be more confusing to tell bats from birds. As bats hunt, they dart here and there chasing insects, so their flying looks erratic and jerky. Night hawks also chase insects at dusk, but they are larger than bats and have a white-colored bar across each wing. If you have the chance to observe bats regularly, you will quickly learn how to identify a bat in the sky in just seconds!

flap their wings, release their grip, and fall slightly to gain speed.

ARE ALL BATS' WINGS THE SAME?

Bats that fly fast have long, narrow wings. For example, free-tailed bats need such wings to quickly chase and capture moths high in the sky. Some bats hover slowly like helicopters to feed at flowers or catch insects from the ground. These bats have short, broad wings.

HOW DO BATS FLY?

Bats move their wings in the same motion that people use to swim the butterfly stroke, cutting through the air the way a person's arms cut through the water. Because they

Overview

Students study the structure of bat wings, then make a glider model of a Mexican Free-tailed Bat.

Skills
Anatomy, flight mechanics, design, following directions

Video Connection
Part One: *Discover Bats!* How They Live, 12 minutes

Time
One activity period

Activity

1 Class views Part One of the *Discover Bats!* video, paying special attention to how different bats fly.

2 Teacher hands out "Read About Bats" background information for students to read aloud or independently.

3 Teacher hands out 7-A: Bat Glider Instructions and 7-B: Bat Glider Pattern. Students color the Mexican Free-tailed Bat and then follow the instructions for cutting and building a bat glider.
Note: See Appendix A for additional detailed folding instructions.

E **Extension**
Challenge students to study differences in the flight, behavior, and habitats of bats with wings that are short and broad and bats with wings that are long and narrow. Compare the wings of bats that migrate long distances such as Mexican Free-tailed Bats with those that don't, such as California Leaf-nosed Bats.

Materials

1 Video, Part One

2 "Read About Bats" background information
(one copy for each student)

3 7-A: Bat Glider Instructions
(one copy for each student)

7-B: Bat Glider Pattern
(one copy for each student)

Colored pencils or crayons, scissors, tape, glue, hobby knife
(optional)

E See "Extension" of Lesson 8: Imitating Echolocation, for a list of bat species to investigate
(page 62)

Instructions:

- **Step 1.** Cut along all solid black lines. A hobby knife (X-acto®) may be useful to cut the U shape of the ears. Otherwise, sharp, pointed scissors will be needed to pierce the paper.

LEGEND	
Cut along these lines	————————
Fold up (printed sides together) along these lines	— – —— – —
Fold down (blank sides together) along these lines	····························

- **Step 2.** Fold up (see legend) along the bat's backbone and crease the center dotted line. Be sure the wingtips match before you crease the paper. Your bat is now folded in half with the blank side of the paper exposed.

- **Step 3.** Choose a side and position your bat so it is flat on the desk or table with its tail pointing toward you. Starting with the first flap, bend each flap down along the dotted lines. Continue folding over each flap until the word "keel" is exposed.

- **Step 4.** Flip the bat over and repeat step 3 on the opposite side.

- **Step 5.** Fold down along the line from the tip of the nose to the shoulder. Allow the ears to remain flat.

- **Step 6.** Flip the bat over and repeat step 5 on the other side.

- **Step 7.** Tape or glue the keel together. The keel is designed like a keel on a boat; it will help weight and balance your bat glider so it will fly correctly.

- **Step 8.** Unfold the bat along its center and place it on its back. Tape or glue each side of the body to the wings.

- **Step 9.** Carefully fold down along the dotted lines on each wing (approximately 45 degrees).

- **Step 10.** Check the symmetry of your bat glider; it should be even on both sides.

- **Step 11.** Flight! Toss your bat glider gently. If it dives into the ground, slightly flatten the creases at the elbows. If it turns to one side, increase the angle of the fold at the opposite wingtip (that is, if it turns right, increase the fold angle of the left wing edge). Have fun!

flap

keel

flap

keel

8 Imitating Echolocation

READ ABOUT BATS

Have you ever been in total darkness? One of the only places you can experience it is in a cave, although a closet or a dark, cloudy night might come close. Can you imagine moving around and finding food in total darkness? Even though you have good eyesight, you would have a hard time. Bats can see as well as other animals, but vision isn't enough. Many bats have a special ability, called **echolocation** (ECK-oh-low-KAY-shun) that helps them **navigate** in total darkness. Echolocation is a way of "seeing" with sound.

Echolocation is a way of "seeing" with sound.

HOW DOES ECHOLOCATION WORK?

Bats use sound as a kind of flashlight in the dark. They send out **high-frequency** sound waves which bounce off all objects in their path and echo back to them. Based on the time it takes for the echoes to return, bats can tell how far away an object is. And, based on the returning sounds, bats can tell the size and shape of an object. Some bats can detect objects as fine as a single hair.

Bats send pulses of sound ("beeps") when they echolocate. Many bats send their "beeps" out through their mouths. Some use their nose and a **nose leaf** to send the sounds. A nose leaf is a fleshy triangle on the nose that the bat uses as a sort of "radar dish" to direct its sound beeps. Most bats use **ultrasonic** sounds to echolocate. These sounds are too high for humans to hear, though young children often hear some bat sounds.

DO YOU WONDER WHY BATS HAVE SUCH STRANGE EARS?

Bat ears are specially designed for echolocation and for hearing faint sounds made by **prey**. A small flap in the ear, called a **tragus**, may help direct the incoming echoes. The tragus may also help protect the bat's sensitive ears from its loud echolocation beeps. Some echolocation calls are so loud that, if we could hear them, they would be as loud as a smoke alarm!

WHICH BATS USE ECHOLOCATION?

All **microbats** use echolocation. Bats that hunt insects and fish use it most. Microbats that eat **nectar** and fruit also use echolocation, but mostly to avoid obstacles as they fly. All bats that enter the total darkness of caves must rely on echolocation to get around inside.

Megabats cannot echolocate, except for one small group that uses a special kind of echolocation. This group produces sounds by clicking their tongues. They use the tongue-click echoes to get around in their dark cave roosts. When they are outside, they rely mostly on their eyes to find fruit and nectar to eat. All megabats see extremely well in the dark.

How Do Bats Hunt Night-Flying Insects?
When an insect-eating bat is searching for prey, it sends out 10 or 20 echolocation beeps per second and listens for returning echoes. These search calls are "broad band," meaning the calls cover a wide range of **frequencies**. Such calls tell the bat about a large area but do not provide many details. When the bat locates prey, it beeps faster and faster and narrows the frequencies to get more information. The bat can speed up its beeping sounds, sometimes up to 200 beeps per second, until it zeroes in for the catch.

You can simulate the difference between broad-band and narrow-band calls with an adjustable-beam flashlight. A wide-angle beam will light a large area, but it is difficult to see details. A narrow beam will light only a small area, but details will be much easier to see.

Some insects can hear echolocation sounds when the approaching bat is still more than 100 feet (30.3 m) away. This gives them a chance to escape by flying away, diving into bushes, or falling to the ground.

Bats have developed some tricks of their own for catching insects. For one thing, some bats, such as the California Leaf-nosed Bat, catch everything they can with vision alone or by listening to footstep or wingbeat sounds made by insects. When these bats do use echolocation, they use faint beeps that cannot be heard from very far. This way, they can catch bugs by surprise. A few bats use far higher or lower echolocation frequencies than most other bats, so insects tuned to listen for typical bats cannot hear

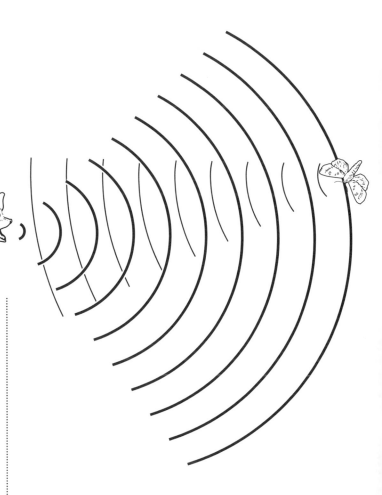

these bats coming and are easily surprised.

WHAT ARE OTHER USES OF ECHOLOCATION?

Some other animals also use echolocation. A few birds, rodents, and insects can echolocate. Whales and dolphins use echolocation to navigate in the ocean. Along with bats, they are the most sophisticated users of this approach to navigation.

Humans have developed machines that imitate echolocation. For example, sonar or "depth-sounding" equipment is used on ships for locating objects under water. Scientists can tell how deep the ocean is, where submarines are, and where fish are by interpreting the echoes from pulses of sound.

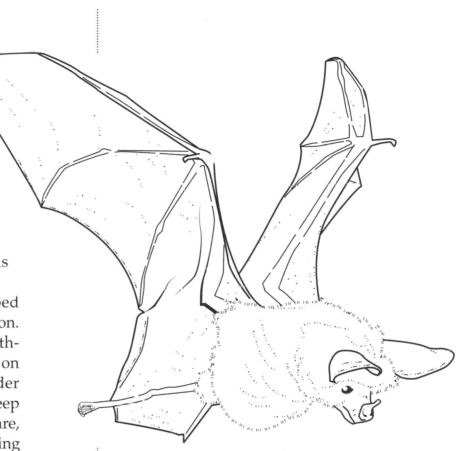

Read More About Echolocation!

Tuttle, Merlin D. 1982. "The Amazing Frog-Eating Bat." *National Geographic*. 161(1): 78-91.

Discover Echolocation on the Internet!

www.batcon.org "BATS *Magazine Archive*."

Fenton, M. Brock. 1991. "Seeing in the Dark." *BATS*. 9(2): 9-13.

Fullard, James H. 1991. "Predator and Prey: Life and Death Struggles." *BATS*. 9(2): 5-7.

Belwood, Jacqueline J. 1988. "Sounds of Silence." *BATS*. 6(2): 4-9.

*Visit BCI's website and search through
25 years of* BATS *magazines.*

Overview

Students participate in an echolocation experiment, using the scientific method to gain an understanding of echolocation and to learn about animal adaptive strategies.

Skills

Conducting an experiment, using the scientific method, participating in a navigation simulation, collecting and interpreting data, analyzing adaptive behavior

Video Connection

Part One: *Discover Bats!* How They Live, 12 minutes

Time

Two activity periods

Activity 1

Materials

1

Class views Part One of the *Discover Bats!* video, paying special attention to the behavior of echolocating bats.

1

Video, Part One

2

Teacher hands out "Read About Bats" background information for students to read aloud or independently.

2

"Read About Bats" background information *(one copy for each student)*

3

Teacher asks the class to identify key points in the video and reading selection. (Teacher may want to include a review of how sound waves form echoes.)

✓ Bats use sounds that *echo* off objects.
✓ Bats can *locate* objects and tell their shape and size from the echoes they hear.
✓ Bats have special ears so that they can hear extremely well.
✓ Bats can change how they echolocate to get general or specific information.
✓ Listening for bats is an *adaptation* that some insects use to avoid being eaten.
✓ Most bats, but not all, use echolocation.
✓ Other animals and humans use echolocation, but humans need machines to do it.

4

Teacher hands out 8-A: Investigate This! (two pages) and tells the class that during the following class period they are going to learn about bat echolocation by conducting an experiment. Teacher then explains that there are two tests in the experiment and that each test will be repeated three times, because scientists repeat tests in order to check results in the same way students might check their math.

4

8-A: Investigate This!, two pages *(one copy for each student)*

8 *Imitating Echolocation/Discover Bats!*

Activity 2

1

When class reconvenes, teacher assigns the following roles to various students for the experiment:

— One to three bats
  (If more than one bat is chosen, each does one hunt in each test.)
— Two to four scientific data collectors
— Four to six observers/boundary guards

—Three or four trees
— One timekeeper
— The rest of the students are insects (four or more)

Note: Students can switch roles, giving them opportunities to play other parts.

2

Teacher reviews the responsibilities and expectations for each of the roles (as they are listed on page 1 of 8-A: Investigate This!). Teacher demonstrates how bats can narrow the band of their echolocation calls to home in on insects and emphasizes how insects and trees within range must respond.

3

Teacher leads a discussion about adaptive behavior which might include the following questions:

✓ What strategies could the "Bat" use that may be the same as strategies that real bats use? (e.g., The "Bat" can use its echolocation sparingly so the "Insects" can't hide as easily. The "Bat" can also speed up the rate of beeps as it gets closer to its prey to track its moves.)

✓ What strategies could each "Insect" use to defend itself that real insects might use? (e.g., The "Insect" can hide behind a tree when a bat approaches, or try to move rapidly to one side to avoid The "Bat's" echolocation calls.)

✓ Can you identify other adaptive behaviors that bats use in predator-prey situations? (e.g., They might listen for footsteps or other sounds from the insect.)

4

Teacher gives each Data Collector and each Observer a copy of 8-B: Calculate This! (two pages) and reviews their responsibilities and where data should be recorded.

5

The class follows the Get Ready, Get Set, and Go steps on 8-A: Investigate This! to conduct the simulations.

6

After the simulations are over, the Observers discuss observations with the class, Data Collectors present the results of the simulations and help lead a discussion of the results with the entire class. Students use the "Discussion and Conclusion" questions at the bottom of 8-B: Calculate This! to review what they have learned about echolocation. The conclusion should be stated in language that directly relates to the question.

Materials

1

A scarf, a stopwatch, clipboards *(optional)*, 3 or 4 chairs to represent trees, and ropes or flagging tape to identify simulation boundaries

4

8-B: Calculate This! *(one copy for each Data Collector and each Observer)*

6

8-B: Calculate This! *(enlarged or rewritten on the board)*

E

Extension

Note: There are two kinds of insect-eating bats: "foliage-gleaners" and "aerial insectivores."

*The **foliage gleaners** hunt stationary prey, using excellent night-vision or listening for mating songs, footsteps, or even chewing sounds. Insects are plucked directly from the ground or from plants. These bats have highly developed vision and/or hearing. They have big eyes or ears and generally use very low-intensity (faint) echolocation calls.*

*The **aerial insectivores** hunt moving prey, catching insects in flight. They have very sophisticated echolocation abilities and generally use high-intensity (loud) echolocation calls.*

Challenge students to observe local insects (e.g., crickets, katydids, moths, flying ants, mayflies, mosquitoes) and predict which ones would be most at risk from foliage-gleaning bats and which would be most at risk from aerial insectivores. Have students research one insect-eating bat from each group (foliage-gleaning and aerial insectivore) and describe how its external characteristics (wing shape, facial features, etc.) help it catch its favorite insect prey.

Bat Species to Investigate:

<u>Foliage Gleaners</u>
- ✓ Northern Myotis
  (Myotis septentrionalis, Myotis keenii)

- ✓ Pallid Bat
  (Antrozous pallidus)

- ✓ California Leaf-nosed Bat
  (Macrotus californicus)

<u>Aerial Insectivores</u>
- ✓ Mexican Free-tailed Bat
  (Tadarida brasiliensis)

- ✓ Little Brown Myotis
  (Myotis lucifugus)

E

Appendix B for bibliography of reference resources

Student "Field Journals"

ROLES FOR THE ECHOLOCATION SIMULATION

Trees (3-4)

- Trees sit on chairs, 6 feet apart, so Insects and Bats can move between them.
- Trees wait to choose a place to sit until after the Bat is blindfolded.
- When the Bat says "beep" in the direction of a Tree, the Tree responds by saying "tree." Trees must watch the Bat's arms to know if they should respond. More than one may respond at once if the Bat's "beam" is very wide.

Insects (4 or more)

- Insects scatter themselves among the Trees.
- When the Bat says "beep" in the direction of an Insect, the Insect responds by saying "insect." Insects must watch the Bat's arms to know if they should respond. More than one may respond at once if the Bat's "beam" is very wide.
- In Test One, Insects cannot move at any time during the simulation.
- In Test Two, Insects may take 3 steps in any direction after responding to the Bat's "beep."
- Insects are "caught" when they are tagged by the Bat.
- Caught Insects must leave the area or sit down along the boundary.

Bat (1-3 — only one bat may participate in each hunt)

- Bat is blindfolded before hunt begins.
- Bat echolocates by saying "beep" and waiting for an answer (either "tree" or "insect").
- Bat "focuses" its call by holding its arms out to symbolize the area over which it is calling. The Bat can narrow its call and "home-in" on an insect by bringing its arms closer together. It can also increase its beep rate.
- Bat must try to avoid Trees. If it runs into a Tree, it is knocked down and the hunt is over.
- Bat catches an Insect by reaching out and tagging it.

Timekeeper (1)

- Timekeeper says "dusk" to start and "dawn" to stop each hunt during both tests.
- Timekeeper has a stopwatch and limits each hunt to 60 seconds (1 minute).

Data Collectors (2-4)

- Before beginning the simulation, Data Collectors record the class predictions about the outcome of each test, and the number of insects available to the Bat during each hunt, on 8-B: Calculate This!
- During each hunt, Data Collectors count the number of insects "caught" and record the totals in the appropriate boxes.
- After each test is complete, Data Collectors calculate the average number of insects caught during the test.
- After both tests are complete, Data Collectors present the results during class discussion.

Observers/Boundary Guards (4-6)

- Boundary Guards hold ropes or flagging tape to designate the simulation boundaries.
- Observers record Insect and Bat behavior during each hunt on 8-B: Calculate This! and share their observations during class discussion.

PERFORMING THE ECHOLOCATION SIMULATION

GET READY

■ Everyone should have a role: Bat, Insect, Tree, Timekeeper, Observer, Boundary Guard, or Data Collector.
■ Each Data Collector and each Observer has a copy of 8-B: Calculate This!
■ The class predicts the outcome for each test. Data Collectors record the predictions on their sheets.

GET SET

■ The Bat is blindfolded.
■ Trees are positioned in the simulation area.
■ Insects are spread out among the Trees.
■ Timekeeper stands on the edge of the simulation area.
■ Data Collectors stand on opposite sides of the simulation where they will have good views of the action.
■ Observers help Boundary Guards set up ropes, and then get set to observe what happens.

GO!

■ Timekeeper says "dusk" to start the hunt.
■ Bat begins echolocating to find Insects and avoid Trees.
■ Trees and Insects respond appropriately to Bat echolocation calls.
■ Data collectors record the numbers of insects caught, and Observers record any notes on bat and insect behavior.
■ Timekeeper says "dawn" to end the hunt.
■ Teacher helps class "Get Set" for the next hunt, until all three hunts in both tests have been completed. After the experiment, Data Collectors present the results to the class, Observers discuss their observations, and the class discusses the questions at the bottom of 8-B: Calculate This!

Instructions:

- Read the Question below aloud to the class, and record the class predictions to fill in the blanks under **Hypothesis** below.

- Data Collectors record the number of Insects available to the Bat for both Tests in the appropriate Data sections below.

- Data Collectors record the actual number of Insects "caught" during each hunt and the average for both Tests using the appropriate boxes in the Data sections below.

QUESTION:

- Will the Bat be able to catch more Insects when the Insects **can** hear a Bat's echolocation call or when the Insects **cannot** hear?

HYPOTHESIS:

- The Bat will catch more Insects when the Insects **can**/**cannot** (*circle one*) "hear" and try to avoid the Bat's echolocation call.

    Test One: The Bat will catch _____ Insects in one minute.

    Test Two: The Bat will catch _____ Insects in one minute.

DATA AND OBSERVATIONS: DATA Test One: Insects **cannot** hear the Bat

Insects	Hunt #1	Hunt #2	Hunt #3	Total	Average (Total ÷ 3)
Available					
Caught					

DATA Test Two: Insects **can** hear the Bat

Insects	Hunt #1	Hunt #2	Hunt #3	Total	Average (Total ÷ 3)
Available					
Caught					

OBSERVER INSTRUCTIONS

- Observers note information about the Bat and/or Insect behavior during the Tests in the appropriate Observation sections that follow.

OBSERVATIONS Test One: Insects **cannot** hear the Bat:

1. Interesting Insect behavior:

2. Interesting Bat behavior:

OBSERVATIONS Test Two: Insects **can** hear the Bat:

1. Interesting Insect behavior:

2. Interesting Bat behavior:

DISCUSSION AND CONCLUSION:

1. How did the number of Insects caught in Test One (Insects **cannot** hear the Bat) compare to the number of Insects caught in Test Two (Insects **can** hear the Bat)?

2. What Bat strategies worked best during the simulations?

3. What Insect strategies worked best during the simulations?

4. Write a conclusion that answers the original question: "Will the Bat be able to catch more Insects when the Insects **can** hear a Bat's echolocation call or when the Insects **cannot** hear?"

9 Comparing How Animals Survive Winter

READ ABOUT BATS

Have you ever wondered what animals do to prepare for winter? Even though they don't have a calendar, they are perhaps more aware of changing seasons than people are. They can detect gradual changes in their **environment** that tell them winter is coming. Most animals are very sensitive to shortening days, because they must prepare far in advance of visible weather changes. When the weather does change, often suddenly, they must be prepared. Each **species** of animal has a slightly different strategy for surviving the winter.

HOW DO ANIMALS SURVIVE COLD WINTERS?

It is hard for animals to survive winter. It takes extra energy to keep warm. New energy can be created only by eating more, but in winter there are fewer food sources. Animals have many ways of dealing with cold weather and less food. Some animals avoid winter by traveling to a place where food is available all winter long. This is called **migration** (my-GRAY-shun). Some animals grow heavy coats of fur to protect them against freezing temperatures. These animals can survive the winter by switching to different food sources that are available during harsh weather. Some animals, like squirrels, store summer foods that they can use during the winter months. Other animals **adapt** physically so they will be able to live on little or no food during this season. Some will save energy by becoming inactive for short periods in a sleep-like state called **torpor** (TOR-pur). Still others will go into a much deeper sleep that lasts most of the winter. This is called **hibernation** (HIGH-bur-NAY-shun).

Animals often use a combination of these strategies to survive winter, and each has different advantages and disadvantages. Many animals migrate long distances and remain active year-round. Some hibernate without migrating and some migrate to find safer places to hibernate. Others remain active in their summer **habitats** all winter, relying on a combination of strategies.

To migrate, an animal needs

> *It is hard for animals to survive winter. It takes extra energy to keep warm, and there is less food. They must adapt or die.*

to know where to go and must have the strength and energy to get there. Mexican Free-tailed Bats migrate as far as 1,000 miles (over 1,600 km) to warmer climates. That's a distance equal to about half the United States from coast to coast, or almost the full distance from North Dakota to Texas! In a car, it would take your family about 15 hours to drive that far. When bats make long trips, they probably watch stars, rivers, and mountains to **navigate**. Migrating bats face many dangers. Some simply run out of energy and die. Others get lost and die when they are blown off course by storms. Still others are caught by **predators**.

By hibernating, animals avoid starving or freezing during extremely cold weather. They also avoid the dangers of migrating. Hibernating animals change their bodies dramatically. Their breathing and heartbeat become very slow, and their body temperature drops to that of the surrounding air. They often look as if they were dead, but in fact, they are just being very careful to use only the energy needed to stay alive until spring comes and food is available again.

HOW DO ANIMALS STORE AND USE ENERGY?

The only energy source most animals have during hibernation is the fat they have stored in their bodies. Some bats will store so much fat that they can actually double their body weights! When a bat is hibernating deeply, it hardly burns any fat. In fact, a Little Brown Myotis stores enough fat each fall to hibernate for more than four years if it only had to wake up once. Waking up costs a lot of fat: an amount that would last for about 30 days of normal hibernation. All hibernating bats must wake up periodically, though. They need to drink water or move to other places within the roost.

If a bat has to wake up just a few extra times during its hibernation period, it may run out of fat before spring. Tens of thousands of bats die every year because disturbances caused by people make them wake up. For this reason, bat caves need protection. Without protection, more bats will become **endangered**. That means there won't be enough bats to do the jobs for which we rely on them, such as eating insects. The good news is that where bat hibernating caves are protected, bat populations are beginning to recover.

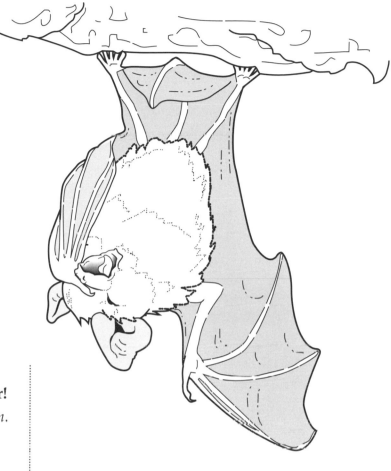

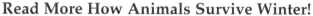

Read More How Animals Survive Winter!

Bennett, Paul. 1994. *Nature's Secrets: Hibernation.* Thompson Learning, 32 pages.

Facklam, Margery. 1989. *Do Not Disturb: The Mysteries of Animals Hibernation and Sleep.* Little Brown and Company, 47 pages.

Pope, Joyce. 1993. *Nature Club: Animal Journeys.* Troll Associates Publishers, 31 pages.

Discover How Animals Survive Winter on the Internet!
www.batcon.org "BATS *Magazine Archive.*"

Tuttle, Merlin D. 1994. "Saving Our Free-tailed Bats." *BATS*. 12(3): 12

Tuttle, Merlin D. 1991. "How North America's Bats Survive the Winter." *BATS*. 9(3): 7-12.

Walker, Steve. 1995. "Mexico-U.S. Partnership Makes Gains for Migratory Bats." *BATS*. 13(3): 3-5.

Visit BCI's website and search through 25 years of BATS *magazines.*

Overview

Students learn that bats and other animals have a variety of adaptive strategies for surviving the hardships of winter and that each of these strategies has advantages and disadvantages. These adaptations allow more animals to share habitats without competing for resources.

Skills

Hypothesizing, comparison, problem solving, discussion, understanding adaptations

Video Connection

Part Two: *Discover Bats!* Where They Live and What They Do, 14 minutes

Time

One activity period

Activity

1 Class views Part Two of the *Discover Bats!* video, paying special attention to how bat hibernate.

2 Teacher hands out "Read About Bats" background information for students to read aloud or independently.

3 Teacher explains that students are going to investigate how different animals survive winter. Teacher hands out 9-A: Investigate This! Students follow instructions on sheet, completing the exercise in small teams or independently.

4 Teacher leads a discussion with class about the advantages and disadvantages for each winter strategy listed. (See Appendix A for answers.) Students should be encouraged to come up with their own ideas about additional advantages and/or disadvantages.

Materials

1 Video, Part Two

2 "Read About Bats" background information
(one copy for each student)

3 9-A: Investigate This!
(one copy for each student or team)

4 Appendix A for answers to 9-A: Investigate This!

5

Teacher explains that bat species use many hibernation strategies. Teacher hands out 9-B: Sharing a Hibernation Cave (two pages) and 9-C: Investigate This! Students follow instructions, completing the exercise independently or in small teams.

6

In summary, teacher leads a discussion with the class about the advantages and disadvantages of each hibernation strategy for the bats listed on 9-B: Sharing a Hibernation Cave.

Emphasize that by adapting different cold tolerance, clustering behavior, and fur types, these three species can live together in a single hibernation cave without competing for food as they come and go in fall and spring, and without competing for roosting space as they hibernate. Furthermore, each species requires about the same amount of fat, relative to its size, to survive winter, meaning that all these strategies work equally well. By the same token, people can be equally happy and successful, despite relying on different occupations or lifestyle strategies. In fact, by being diverse, more of us can share the same town, just like more bats can share the same cave.

E

Extension

Challenge students to investigate how humans are adapted for different habitats. For example, have them find photographs of Eskimos (who live in very cold climates) and Masai (who live in very hot climates). What physical differences are immediately apparent? The chunky bodies and short arms and legs of Eskimos expose less skin surface in relation to body mass to the air and thus help them stay warmer. Conversely, the extremely slender Masai, with their long arms and legs, are adapted to survive better in hot deserts. Their darker skin color also helps protect them from intense equatorial sun. Students can design research projects to investigate how physical differences seen in humans provide special advantages. Can students correlate temperature or other tolerances with body types? Results can be presented in an oral or written report or as a science fair topic.

5

9-B: Sharing a Hibernation Cave, two pages
(one copy for each student)

9-C: Investigate This!
(one copy for each student or team)

6

Appendix A for answers to 9-C: Investigate This!

E

Appropriate reference articles from natural history magazines *(e.g.*, National Geographic, *etc.)*

Student "Field Journals"

Instructions: Read about animal **adaptations** for surviving winter (1-3) below. Consider the possible advantages and disadvantages of each adaptation. Then read the listed advantages and disadvantages (A-D) and match them to the adaptations (1-3). Some of the listed advantages and disadvantages could apply to more than one of the animals.

I. HOW DIFFERENT ANIMALS SURVIVE THE WINTER

ADAPTATIONS

1. Tri-colored Bats hibernate deep in a cave near where they live in summer. In late summer, they must store enough fat to last for six to eight months, thus avoiding the need to find food in winter.

1. Tri-colored Bats		2. Purple Martins		3. Red Squirrels	
Advantage	Disadvantage	Advantage	Disadvantage	Advantage	Disadvantage

2. Purple martins migrate one to two thousand miles south into Central and South America where they find warm climates and plenty of food in winter. They must store fat for their long trips.

3. Red squirrels rely on several strategies. They put away extra food in summer, store fat and grow heavy fur coats in fall, and live in warm nests and occasionally enter torpor during extremely cold weather in winter.

---

*Match an Advantage
with the Animals Listed Above*

A. These animals usually have enough food in winter.

B. These animals don't have to eat in winter.

C. These animals are especially safe from storms and predators.

D. These animals have more active time to rear young.

*Match a Disadvantage
with the Animals Listed Above*

A. These animals may die before spring if fat is used up during an extra long winter.

B. These animals may run out of energy or get lost before reaching their winter home.

C. These animals may freeze to death or run out of food during extra cold winter storms.

D. These animals may be found and caught by predators at any time of year.

Far more bats can hibernate in a single cave if they have adaptations that permit them to arrive at different times and roost in different places. They need to eat as they arrive and depart, and during hibernation, they must wake up as little as possible so their stored fat can last until spring. If bats have to wake up just once, it will cost them as much stored fat as they would use if they were to remain asleep for two full months. While hibernating, a bat's metabolism and fat use is lowest at the coldest temperatures, but cold air is also the driest. Bats in especially cold places must be very careful not to expose too much body surface to the dry air. Drying out forces bats to waste lots of extra energy waking up to drink. By using different adaptations and behavior, up to eight species of bats can hibernate in a single cave. Let's compare how Big Brown Bats, Tri-colored Bats, and Indiana Myotis do this without competing.

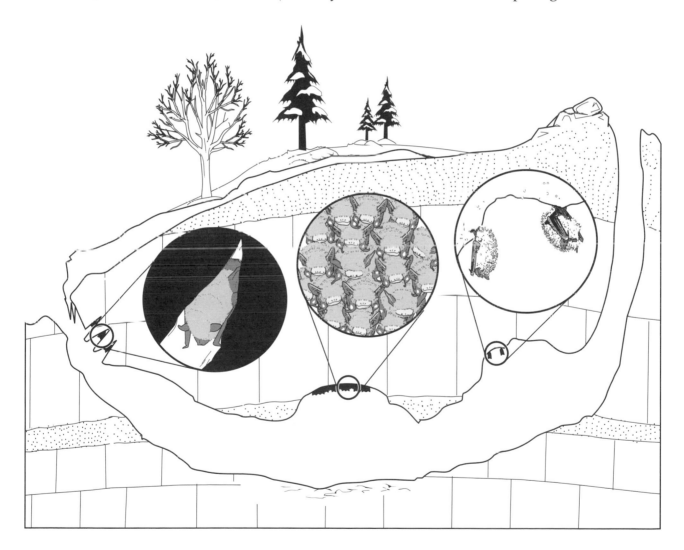

WINTER AIR FLOW IN HIBERNATION CAVES

Cold winter air is heavy and sinks into the lowest entrance, while air warmed by cave walls is lighter and rises from the upper entrance. This causes air to flow through the cave. No bats can hiberate near the second entrance, because it is too warm there.

Big Brown Bats can survive freezing temperatures, enabling them to feed and store fat until December and emerge from hibernation in early March. They squeeze into narrow rock crevices in cave entrances where the temperature is close to 32° F (0° C). Low temperatures keep their metabolism exceptionally low, and crevices help protect them from temperature extremes and from drying out. Nevertheless, they still have to wake up more than any other bats because of the big temperature changes that occur in cave entrances.

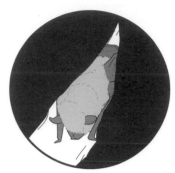

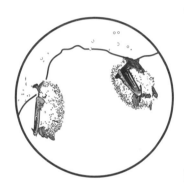

Tri-colored Bats easily freeze to death in cold weather. They must finish storing fat and enter hibernation caves by September or October and can't leave until April or May. They hibernate alone, deep inside, where temperatures are close to 50° F (10° C). Such places are moist with few temperature changes. Tri-colored Bats also have special fur that catches and covers them with tiny water droplets which prevents them from drying out. This enables them to save energy by waking up less than other bats.

Indiana Myotis are less hardy than Big Brown Bats, but less vulnerable than Tri-colored Bats. They enter hibernation caves in October or November and leave in late March or early April. They cluster together at 300 per square foot (over 3,000 per square meter) on cave walls, exposing only their noses, wrists, and ears to dry air. Being so close together, when one wakes up, they all do, but this allows them to share body heat and save energy. They choose temperatures close to 45° F (7° C), where temperature changes are less than in cave entrances, but more than farther inside.

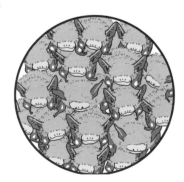

Instructions: Use 9-B: Sharing a Hibernation Cave to answer the following questions. Be sure to explain your answers.

1. Are Big Brown Bats, Tri-colored Bats, and Indiana Myotis likely to compete much for food as they arrive and depart from their cave?

2. Would these three species ever compete for roosting space?

3. Which two species wake up the most often, and which one of these species uses the most fat each time?

4. Which of these three species can sleep the longest without waking up?

5. Which of these three species uses the least fat while asleep?

6. Which species requires the most fat each time it wakes up?

7. Which species uses the most fat during its entire winter period of hibernation, and how does it solve that problem?

8. Based on the length of its hibernation period, which species do you think uses fat the least rapidly, and how does it accomplish this?

10 Recognizing Bats in the Balance of Nature

As bats take what they need from their habitats, they also play a major role in keeping ecosystems healthy and in balance.

READ ABOUT BATS

Did you ever wonder what would happen if there were suddenly no more hawks, owls, or snakes to eat rats and mice, or if there were no more birds or bats to eat insects? The truth is, all animals and plants have important roles in the balance of nature.

Throughout the world, animals and plants live together in a variety of communities called **ecosystems**. The actual area within an ecosystem where an animal lives is called its **habitat**. Many plants and animals share unique habitats within each ecosystem, and they all must interact to take care of their basic needs—food, water, shelter, and space. No animals could survive without plants. Animals, from insects to deer, eat plants directly, and they in turn become food for other animals. In each ecosystem, plant-eaters keep the plants in balance, and **predators** keep the plant-eaters in balance.

HOW DO SCIENTISTS STUDY THE BALANCE OF NATURE?
Scientists called **ecologists** have placed all living organisms into categories based on how they produce or consume energy. Plants are the **primary producers** of energy. Animals that eat plants directly, such as insects and rabbits, are called **primary consumers**. Bats and hawks that eat these primary consumers are **second-level consumers**. If a hawk catches an insect-eating bat instead of an insect or a rabbit, in that case, the hawk becomes a **third-level consumer**. Finally, if the hawk is then eaten by a bobcat, the bobcat becomes what ecologists call a **top-level carnivore**. For nature to stay in balance, there must always be fewer **predators** than **prey** at each level. A bat may require thousands of insects daily to stay alive, or a hawk may have to eat a dozen mice. Very few animals can find enough energy by feeding as top carnivores.

Finally, even carnivores die, and all organisms that die are recycled into new energy for the plants. The almost countless numbers of organisms that recycle energy are called **decomposers** or **detritivores** (dee-TRIT-ih-vores). Bacteria, **fungi**, fly maggots, and other decomposers break down organic matter, dead plants, and animals into new energy that can be used again by primary

area, because they have at least slightly different requirements. Some are carnivores that eat fish, while others eat lizards or frogs. *Carollia* (kah-ROLL-ee-ah) bats eat mostly **piper** fruits near the forest floor, while Jamaican Fruit-eating Bats eat mostly figs in the forest **canopy**. Nectar bats with different shaped noses visit different kinds of flowers. Broad-winged *Tonatia* (toe-NAH-tee-ah) bats pluck katydids from foliage, while narrow-winged free-tailed bats hunt only flying insects above the forest.

In addition to targeting different foods, bats also avoid competition by selecting slightly different kinds of **roosts** in the habitats where they live. For example, in the Costa Rican rain forest several species of bats live in tents they make from leaves, but each prefers to cut a different kind of leaf. *Tonatia* bats live in hollow termite nests. Sac-winged bats live beneath strangler fig vines, and many others live in hollow trees or caves. Those that live in hollow trees have many different requirements. Free-tailed bats like small holes and crevices in the tops of dead trees that rise above the canopy, while *Carollia* bats live in larger hollows near the ground. The more animals specialize in unique lifestyles, the more species can live together in a single area. Bats have **adapted** to live in a wider variety of places and eat a wider variety of foods than any other group of

producers. Scientists who study animal relationships in ecosystems sometimes show the flow of energy from producers to consumers and **carnivores** by drawing **food chains**. To illustrate the role of all of these animals in the flow of energy from plants through consumers to top carnivores, they place the different categories of animals in a **food pyramid**. You can produce your own food chains and pyramids for plants and animals in a Costa Rican **rain forest** or even for those in your own backyard.

How Do Bats Share Similar Habitats in a Rain Forest Ecosytem?

In a Costa Rican rain forest, dozens of species of bats can live in the same small

mammals. Do you suppose that might help explain why there are so many types of bats?

What Rain Forest Animals Eat Bats?

Bats aren't the only animals hunting in the rain forest. Many other predators exist. Hawks can catch bats as they emerge from their roosts at dusk. Later in the evening, owls, snakes, and other **nocturnal** predators hunt bats. Some predators sneak up on roosting bats during the day. A **coati** (coh-AH-tee) is an **omnivorous** raccoon-like mammal that eats a wide variety of food, including plants, fruits, snakes, and even bats. Like all animals, bats face the problem of finding enough to eat while avoiding predators that are trying to eat them.

Does the Variety of Bats Make a Difference for Other Animals?

As bats take what they need from their habitats, they also play a major role in keeping ecosystems healthy and in balance. Lesser Long-nosed Bats are important **pollinators** and **seed dispersers** for night-blooming cactus plants in the Sonoran Desert. Epauletted bats pollinate **baobab** (BAY-oh-bab) trees and are important carriers of seeds for many other trees in African **savannahs**. As pollinators, bats help plants to produce fruits and seeds. And as fruit-eaters they help carry seeds to places where they can grow. Plants, such as the baobab, rely on bats and are essential to the survival of countless other animals. Bats are also important to many of the world's most economically valuable plants. Their products include timber, balsa wood, and medicines, as well as many fruits in our local grocery stores.

In climates with cold winters, only insect-eating bats can survive, but even here they are very important. Without bats by night and birds by day, we could be overwhelmed by insects that eat our crops and destroy our forests. What do you think would happen to us, and to other animals, if insects ate all the plants?

Read More About
Bats in the Balance of Nature!

Sunquist, Fiona. 1992. "Blessed Are the Fruit Eaters." *International Wildlife*. 22(3): 4-10.

Tuttle, Merlin D. 1982. "The Amazing Frog-Eating Bat." *National Geographic*. 161(1): 78-91.

Tuttle, Merlin D. 1986. "Gentle Flyers of the African Night." *National Geographic*. 169(4): 540-558.

Tuttle, Merlin D. 1991. "Bats: The Cactus Connection." *National Geographic*. 179(6): 131-140.

Discover Bats in the Balance of Nature on the Internet!
www.batcon.org "BATS *Magazine Archive*."

Fleming, Theodore H. 1991. "Following the Nectar Trail." *BATS*. 9(4): 4-7.

Thomas, Donald W. 1991. "On Fruits, Seeds, and Bats." *BATS*. 9(4): 8-13

Visit BCI's website and search through
25 years of BATS *magazines.*

Overview

Students learn about ecosytems, habitats, and food chains and how bats help keep ecosystems healthy.

Skills

Listening, reading comprehension, drawing conclusions, analysis, interpretation, plant/animal interactions, predator/prey interactions, food chains

Video Connection

Part Two: *Discover Bats!* Where They Live and What They Do, 14 minutes

Time

Two activity periods

Activity 1

1 Teacher tells students they are going to learn how we and other animals rely on plants and each other to survive. Students are asked to get out a piece of paper, fold it length-wise into thirds, and unfold it to label each third with the following headings: 1) bat species, 2) bat foods, and 3) bat predators.

2 Teacher hands out "Read About Bats" background information for students to read aloud or independently, recording different examples of: 1) bat species, 2) bat foods, and 3) bat predators.

3 Class views Part Two of the *Discover Bats!* video, closely watching and recording different examples of 1) bat species, 2) bat foods, and 3) bat predators.

4 Teacher leads a discussion about the observations students have made regarding the diversity of bat species, bat foods, and bat predators, making a class list on the board or on an overhead transparency *(optional)*.

5 Teacher reviews the concept of "Food Chains" and has students identify the feeding relationships among bats and their prey and among bats and their predators. During the remainder of class time, or as homework, teacher has students identify as many "Food Chains" as possible among their lists of: 1) bat species, 2) bat foods, and 3) bat predators. Students save their lists in their "Field Journals" or on a new sheet of paper.

Materials

1 paper and pencils

2 "Read About Bats" background information *(one copy for each student)*

3 Video, Part Two

4 Overhead projector and transparency *(optional)*

5 Student "Field Journals" *(optional)*

10 Recognizing Bats in the Balance of Nature/Discover Bats!

1

Teacher reviews the concepts of Trophic Levels: Primary Producers, Primary Consumers, Second-Level Consumers, Third-Level Consumers, Top-Level Carnivores, and Detritivores, giving examples of each on the board or on an overhead transparency, such as:

Primary Producers	(autotrophs)	=	algae, fig trees
Primary Consumers	(herbivores)	=	minnows, fruit bats
Second-Level Consumers	(carnivores)	=	fishing bats, tree snakes
Third-Level Consumers	(carnivores)	=	tree snakes, coatis
Top-Level Carnivores	(carnivores)	=	owls, jaguars

Detritivores can derive their energy from any trophic level and include organisms such as bacteria, fungi, earthworms, and scavengers (crayfish, cockroaches, and vultures). Some detritivores can also become food sources for second-, third-, or top-level consumers.

2

Teacher explains how the transfer of energy from one trophic level to another represents a food chain, similar to the food chains that they developed in Activity 1. The actual feeding relationships in any environment involve many organisms at each trophic level, many of which can function in more than one trophic level, depending upon their food source at any given time. All organisms in a habitat or ecosystem can be compared in a complex "Food Pyramid."

3

Teacher has students refer to their "Food Chains," developed in Activity 1, and list other organisms at either end of the chain that may feed on or be fed by the other members of the chain. Now they are beginning to gather information for a "Food Pyramid."

4

Discuss how different species of bats can exist at different trophic levels. This could include:
- ✓ Primary consumers = fruit- and nectar-eating bats
- ✓ Second-Level consumers = insect- and fish-eating bats
- ✓ Third-Level consumers = carnivorous bats

5

Teacher hands out 10-A: Investigate This! and instructs students to identify members of their extended food chains and place them in the proper trophic level on the "Food Pyramid." To simplify the activity, students can concentrate on the Costa Rican rain forest or on animals from a habitat or ecosytem near where they live. See 14-A: Investigate This! and 14-B: Rain Forest Plants and Animals for descriptions of producers and consumers found in a Costa Rican rain forest habitat and see Appendix A for answers to 10-A Investigate This! using organisms found in a Costa Rican rain forest.

Materials

1
Overhead projector and transparencies
(optional)

5
10-A: Investigate This!
(one copy for each student)

14-A: Investigate This! and 14-B: Rain Forest Plants and Animals
(optional)

Appendix A for answers to 10-A: Investigate This!

E1

Extension 1

Challenge students to think about how human actions toward bats can affect food pyramids (i.e., what happens when bats are taken out of an environment). Have students look at their completed food pyramids and answer the following questions for each situation listed below:

✓ Which community members are most affected?
✓ Are effects always negative?
✓ How are bats in particular affected?

Situations:
✓ An important cave for insect-eating bats is destroyed.
✓ The oldest trees in a forest are cut.
✓ Crops are sprayed with pesticides that can kill bats.
✓ Bats are excluded from attics and old buildings.
✓ Too many wild agaves are harvested to make tequila.

E1

Completed copies of 10-A: Investigate This! *(from Activity 2)*

E2

Extension 2

Challenge students to identify the different members of a community of plants and animals in a local habitat, paying special attention to the roles of local bats. Have them list those plants and animals that directly interact with each other by making food chains and food pyramids. (Students may use copies of 10-A: Investigate This! to describe their findings.) Encourage students to explore situations that would interfere with these interactions. What would be the result? How can problems be avoided? Students can summarize their findings in a poster, written or oral report, or as a science fair project. Creative students can present their findings as a mobile with each member of an interaction sharing a balance bar. By removing members from an interaction, students can see what would happen if an organism becomes endangered or extinct.

E2

Student "Field Journals"

10-A: Investigate This! *(optional)*

Food Pyramid

for the _____ Habitat

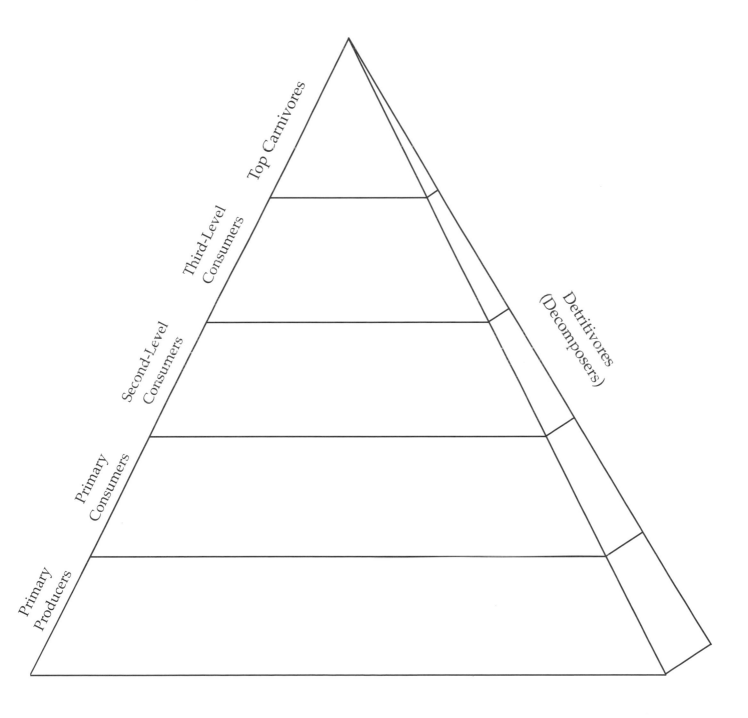

11 Examining Bats in a Desert Ecosystem

READ ABOUT BATS

The Sonoran Desert has big mountain ranges, green river oases (plural of oasis), sand dunes, marshlands, and volcano fields. Most plants that live there, including the **agaves** (ah-GAH-vays) and giant **saguaro** (sah-WAR-oh) and organ pipe **cacti** (CAK-tie, plural of cactus) are tough and spiny. The weather is mostly dry, except for a few weeks each year when heavy rains cause the desert to turn green and burst with flowers overnight. It is scorchingly hot during the day but cold at night.

Desert animals normally avoid the most intense midday heat by being active only at night (**nocturnal**) or at dusk and dawn (**crepuscular**). Ground squirrels, tortoises, and large lizards called Gila (HEEL-ah) monsters often escape into cool burrows. Pack rats build large nests in rocky areas, and coyotes and many birds simply retreat to the shade of trees and shrubs.

ARE CACTUS PLANTS IMPORTANT?

As in all ecosystems, plants and animals depend on each other for survival. The Sonoran Desert is famous for its giant cacti, which include the saguaro and organ pipe. These plants stand 15 to 40 feet (13.5-36.5 m) tall and provide essential homes, food, and moisture for many animals. Hawks and owls nest in their branches, and Gila woodpeckers and other birds nest in their hollowed-out trunks. Many kinds of animals, from hummingbirds, doves, and finches, to bats, pack rats, and squirrels, obtain food and water by drinking nectar or eating the fruits of saguaro and organ pipe cacti.

WHAT DO CACTUS PLANTS NEED?

Giant cacti begin life as tiny seedlings, and in order to survive, they need the shade of desert shrubs, often referred to as **nurse plants**. When the cacti become adults, they rely heavily on bats to **pollinate** their flowers and carry the seeds of their fruits to new locations where they can grow.

The special relationship between **endangered** Lesser Long-nosed Bats and giant saguaro and organ pipe cacti is an excellent example of just how much plants and animals have come to depend on each other. These cacti produce flowers that

The special relationship between endangered lesser long-nosed bats and desert cacti is an excellent example of just how much plants and animals have come to depend on each other.

are perfectly shaped to fit a bat's head like a lock and key. The flowers produce special sugars and odors that appeal to bats, and they open at night to take advantage of the bats' nocturnal habits.

The organ pipe cactus blooms mostly from dusk to dawn and relies primarily on bats to pollinate its flowers. However the saguaro cactus doesn't open its flowers until midnight and keeps them open until the following afternoon. It relies on a combination of bats, doves, hummingbirds, and bees for pollination. This enables it to live farther north where there are fewer nectar-eating bats.

When organ pipe and saguaro cacti produce fruit, bats are attracted from caves up to 30 miles (over 48 km) away. The bats eat the fruits and drop seeds all the way home. This gives the seeds an exceptionally good chance of falling where they can grow. Birds and other animals also eat cactus fruit, but they typically drop seeds nearer to the parent plant.

WHAT DO THE BATS NEED?

In turn, the bat's life is affected by the cacti and agaves. The bats need to find a roosting cave that is as near as possible to the cacti and agaves. Also, because these bats **migrate** north with the advancing season each year, they need to travel through areas where

there will be enough flowering and fruiting plants to fuel their journeys. The bats and the organ pipe cacti and agaves now rely so much on each other that the loss of either could be a serious problem for the other. The saguaro also provides important food for bats. However, it can survive without bats when enough day-time pollinators are present.

How Do Plants and Animals Help Each Other?

The Sonoran Desert **ecosystem** relies on hundreds of kinds of plant and animal relationships. A few are clearly defined. Others are more difficult to understand, and many may still be completely unknown to us. But this is one reason why studying the plant and animal relationships in a desert is so fascinating. More than 60 **species** of agave bloom at night and rely on bats as pollinators. In contrast, the old man's beard cactus also blooms at night, but it produces different odors and nectar and is visited only by moth pollinators. Beautiful red **ocotillo** (oh-coh-TEE-yo) flowers open by day and rely on hummingbirds for pollination. Other day-blooming plants, including the **mesquite** (mess-KEET) and **paloverde** (pal-oh-VER-dee) nurse plants rely on bees and a wide variety of other insects to pollinate their flowers.

In turn, each plant helps feed or shelter different kinds of animals who might not survive without them. Sometimes these animals also help the plants, but sometimes they don't. When deer eat agave flower stalks before they bloom, this harms the plant by preventing seed production. Many hummingbirds, bees, and wasps that visit agave flowers in the morning obtain lots of **nectar** and **pollen** to eat but often provide little pollination service. However, they are not harming the plant, since it has already been pollinated the night before by bats. As you can see, life in the desert depends on a delicate balance of many kinds of animals and plants, all relying upon each other to different degrees as members of a unique ecosystem.

Read More About Desert Ecosystems!

Tuttle, Merlin D. 1991. "Bats: The Cactus Connection." *National Geographic*. 179(6): 131-140.

Discover Desert Ecosystems on the Internet!

www.batcon.org "BATS *Magazine Archive*."

Fleming, Theodore H. 1989. "Climb Every Cactus." *BATS*. 7(3): 3-6.

Fleming, Theodore H. 1991. "Following the Nectar Trail." *BATS*. 9(4): 4-7.

Visit BCI's website and search through 25 years of BATS *magazines.*

Overview

Students will learn about the relationships between plants and animals in a desert ecosystem and the important roles that bats play. To better understand the delicate balance of nature, students will identify various relationships from a drawing and determine whether there are positive, negative, or no effects within each relationship.

Skills

Observation, reading comprehension, critical thinking, hypothesizing

Video Connection

Part Two: *Discover Bats!* Where They Live and What They Do, 14 minutes

Time

Two activity periods

Activity 1

1 Teacher hands out "Read About Bats" background information for students to read aloud or independently.

2 Class views Part Two of the *Discover Bats!* video, looking for realtionships between bats and desert plants.

3 Teacher hands out 11-A: Investigate This! Students are asked to draw lines between animals and plants depicted in the picture that have relationships with each other. They should look for different relationships and not draw lines between every possible combination depicted. For instance, if they draw a line between a bat and a cactus flower, they should not draw a second line between another bat and a second cactus flower of the same kind.

Materials

1 "Read About Bats" background information *(one copy for each student)*

2 Video, Part Two

3 11-A: Investigate This! *(one copy for each student)*

Activity 2

1

Teacher hands out 11-B: Investigate This! Teacher asks students to write down the effects desert animals have on desert plants and the reciprocal effects desert plants have on desert animals by filling out the table. (See Appendix A for answers.)

2

(Optional) Teacher leads further discussion of the roles of different animals in ecosystems, using 11-C: Discuss This!

E

Extension
Challenge students to list the plant/animal relationships in their backyard, local park, or nearby nature area.

✓ Which relationships are positive for both plant and animal?
✓ Are some relationships negative?
✓ What other forces affect each relationship?
✓ What can you do in your yard to encourage positive relationships?

Ask students to summarize their findings in a poster or report.

Materials

1

11-B: Investigate This!
(one copy for each student)

Appendix A for answers to 11-B: Investigate This!

2

11-C: Discuss This! *(optional)*
(one copy for each student)

E

Student "Field Journals"

Instructions: Draw lines between plants and animals that rely on each other. Be prepared to discuss the relationships you have drawn with the class.

❶ Agave, ❷ Mesquite, ❸ Ocotillo, ❹ Old Man's Beard,
❺ Organ Pipe, ❻ Prickly Pear, ❼ Saguaro

Instructions: Write down the effect each member in the plant/animal pairs listed below has on the other, choosing from the following list:
- very positive effect
- little positive effect
- no effect
- negative effect

Pair:	Plant	Animal	Effect of Plant on Animal	Effect of Animal on Plant
1.	organ pipe cactus flowers	bats		
2.	organ pipe cactus flowers	moths		
3.	organ pipe cactus flowers	hummingbirds		
4.	saguaro cactus flowers	birds		
5.	saguaro cactus flowers	bees		
6.	saguaro cactus fruits	bats		
7.	saguaro plants	hawk nests		
8.	old man's beard cactus flowers	bats		
9.	old man's beard cactus flowers	moths		
10.	nurse plant flowers	bees		
11.	nurse plant flowers	bats		
12.	agave flowers	bees		
13.	agave flowers	deer		
14.	agave flowers	bats		
15.	agave flowers	hummingbirds		

Animals and plants affect each other in many ways.

1. Does a mouse, pack rat, or squirrel that eats a plant's seeds harm the plant? What about when they carry seeds off and lose them?

2. What if a deer eats, and thus kills, the first new sprouts of a potential nurse plant, but also eats grass that might have kept other nurse plants and young saguaro cactus from surviving?

3. Is a moth "good" when it pollinates flowers but "bad" when its caterpillar **larva** eat plants?

4. Can you judge whether an animal is "good" or "bad?" Explain.

5. What is the role of humans? What might happen if we:

— disturb or destroy bat caves?

— protect too many deer?

— carelessly allow our pesticides to kill off insects needed to help desert plants reproduce?

12 Exploring Bat Caves

READ ABOUT BATS

Most **species** of bat do not live in caves, but the largest bat **colonies** do. Those that live in caves have very specific requirements. To **hibernate** in caves, bats must find **roosting** places that are quite cool, but safe from freezing. To rear young in caves, they must find places that trap heat so the babies can stay warm while their mothers are out finding food.

The size and shape of a cave makes a big difference in whether or not it meets the needs of bats.

WHAT CHARACTERISTICS MAKE THE BEST BAT CAVE?

In northern or mountain climates of North America, many caves are cool enough for bats to hibernate in during the winter, but they are not warm enough for bats to rear young in summer. In southern areas, many caves are warm enough for rearing young, but are too warm for hibernation. Most caves located in the **temperate** areas in between are neither warm enough nor cold enough for bats to use them. For this reason, bats often **migrate** back and forth between their hibernation caves and those in which they rear young.

The shape and size of a cave makes a big difference in whether or not it meets the needs of bats. A few caves are shaped so they trap either cold or warm air, sometimes both, and this determines how bats can use them. Scientists who have studied **endangered** Gray Myotis have observed that these bats die if they cannot find roosting caves with the right shape and temperature.

DO BATS HAVE DIFFERENT HOMES FOR DIFFERENT SEASONS?

Let's follow a year in the life of the endangered Gray Myotis to understand bats' different needs throughout the seasons. Gray Myotis live in the southeastern U.S., mostly from Kentucky to Tennessee and Alabama, and from Missouri to Arkansas. Each spring, as they leave their cool hibernating caves, they travel to the nearest caves they can find that have temperatures warm enough to raise their **pups**. The warmest caves are usually south of where the bats hibernated. Sometimes, however, there are caves to the north that are shaped to trap warm air and are warm enough for rearing young. Thus, unlike most birds that migrate south in fall and north in spring, Gray Myotis sometimes travel in all directions!

Each mother Gray Myotis bears one baby in early June. A baby will grow most rapidly if it is lucky enough to live either in an extra warm cave or an extra large colony. In the warmest caves, bat pups do not waste energy shivering when their mothers leave to hunt at night, and those that live in the biggest colonies can huddle together with other babies to keep warm. Gray Myotis can use temperatures between 57° and 85° F (14-27° C). Even 57° F (14° C) is too cold for a roost unless the bats are in a large colony where pups can huddle together.

Pups that keep warm grow faster and gain more fat than those that are shivering cold. The fat gives them a supply of energy critical to their survival during fall migration and winter hibernation. It is still hot outside when the bats begin to hibernate, but the caves they seek must already be cool enough to allow bats to lower their body temperatures and save energy. Their roosting sites within the cave need to be cold but not freezing—about 40° to 50° F (4-10° C)—similar to the temperature of your refrigerator at home.

WHAT MAKES A CAVE HOT OR COLD?

To understand why some caves are much warmer or cooler than most, we must first understand that all caves get their internal temperature from the ground around them, unless cooler or warmer air enters from outside. Also, you may be wondering how the ground gets its temperature. If you live in an area where the lowest temperature in winter is about 10° F (-12° C) and the hottest in summer is 100° F (38° C), the ground temperature several feet below the surface will be the average of these. To calculate the approximate ground temperature, we simply add 10 plus 100 (=110) and divide by 2 (=55). This means the ground temperature would be 55° F (13° C). That is the temperature we could expect in all the caves of your area unless they were able to trap cool or warm air from outside. Even if they do trap air inside, the caves will still always be warmer than outside on cold winter days and cooler than outside on hot summer days.

To understand how air enters caves and becomes trapped, you must know two basic facts of science—that warm air is lighter than cool air; and that, therefore, warm air rises when possible. If you have a fireplace at home, notice that the smoke goes up the chimney because it is carried by very hot, very light air that rises straight up. Cooler air is heavier and tends to flow down into low areas. Next time you are at your local grocery store, go to the frozen food section. Many of the frozen foods are kept in long, low containers that are open only at the top. These containers trap cold air, because the refrigerated air is much cooler and heavier than the normal, warmer air in the store.

Caves that slope upward tend to trap warm air, and those that slope downward trap cool air. If they have two entrances, like your chimney at home, which is open at the bottom and at the top, the warm air will rise much more rapidly. This is called a "chimney effect." Also, when warm air rises, it may create a vacuum—an area with less air pressure. The vacuum will draw in any cooler, and thus heavier, air. This explains how some caves "breathe" in different seasons. They draw warm air into high areas where it is trapped because it is lighter, or, they draw cold air into low areas, where it is trapped because it is heavier.

What Do We Need to Know About Caves to Protect Bats?

Understanding how cave shapes affect temperature, scientists can tell which caves are valuable to the endangered Gray Myotis for hibernation or for rearing young. Caves that are exceptionally warm or cool are more valuable to Gray Myotis, and when warm and cool caves are located near each other, they are especially valuable—because the bats do not have to spend as much energy traveling between them during spring and fall migration. The most valuable summer nursery caves are those that are closest to rivers or lakes, because Gray Myotis feed over water. Having water nearby means they do not have to spend as much energy traveling to find food.

For these reasons, summer caves shaped to trap warm air and located near both cool hibernation caves and rivers or lakes for feeding, are the very best for Gray Myotis. Bats living in these caves save much energy because they travel shorter distances while migrating, as well as while going go out to feed each night.

Gray Myotis have become endangered because people have destroyed or disturbed too many of their special caves. Disturbance of a roosting cave during hibernation forces bats to wake up too often. When they wake up, they waste energy from their stored fat, which must last until spring. If too much energy is wasted, they starve to death. When a cave is disturbed too often, the bats die.

The special cool-air-trapping caves that Gray Myotis must have to hibernate are so rare that almost every bat of this species—every Gray Myotis on earth—lives in one of only nine such caves each winter. In fact, more than half live in just one. That means that just a few careless people entering this one cave in winter could kill more than half of all the remaining Gray Myotis. No wonder this species is endangered!

Fortunately, many of the Gray Myotis' most important caves are now protected by special gates, fences, or warning signs that allow bats to use them while keeping disruptive people out. Such protection is very important to this species' survival, since fewer than five percent of all available caves meet their needs. Where these caves are being protected, colonies of this endangered bat are growing, meaning that with continued help, the species can recover.

Read More About Bat Caves!

Gunzi, Christiane. 1993. *Cave Life: Look Closer*, Dorling-Kindersley, New York, 29 pages.

Julivert, Maria Angels. 1994. *The Fascinating World of Bats*, Barrons Juveniles, New York, 31 pages.

Discover Bat Caves on the Internet!
www.batcon.org "BATS *Magazine Archive."*

Anon. 1992. "Protection for Critical Bat Caves in New Mexico." *BATS*. 10(3): 17-18.

Gore, Jeffery A. and Julie A. Hovis. "The Southeastern Bat: Another Cave-Roosting Species in Peril." *BATS*. 10(2): 10-12.

Thorne, Janet. 1990. "Bats and Cavers." *BATS*. 8(1): 10-14.

Visit BCI's website and search through 25 years of BATS magazines.

Overview

Students will learn how knowledge of an endangered species' habitat needs can help scientists save it from extinction. Students will also learn how unique cave shapes trap air of differing temperatures, making some caves cool enough for hibernation and others warm enough for rearing young.

Skills

Experimenting, hypothesizing, introduction to thermodynamics

Video Connection

Part Two: *Discover Bats!* Where They Live and What They Do, 14 minutes

Time

Two activity periods

Activity 1

Materials

Note: These activities would be best to do in a chemistry or science lab where teacher has access to materials and lab tables. Dry ice should be handled with gloves.

1 Class views Part Two of the *Discover Bats!* video.

1 Video, Part Two

2 Teacher hands out "Read About Bats" background information for students to read aloud or independently. Teacher can condense and simplify this information for lower grade levels.

2 "Read About Bats" background information *(one copy for each student)*

3 Teacher demonstrates that cool air is heavier than warm air with the following procedure. First, teacher places about a pound of dry ice in a pitcher of water. (Teacher should wear gloves or use tongs when handling the ice.) As the CO_2 vapor forms in the pitcher, teacher pours the vapor into a clear glass. As soon as the glass is full, the teacher shows how the cold vapor is trapped, too heavy to escape until it is poured out. Next, heat a glass of water until the glass is too hot to hold without a glove. Quickly pour the water out, and while the glass is still hot, pour it full of the CO_2 vapor. As the glass heats the vapor, it will rise out of the glass, and even if poured, continues to rise (for as long as the glass is hot enough to warm it). Changing the water around the ice about every two minutes will keep up a steady production of vapor for 10 minutes or more.

3 about one pound of dry ice

clear pitcher

gloves or tongs for handling ice

Clear drinking glass

1

Teacher fills a clear gallon jug with water, and while partially obstructing the mouth with two fingers, allows the water to slowly pour out, showing the students that as water flows out, a vacuum is created inside, drawing equivalent amounts of air inside. This demonstration shows what happens during summer with airflow through the entrance to Cave I in 12-A: Investigate This! As air is cooled by the cave walls (which are cooler than the outside air), the cooled, heavier air flows out, creating a vacuum which sucks warmer air in along the ceiling. The warmer air is trapped at the highest place in the cave, making that location best for providing the warmth that mother bats need for rearing young. (The reverse occurs in Cave II in winter: heavy, cool air flows in, and is trapped in low places, while it forces warmer air out along the ceiling. This interaction provides a cool hibernating site.)

1

narrow-necked gallon jug of water
(container must be transparent)

2

Teacher hands out 12-A: Investigate This! and 12-B: Investigate This! Students follow instructions to investigate how cave shapes affect airflow, interior temperature, and potential bat use.

Note: It might be easier for students to make determinations about airflow patterns if you tell them that the average ground temperature where these caves are located is 55° F (13° C), an average summer day is 85° F (29° C), and an average winter day is 25° F (-4° C).

2

12-A: Investigate This!

12-B: Investigate This!

3

Students exchange papers and then discuss the correct answers while the teacher uses an overhead projector and transparency copies of 12-A: and 12-B: Investigate This! to explain the airflow in each cave diagram and how it affects bat use. (See Appendix A for answers.)

3

12-A: Investigate This! transparency

12-B: Investigate This! transparency

Appendix A for answers to 12-A: and 12-B: Investigate This!

E1

Extension One
Students estimate the lowest winter and highest summer temperatures for their local area. Students average these numbers to determine the approximate local ground temperature. Teacher explains that most cave-dwelling bats require temperatures of 40° to 50° F (4-10° C) for hibernation and 57° to 85° F (14-29° C) for rearing young. Given their estimates of local ground temperatures, students decide if caves in their area would need to trap cool air to be used for bat hibernation, or trap warm air for rearing young? Could this help explain why bats don't use local caves or which ones they use and when?

E1

Student "Field Journals"

E2

Extension Two

Independently, students can set up a temperature monitoring project at their home to see how their home compares to a bat cave. Have students record the daily maximum and minimum outside temperature at their house using a thermometer. Minimum temperatures should be taken near dawn and maximum temperatures taken in the mid-afternoon (or just use a maximum/minimum thermometer). Next, have students set up monitoring stations in their houses, using two monitoring points, one near the floor and one near the highest point of the ceiling (or in a basement and in an attic). The interior temperatures should be compared with the outside temperatures for each monitoring period. Have students graph their results over a 24-hour or one-week period. Encourage students to predict what their temperature profiles would look like in different seasons (i.e., winter vs. summer, spring vs. fall). Based on what students have learned during this activity, could bats rear young or hibernate anywhere in their house? Why or why not?

E2

Student "Field Journals"

Thermometers
(one for each monitoring point chosen)

graph paper

Instructions: Examine the Cave Diagrams, I through IV, below. Based on what you have learned, circle the correct answer for each of the three choices listed to the right of the cave diagrams, I through IV. In the places where you predict airflow will occur, mark its direction with a blue arrow for cold airflow and a red arrow for warm airflow.

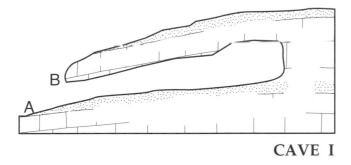

CAVE I

1. Most air flow (in and out) occurs in *summer* or *winter*?

2. Cave will trap air that is *cooler* or *warmer* than the ground temperature?

3. Bats could use this cave for *rearing young*, *hibernation*, or *both*?

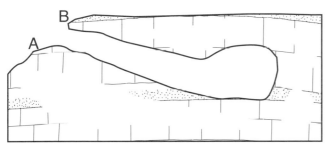

CAVE II

1. Most air flow (in and out) occurs in *summer* or *winter*?

2. Cave will trap air that is *cooler* or *warmer* than the ground temperature?

3. Bats could use this cave for *rearing young*, *hibernation*, or *both*?

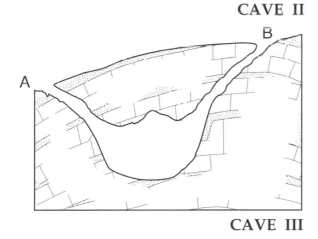

CAVE III

1. Most air flow (in and out) occurs in *summer* or *winter*?

2. Cave will trap air that is *cooler* or *warmer* than the ground temperature?

3. Bats could use this cave for *rearing young*, *hibernation*, or *both*?

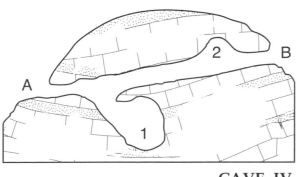

CAVE IV

1. Most air flow (in and out) occurs in *summer*, *winter*, or on the *hottest and coolest days* year round?

2. Cave will trap air that is *cooler*, *warmer*, or *both cooler and warmer* than the ground temperature?

3. Bats could use this cave for *rearing young*, *hibernation*, or *both*?

Instructions: Your job is to predict which caves on 12-A Investigate This! should be protected to help save endangered Gray Myotis. Refer to the cave diagrams I-IV to answer the following questions:

1. Which caves are most suitable for Gray Myotis hibernation? _____

2. Which caves are most suitable for Gray Myotis rearing young? _____

3. In CAVE IV, which location will trap the coolest air and be best for hibernation?

_____

4. In CAVE IV, which location will trap the warmest air and be best for rearing young?

_____

5. Assuming all these caves are located near where Gray Myotis can feed over water, which one would be best for them, considering the energy they must spend to migrate?

_____

6. Can you think of a reason why cold air traps that also have domed ceilings provide bats a safer place to escape freezing during especially cold winter weather?

_____

BONUS QUESTION:

What would happen to the airflow in Cave IV if entrance B were bulldozed shut? How would this affect its usefulness for Gray Myotis to hibernate or rear young?

_____

_____

_____

13 Studying Neighborhood Bats

READ ABOUT BATS

Have you ever seen bats flying around your house at dusk? You probably have bats as neighbors even if you've never seen them. As they flit through the sky, most bats look alike, but it's possible that you may have a dozen different kinds living nearby. Forty-six different **species** live in the United States and Canada. How can you tell which ones live near you?

The first step is to study **range maps**. These are special maps that scientists make to show which species are found in which areas. A bat's "range" is described as how far north, south, east, and west it is found. After you have studied range maps, you can make a list of the different species of bats that live in your area.

Just because a species is known to live in your area, however, doesn't mean that it lives in your neighborhood. The next thing you must consider is your neighborhood **habitat**. Does your habitat have the kinds of **roosts** that bats like? Are there warm roosts for rearing young and cool roosts

for **hibernation** not too far away? Does the habitat support the kinds of insects bats eat?

HOW IS YOUR HABITAT?

Some bats will live in a variety of habitats and can adapt to many different local conditions. For example, Big Brown Bats can be found in all major North American habitats including arid **deserts**, **chaparral** and oak woodlands, grasslands, and both **deciduous** (dee-SID-your-us) and **coniferous** (kho-NIF-er-us) forests. Red Bats, on the other hand, **roost** only in deciduous forest habitats. Gray Myotis have one of the most restricted ranges of all. They live only in deciduous forest habitats along rivers where there are caves.

Good habitats must combine both the roosts and foods that a bat species needs. Some bats, such as the Gray Myotis, roost only in certain kinds of caves. In the summer, they must rear young in warm caves that are 57° to 80° F (14-27° C). In the winter they have to hibernate in cooler caves that stay at 40° to 49° F (4.5-9.5° C). Other bats, such as Pallid Bats, will roost in many different places, from caves and old mines to cliffs, buildings, and tree cavities.

There are some bats that will roost only in trees. Red Bats and Hoary Bats hang in tree **foliage**.

WHAT'S FOR DINNER?

Nearly all North American bats eat insects, though not all bats will eat all insects. Most eat a wide variety of bugs from beetles and moths to mosquitoes and mayflies, but they prefer certain types. Big Brown Bats eat many kinds, but prefer beetles. Red Bats and Mexican Free-tailed Bats prefer moths. Other species, such as the Yuma Myotis and the Little Brown Myotis feed over water on **aquatic** insects, such as tiny flies, mosquitoes, and mayflies. Bats that eat aquatic insects must live near rivers or lakes. Thus, you would not expect to find the Yuma Myotis and the Little Brown Myotis in dry desert habitats that are far away from streams or ponds.

Pallid Bats feed on scorpions and centipedes as well as a wide variety of large, ground-dwelling insects, such as grasshoppers, katydids, and crickets. Instead of catching their **prey** straight out of the air the way a Mexican Free-tailed Bat does, the Pallid Bat picks its prey off the ground or vegetation. The Pallid Bat is not as dependent upon water for finding insects or for drinking, so it can be found in more extreme desert habitats.

Some bats eat insects that are common in forests; other bats eat insects that prey on farmers' crops. Wherever there are roosts near where an abundance of insects can be found, bats are sure to be there. The greater the variety of insects you can find, the greater the variety of bat species.

WHERE CAN I WATCH BATS?

Now that you know more about what kinds of habitats, roosts, and insects bats like, you can decide if your local neighborhood offers a good home for bats. Walk around at dusk on a warm evening to see if bats are catching bugs in the light of a streetlamp, or swooping low over ponds, lakes, or streams. Some bats

might be drinking out of your backyard swimming pool!

If you don't see bats in your neighborhood, it may be because the habitat is not adequate. Sometimes bats can't live where too many **pesticides** are sprayed. Pesticides reduce the amount of food available and may poison the bats. Smoke from fireplaces, campfires, and even exhaust from cars may be driving insects away. Sometimes a habitat might not have enough roosts for bats. Prairies and grasslands have few caves or suitable tree roosts. Bats that live in these areas tend to live in buildings or other man-made structures. New neighborhoods that have few large trees and few crevices in old buildings also may lack roosts for bats. But if you are a patient and careful observer, and understand bat needs, you should be able to find appropriate bat habitat.

Bats are fun to watch, but you should never try to catch bats or handle those that you find. *Any wild animal that can be approached is likely to be sick, and could bite in self-defense. Also, never disturb bats where they are roosting.* This may cause them to abandon their roost and die. When we remember to simply watch from a distance, bats make excellent neighbors.

Read More About Neighborhood Bats!

Ackerman, Diane. 1997. *Bats: Shadows in the Night*. Crown Publishers, New York, 31 pages.

Tuttle, Merlin D. 1997. *America's Neighborhood Bats*. (Rev. Ed.) University of Texas Press, Austin, 98 pages.

Discover Neighborhood Bats on the Internet!
www.batcon.org "BATS *Magazine Archive.*"

Anon. 1991. "A Vacationer's Guide to Bats." *BATS*. 9(1): 3-7.

Fenton, M. Brock. 1991. "Tuning in with a Bat Detector." *BATS*. 9(2): 12.

Tuttle, Merlin D. 1989. "If You Have Bats in Your Bat House and Want to Know What Kind They Are." *BATS*. 7(2): 7.

Visit BCI's website and search through 25 years of BATS *magazines.*

Overview

Students use maps to determine which common bat species might live in their neighborhoods and then assess habitat for different bat needs.

Skills

Data analysis, charting, investigation of resources, evaluating habitats, understanding animal ranges and use of maps

Video Connection

Part Four: *Discover Bats!* Valuable Neighbors, 8 minutes

Time

Two activity periods plus homework

Activity 1

1 Class views Part Four of the *Discover Bats!* video.

2 Teacher hands out "Read About Bats" background information for students to read aloud or independently. Teacher then leads a discussion about the factors that affect where a bat lives: roosts, access to water, type of food, pesticides, etc.

3 Teacher helps students to identify the exact location of their town on a map.

4 Teacher hands out 13-A: Range Maps for Common North American Bat Species (two pages). Students mark each bat range map with an "X" representing the location of their town.

5 Teacher explains that if the "X" falls within the shaded area of the range map, then the bat species for that map is likely to occur nearby.

6 Students compile a written list of all the bat species likely to occur in their area. Students should be prepared to discuss their findings with the entire class during the next activity period.

Materials

1 Video, Part Four

2 "Read About Bats" background information *(one copy for each student)*

3 Map of North America

4 13-A: Range Maps for Common North American Bat Species, two pages *(one copy for each student)*

6 paper and pencil

1

Teacher leads a discussion of North American habitat types and locations mentioning indicator species in each habitat including:

✓ deserts—arid areas, yucca, agave, cacti, thorny bushes; southwest

✓ grasslands—prairies and other mostly grassy areas; midwest

✓ chaparral and oak woodlands—relatively short trees, live oak, evergreen shrubs, juniper; southwest

✓ deciduous forests—tall trees, oak, maple, birch, hickory; east

✓ coniferous forests—tall trees, pine, spruce, fir, cedar, hemlock; north and mountains

2

After the class determines the prominent habitat type in their area, teacher explains different groupings of insects, giving examples of familiar species contained within each, including:

✓ aquatic insects (mosquitoes, caddis flies, mayflies)

✓ flying insects (moths, beetles, flies)

✓ ground-dwelling insects (crickets, katydids)

3

Teacher hands out 13-B: Investigate This! Students work independently or in small groups, following the instructions on the sheet, first crossing out bat species NOT on the class-generated list (from Activity 1) and then making decisions about the types of habitats, food resources, and roosts available to bats in their area, crossing out any other species excluded from the area due to habitat and/or food resource limitations.

3

13-B: Investigate This!
(one copy for each student)

4

Teacher reconvenes the class to discuss the results and to enter the species on 13-C: Investigate This! Teacher writes the list on the board or on an overhead transparency and students work independently or as a group to identify local areas which might include good bat habitat.

4

13-C: Investigate This!
(one copy for each student)

E

Extension

Challenge students to characterize their neighborhood habitat, possible bat roosts, insect diversity, and water resources to predict where good areas to observe bats might be located. During the late spring or early fall, have students monitor these areas on a regular basis for a week, a month, or a season to record bat sightings in their "Field Journals." Encourage students to summarize their findings in a report, science fair project, or oral presentation. How does temperature affect insect and bat activity?

E

Student "Field Journals"

Hoary Bat
Lasiurus cinereus

Silver-haired Bat
Lasionycteris noctivagans

Little Brown Myotis
Myotis lucifigus

Cave Myotis
Myotis velifer

Yuma Myotis
Myotis yumanensis

Evening Bat
Nycticeius humeralis

Pallid Bat
Antrozous pallidus

Canyon Bat
Parastrellus hesperus

Tri-colored Bat
Perimyotis subflavus

Big Brown Bat
Eptesicus fuscus

Red Bat
Lasiurus borealis

Mexican Free-tailed Bat
Tadarida brasiliensis

Bat Food and Habitat Requirements

Instructions: Using 13-A: Range Maps for Common North American Bat Species, locate your town on each range map and decide if the bats from the following list might occur in your area. Cross out the bat species names and the entire row in the table below for all species that do NOT occur in your area. Review the habitat types listed for the bats you have not yet crossed out. Are there any habitat types listed that you know do NOT occur where you live? If so, cross those out as well. Do the same for the roost types and food types that you are sure do NOT occur where you live. Does this eliminate any other species from the list? The remaining bats are the common species which can be found in your area.

Species	Food	Summer Roost	Winter Roost	Habitat Type
Pallid Bat	walking insects	caves/mines, cliffs, tree hollows, buildings	caves/mines, cliffs	desert, oak woodland and chaparral
Big Brown Bat	flying beetles	buildings, tree cavities	caves	all habitat types
Silver-haired Bat	flying flies	tree foliage or cavities	unknown	deciduous and coniferous forest
Red Bat	flying moths	tree foliage	leaf litter, tree hollows	deciduous forest
Hoary Bat	flying moths	tree foliage	tree trunks and cavities	deciduous and coniferous forest
Little Brown Myotis	water insects	buildings, caves	caves/mines	coniferous and deciduous forest, chaparral
Cave Myotis	flying moths	caves	caves	desert, chaparral
Yuma Myotis	water insects	caves/mines, buildings	unknown	desert, grasslands, chaparral
Evening Bat	flying insects	tree cavities, buildings	unknown	deciduous forest
Canyon Bat	flying insects	cliffs, rock crevices	caves	all western habitat types
Tri-colored Bat	flying insects	tree cavities	caves	chaparral and deciduous forest
Mexican Free-tailed Bat	flying moths	caves, buildings	caves (migrates to warm areas and doesn't hibernate)	oak woodlands and chaparral, desert

Needs of Local Bats

Instructions: List the species that occur in your area in the first column below. Then, for each species, fill in the next two columns with what you think they would eat and any specific roosts in your area (for both summer and winter) where they might live.

Species	Food Options	Roost Options
1.		S: W:
2.		S: W:
3.		S: W:
4.		S: W:
5.		S: W:
6.		S: W:
7.		S: W:
8.		S: W:
9.		S: W:

14 Observing How Bats Help Rain Forests

READ ABOUT BATS

Anyone that is fascinated by unique plants and animals would find no place more exciting than a **tropical rain forest**. Can you imagine finding close to 200 kinds of trees and thousands of other plant and animal species in an area the size of an average shopping mall? In fact, you could spend your entire life in a shopping mall-sized section of rain forest and never find them all!

Tropical rain forests grow near the equator, mostly in Africa, Asia, and South America. About half of the world's plant and animal species—more than two million different kinds—live there. The climate is warm and moist. Trees are huge, blocking nearly all sun from reaching the ground. Green leaves, flowers, and fruits are mostly in the treetops, and that is also where most of the animals live. Animals easily climb from tree to tree on vines and large branches that form a network called a **canopy**. This interlocking network also holds the trees together, so they rarely blow down during storms.

All rain forest species have unique roles to play, but no group of animals is more important than bats.

DO ALL RAIN FORESTS HAVE THE SAME KINDS OF ANIMALS?

Each rain forest has its own unique animal **species** that are found nowhere else—for example, pythons and tigers are found in Asian rain forests and boa constrictors and jaguars are found in **Latin American** rain forests. The Amazon rain forest in Brazil and Peru is the largest of all. There, you might see monkeys and marmosets (small, colorful monkeys), parrots and toucans, jaguars and giant anteaters, 500-pound (225 kg) snakes, and toads the size of your head. At night, you would also find an incredible variety of bats. It's a biologist's paradise!

Rain forests are the world's richest **habitats**, but they are also the most fragile. The plants and animals that live there are very dependent on each other. Some flowers, for example, appear to be **pollinated** by just one species of bat. Others require a single species of bee. Round-eared Bats live only in hanging termite nests that they hollow out for homes. Fig trees offer one of the best examples of special relationships between plants and animals. There are more than 750 types of fig trees, and each one is pollinated by a different species of wasp. Each kind of fig tree would die without its one kind of wasp, and the wasps would die without their one kind of fig.

Figs are among the most important foods for rain forest animals, and they rely on bats more than any other animal to spread their seeds around the forest. Bats often eat hundreds of pounds of figs from a single tree, and most have to carry the fruits away before eating. This is because snakes, owls, and other **predators** wait by ripe fruits to catch and eat bats. In order to avoid this danger, bats have to carry fruit to new locations before they eat it. In this way, countless thousands of tiny seeds are transported as well. Seeds that fall directly beneath the parent tree seldom survive, so carrying them away to new places is important.

Many of the largest and most valuable rain forest trees are also pollinated by bats. The giant **kapok** tree blooms at night, and relies mostly on bats to visit its flowers. The tree's many huge, leafy branches and hollow trunk provide homes for hundreds of kinds of insects, frogs, lizards, snakes, birds, and small mammals. But no animal is more important to the kapok than bats. Not only do they pollinate the tree, they **fertilize** it as well. The droppings from bats that live in the kapok's hollow trunk contain nutrients that help the tree grow faster.

All rain forest species have unique roles to play, especially the bats. Approximately half of all the **mammal** species that live in rain forests are bats. In numbers of individuals, they often outnumber all other mammals combined. Bats are as important by night as birds are by day in keeping insect populations in check, and like birds, they are essential pollinators and **seed-dispersers**. In fact, many of the most important rain forest trees and shrubs rely on bats.

Scientists are worried about how to save these complex and threatened **ecosystems**. Rain forests produce so much oxygen that they have been called the lungs of our planet. The giant trees cool the earth and give off huge amounts of water that falls in other areas as rain. Many valuable medicines, food, and other products come from these forests. Without healthy rain forests to restore the earth, we ourselves could become **endangered**.

HOW COMPLEX ARE RAIN FOREST ECOSYSTEMS?

In a tropical rain forest, thousands of kinds of plants and animals depend on each other to survive. Not only do giant kapok and fig trees provide support that helps protect all trees from being blown over in storms, but they also protect trees that grow beneath the canopy from hot sun and wind. In addition, kapok trees provide treetop homes for thousands of kinds of **epiphytic** (EP-ih-FIT-ick) plants (plants that grow on other plants), including many beautiful **bromeliads** (broh-MEE-lee-adds) and orchids. One large tree may support thousands of smaller plants and over a hundred species. In turn, these plants feed thousands of insects that eat their leaves, fruits, or flowers. They also catch rainwater that frogs and insects use for breeding.

Birds, bats, spiders, and other predatory insects consume plant-eating insects so the forest is not overwhelmed by them. Each flowering and fruiting plant feeds some animal that helps pollinate it or spread its seeds, but few benefit as many animals as do fig trees. Many of the animals that eat figs also become food for predators, such as hawks, owls, and jaguars.

WHY SAVE RAIN FORESTS?

Rain forest plants and animals produce numerous unique chemicals that can save human lives. In fact, new medicines from rain forests are constantly being discovered.

Countless other valuable products for people also come from rain forests. Even more important, rain forests have an enormous impact on world weather and oxygen production essential to human life all over the planet. An area of rain forest as large as an average U.S. state is destroyed each year. At this rate, humans may not enjoy the benefits of the rain forests for much longer, unless something is done to preserve this important and beautiful ecosystem.

Read More About Bats and Rain Forests!

Tuttle, Merlin D. 1986. "Gentle Flyers of the African Night." *National Geographic.* 169(4): 540-558.

Discover Bats and Rain Forests on the Internet!
www.batcon.org "BATS Magazine Archive."

Fleming, Theodore H. 1987. "Fruit Bats: Prime Movers of Tropical Seeds." *BATS.* 5(3): 3-5.

Fujita, Marty. 1988. "Flying Foxes and Economics." *BATS.* 6(1): 4-9.

Tuttle, Merlin D. 1983. "Can Rain Forests Survive Without Bats?" *BATS.* Premier Issue (1): 1-2.

Visit BCI's website and search through 25 years of BATS magazines.

Overview

Students learn about the complex interdependence of plant and animal species in a tropical rain forest ecosystem, including the roles of animals as seemingly insignificant as tiny fig wasps.

Skills

Ecology and math, reading comprehension, understanding rain forest ecosystems, calculating animal impacts, introducing global environmental concerns

Video Connection

Part Two: *Discover Bats! Where They Live and What They Do*, 14 minutes

Time

Two activity periods plus homework *(optional)*

Activity 1

1

Class views Part Two of the *Discover Bats!* video, paying special attention to how rain forest plants and animals rely on each other.

2

Teacher hands out 14-A: Investigate This! and the "Read About Bats" background information for students to read aloud or independently. Teacher leads a discussion about rain forest ecosystems including:

✓ Where rain forests are on a world map

✓ The great diversity of species found in rain forests

✓ The fact that different animals are found in all levels of the rain forest from the forest floor to above the forest canopy

✓ The interdependence of rain forest species

✓ The value of the rain forest for weather, oxygen, species richness, medicines, and other products

✓ Threats to the rain forest

3

Teacher hands out 14-B: Rain Forest Plants and Animals (two pages). Students follow instructions to learn about rain forest plants and animals pictured on 14-A: Investigate This! They can work individually or in groups to complete their identifications. Then they trade papers and check their identifications as a class with the teacher, using an overhead transparency copy as a guide. Students keep their corrected copies of 14-A: Investigate This! to use in Activity 2.

Materials

1

Video, Part Two

2

"Read About Bats" background information *(one copy for each student)*

14-A: Investigate This! *(one copy for each student)*

3

Transparency copy of 14-A: Investigate This!

14-B: Rain Forest Plants and Animals *(one copy for each student)*

Appendix A for answers to 14-A: Investigate This!

Activity 2

1

Teacher hands out 14-C: Discuss This! to complete in class (or for homework). Students follow instructions on sheet.

2

Class discusses answers to questions on 14-C: Discuss This!

E

Extension

Challenge students to do research to identify which rain forests are most endangered and why. Hold a discussion to see how important your students think it is to save rain forests. Talk about what each of us and our government can do to help. Students might want to write letters to government agencies, companies, or other groups they believe are most able to help. They could also write letters of appreciation to those groups that are already helping.

Materials

1

14-C: Discuss This!
(one copy for each student)

2

Appendix A for answers to 14-C: Discuss This!

E

Appropriate environamental publications and encyclopedias

Instructions: Learn about the following rain forest plants and animals on 14-A: Investigate This! by labeling all the plants and animals you can find with their identifying numbers and letters.

PLANTS

1. Kapok Tree — a rain forest giant; it provides hollow cavities for many animals to live in, huge branches for epiphytes to grow on, and flowers with nectar to feed bats.

2. Fig Tree — some are giants, others are small; they provide essential food for many rain forest animals, hollows and crevices for homes, and big branches for epiphytes to grow on. Some, like strangler figs, have twisted trunks.

3. Palm Trees — often found beneath the forest canopy; they provide fruits for many animals including birds and people. Bats and other animals often carry their seeds.

4. Epiphytes — plants that grow on the branches and trunks of other plants. Many catch water that is used by tree-top animals and provide homes for many kinds of insects, spiders, and frogs.

   4a. Bromeliads — leafy plants that look like pineapple tops
   4b. Orchids — spindly plants with flowers on stalks

ANIMALS

5. Harpy Eagle — a predatory bird that eats monkeys and other small animals; nests atop tall trees

6. Toucan — a large-billed bird that eats figs and other fruits; nests in tree cavities

7. Parrot — a strong-billed bird that eats figs, seeds, and other fruits; nests in palm tree cavities

8. Flycatcher — a quick bird that eats flying insects; builds nests in branches

9. Owl — a nocturnal bird with big eyes that eats bats and other small animals; nests in hollow trees

10. Jaguar — a large spotted cat that eats many kinds of animals including agoutis; raises its young in hollow logs or rock cavities

11. Monkey — a primate that eats a wide variety of fruits and leaves; lives in the forest canopy

12. Agouti — a large Guinea-pig-like rodent that eats fruits that fall to the forest floor; lives in burrows in the ground

13. Coati — a racoon-like animal that is omnivorous and eats everything from plants and fruits to bats and snakes; an excellent climber and lives in treetops, rock crevices, and caves

14. Nectar-feeding Bats — long-tongued bats that eat nectar; live in caves

15. Fruit-eating Bats — broad-winged bats that eat fruit, especially figs; live in caves and hollow trees

16. Free-tailed Bats — narrow-winged and fast-flying bats that eat insects above the forest canopy; live mostly in caves, sometimes in old dead trees

17. Round-eared Bats — big-eared, maneuverable bats that pluck katydids from the foliage under the canopy; live only in termite nests

18. Gecko — a small lizard that eats insects attracted to bat droppings; lives in hollow trees

19. Tree Snake — a climbing snake that eats small animals like birds, mice, and bats; lives in tree hollows

20. Termite Nest — a large, muddy-looking home built on tree limbs by termites, which eat dead and dying wood.

21. Bees — insects that can be either solitary or social and eat nectar or pollen from orchids and other flowers, often relying on only one or a few species as their main food source; live in tree hollows and build honeycomb nests.

22. Fig Wasps — tiny insects that pollinate the flowers of more than 750 species of fig trees. The majority of fig trees each rely on a different species of wasp for pollination.

Instructions: Using what you have learned about rain forest ecosystems, answer the following questions. Be prepared to discuss your answers with the class.

1. Imagine what might happen if the caves where nectar-feeding bats live were destroyed. With less bat pollinators, kapok trees would produce fewer seeds and might die out. If this happened, how many of the plants and animals in the picture (14-A: Investigate This!) would be affected? Explain.

2. If pesticides accidentally killed fig wasps, would there be any more figs produced? Name the animals in the picture that rely on figs for food. What would happen to them?

3. Name the animals from the picture that do not need to eat figs, but that also would decline if fig wasps were killed.

4. Do predators that eat fruit bats help or harm fig trees? Explain.

5. Insect-eating bats and birds help to control the number of insects. If all the bats died, could the birds still keep insects in balance? What if only birds were lost, could bats keep insects in balance? Explain.

6. If all the rain forests were cut down, could we simply plant more and expect the rain forest to grow back? Why?

7. Most tropical rain forests are a long way away from North America. Why should we worry about losing them?

Bonus Question:
One Short-tailed Fruit Bat can spread up to 60,000 seeds in a night. Assume that on an average night it carries half this number. How many would it then carry in a night? If only one out of every 100 seeds carried lands where it can grow, how many new seedlings will this bat be planting each night? How many new seedlings would be planted by this bat in a year (365 days)? How many would a colony of 100 Short-tailed Fruit Bats plant in a year?

15 Saving a Tropical Rain Forest

READ ABOUT BATS

Most of the world's **rain forests** are in countries too poor to protect the incredible trees, plants, and animals that live in them. The populations of these countries are growing so rapidly that people are cutting down as much as 70 football fields worth of rain forest every minute. At this rate, we are rapidly running out of time to save these forests.

In Brazil, there are still spectacular forests with porpoises and giant otters in the rivers and scarlet macaws, parrots, toucans, and monkeys in the treetops. Nevertheless, these forests are being cut by people forced to leave over-populated cities to find new ways of making a living. They work very hard every day, but they find it extremely difficult to feed their families. To survive, they constantly cut forests to grow crops or raise cattle.

CAN PEOPLE USE FORESTS BETTER?
Have you ever thought about what advice you might give to help frontier villagers survive without harming their forests so much? Nobody wants to see another tree cut or another animal harmed, but people have to survive too.

New ways are being discovered to help people earn a living harvesting forest products without actually cutting so many trees. Also, when they do have to cut forests, there are things they can do to help them regrow.

HOW CAN BATS HELP?
Efforts as simple as protecting bat **roosts**, such as caves, can help. Bats are especially good at helping damaged rain forests regrow because they are the only animals that frequently carry seeds into rain forest clearings. The plants whose seeds bats carry are called **pioneer plants**, because they are the only ones able to survive the extremely hot, dry conditions in clearings.

Fruit bats often eat more than two times their body weight in a night, and they need to drop seeds as quickly as possible to lighten the load. Huge numbers of seeds are dropped as they fly. In fact, just one small bat can drop up to 60,000 seeds in a single night! As long as forest clearings are not too large, bats will cross them to reach fruit trees on the other side.

Bats are especially good at helping damaged rain forests regrow because they are the only animals that frequently carry seeds into rain forest clearings.

ARE BIRDS AND MONKEYS NEEDED TOO?

Birds and monkeys are also important **seed dispersers**. However, there isn't enough food or shelter to attract them into clearings until seeds dropped by bats begin to grow. Then, small birds begin to visit. They drop seeds mostly beneath perches in trees and shrubs, and this works out very well for forest regrowth as long as there are plenty of bats to plant the first seeds. The birds drop seeds of trees and shrubs that need shade to survive, and these now can grow in the shade of plants brought by bats. As the new trees and shrubs from birds grow taller, they attract monkeys and many other animals that bring additional seeds. All these animals are needed to make a new rain forest complete.

Now that you know more about how rain forests grow, perhaps you can make some suggestions on how to help them recover.

Read More About Tropical Rain Forests!

Cherry, Lynne. 1990. *The Great Kapok Tree: A Tale of the Amazon Rain Forest*. Harcourt Brace Publishers, New York, 36 pages.

Goodman, Billy. 1992. *The Rain Forest: A Planet Earth Book*. Little Brown and Co., New York, 96 pages.

Discover Tropical Rain Forests on the Internet!

www.batcon.org "BATS *Magazine Archive*."

Estrada, Alejandro and Rosamond Coates-Estrada, 1993. "Bats and the Vanishing Rain Forests of Mexico." *BATS*. 11(3): 6-11.

Fleming, T.H. 1993. "Fruit Bats: Prime Movers of Tropical Seeds." *BATS*. 5(3): 3-8.

Montgomery, Sy. 1991. "Into the Rain Forest." *BATS*. 9(4): 14-15.

Visit BCI's website and search through 25 years of BATS *magazines.*

Overview

Students learn about balancing human and wildlife needs to save a tropical rain forest. They also learn about natural reforestation processes.

Skills

Ecology, social studies, problem solving, land management, reforestation, global environmental awareness

Video Connection

Part Two: *Discover Bats!* Where They Live and What They Do, 14 minutes

Time

One activity period

Activity

1 Class views Part Two of the *Discover Bats!* video, to better understand rain forests and their reliance on bats.

2 Teacher hands out "Read About Bats" background information for students to read aloud or independently.

3 Teacher hands out 15-A: Discuss This! and 15-B: Tropical Forest Regrowth. Students answer questions and participate in a class discussion about ways to save rain forests.

Materials

1 Video, Part Two

2 "Read About Bats" background information
(one copy for each student)

3 15-A: Discuss This!
(one copy for each student)

15-B: Tropical Forest Regrowth
(one copy for each student)

4

4

Class discusses answers to 15-A: Discuss This! and the role of bats in rain forest regrowth illustrated in 15-B: Tropical Forest Regrowth. Teacher can offer additional questions for discussion, which might include:

✔ Have students make lists of their favorite places, and ask them to decide what would happen to these places if there were twice as many people. What can be done to keep such places special?

✔ Ancient humans, such as the Mayans, successfully practiced what is called "slash and burn" agriculture in the rain forests of Central America. They cut plots for gardens, grew crops for several years until the soil was depleted, then cut new plots and allowed the first ones to regrow into rain forest over long periods of time before cutting it again. This apparently worked quite well until human populations grew too large. Then they tried to cut too much of the forest too often. This depleted the soil and the animals that help regrow rain forests. As a result, most of the people starved to death, even their wealthy rulers. What should we learn from this?

✔ What are the advantages and disadvantages of attracting tourists to enjoy the wildlife of a rain forest? Who would build hotels and provide transportation? Could the local people be trained as drivers, managers, or guides? If not, where would the tourist dollars go?

✔ As human population pressures grow, there will also be more and more pressure to make all land and wildlife pay for itself. Ecotourism can help, but more sources of income will be needed in many places. Finding ways to keep native wildlife is always ecologically preferable to replacing them with domestic livestock. What can be done to encourage protection of native wildlife?

Appendix A for answers to 15-A: Discuss This!

E

E

Extension

Challenge students to find out what kinds of products come from rain forests and which of these could be harvested without harming rain forest ecosystems. Rain forest products that are sometimes sold include: 1) plants used in medicines; 2) orchids and bromeliads used as house plants; 3) fruits, nuts, and herbs; 4) butterflies and other insects sold to collectors and artists; 5) tropical fish for aquariums; 6) exotic woods for carving; 7) wood for paper pulp; 8) timber for building; 9) animals sold as pets; 10) animals hunted as game; and 11) animals harvested for food. How many of these could be used without seriously harming the forest? What items on our list might earn the most income with the least damage? What planning and management rules would be necessary? Keep in mind that one of the most common alternatives is to clear the entire forest and replace the native animals with cattle.

Appendix B for bibliography of reference resources

Instructions: Read the paragraph below and then answer the questions. Be prepared to discuss your answers in class.

Pretend that you are in charge of advising frontier people in Brazil on how to manage their rain forests. You can't stop all the forest cutting, but you at least want to help find ways to do the least damage possible until better ways to save the forests and their wildlife are found. You know that several years after a rain forest is cut the soil often becomes too poor to grow crops or support people. In fact, if too much is cut, the animals required to regrow rain forests would be lost, and then the forests could never be replaced.

Answer the following questions to decide how you will advise these people and explain each of your decisions.

1. Would it be best to cut trees from several places in the rain forest or all from one place? What if trees were cut along an outer edge versus in the interior?

2. Should some area be set aside as a completely protected wildlife sanctuary? What are the possible advantages of having a sanctuary?

3. Suppose there is a cave with a large colony of fruit and nectar bats. Why might it be especially important to include the cave in the sanctuary?

4. Assuming that you can plan a pattern of cutting that leaves a mixture of forested and cleared areas where wildlife can survive and forests can regrow, what would be the short- and long-term advantages and disadvantages for these people?

5. Suppose that a group of hunters offers to hire wardens to keep the rest of the animals safe if they are allowed to shoot one each of four kinds of game animals each year. Explain why this is a good or a bad idea.

Year 1
Immediately after clearing, bats begin dropping seeds of the first pioneer plants.

Year 3
Bat pioneer plants are well established and now attract birds and mammals carrying seeds that can grow in the shade of the pioneer plants.

Year 20
The forest continues to grow and is beginning to develop distinct layers of vegetation, including trees that will someday be as tall as the uncut forest around them.

Year 50
To the untrained eye, the clearing cannot be distinguished from the rest of the forest. However, it will take many more years before the soils, plants, and animals are as diverse as in the undisturbed forest.

16 Counting Bats

READ ABOUT BATS

People often wonder how many bats live in a cave. This is very important information for scientists and conservationists. To better understand our **environment**, we must know whether animal and plant populations are stable, growing, or declining. Such information helps us protect them and keep **ecosystems** healthy.

Scientists count bats in several ways. When a **colony** is small, they can count each bat as it emerges from its **roost**. When colonies contain hundreds or thousands of bats, this becomes difficult. When there are millions of bats, it is nearly impossible.

At some medium-sized colonies, scientists estimate the number of bats by using simple math. First, they count how many bats leave during exactly one minute. They repeat this one-minute count several times during the **emergence**. Then they calculate the average number that left each minute, by adding up the numbers of bats in each one-minute sample, and dividing by the number of samples. For example, if they had counts of 10, 5, 10, and 15, their average would be 10. (10 + 5 + 10 + 15 = 40 divided by 4 = 10). They multiply this average times the number of minutes it took all the bats to leave. If 10 bats left per minute, and it took 20 minutes to leave, the approximate colony size is 10 times 20, or 200 bats.

Scientists can sometimes count bats in a cave without even seeing them. Large bat colonies often stain cave ceilings or walls where they roost. The stains are reddish brown and take many years to form, but they can still be seen hundreds of years later. Scientists measure these stains to estimate the size of past populations.

For many bat species, scientists already know the number of bats that normally roost together in a square foot. For example, scientists know that a cluster of **endangered** Gray Myotis contains approximately 200 individuals in each square foot (over 2,000 per square meter). To calculate the sizes of past populations of Gray Myotis, researchers

To better understand our environment, we must know whether animal and plant populations are stable, growing, or declining.

simply measure the area of cave wall or ceiling that was stained by roosting bats and multiply the number of square feet covered times 200. If a stained area is 10 feet long by 3 feet wide, we can multiply 10 times 3 and know that the clustered bats covered 30 square feet. Then, by multiplying 30 times the known roosting density of 200 bats per square foot, we find that 6,000 bats once used this roost.

To estimate the number of Gray Myotis that used a roost during the most recent nursery season, researchers simply enter a cave after the

bats have left in fall and measure the area covered by fresh droppings that have fallen straight down from the roosting bats.

The droppings, also called **guano**, form an outline on the ground of where the bats roosted up on the ceiling. If we measure the droppings and find they cover 5 feet by 3 feet, using the same calculations as we did previously for the stained roost surface, we know that the colony has declined to just 3,000, half its former size.

What would it mean if the area of the droppings was greater than the area of the roost stains on the cave ceiling? Because roost stains take many years to form, measuring guano piles gives a more accurate estimate of the current population size. If the area covered by new guano is greater than that of the ceiling stain, it means that the population is increasing!

Counting exiting bats and measuring ceiling stains or guano deposits are good ways to learn about bat population sizes, because these techniques can be used without disturbing bats.

Read More About Bat Populations!

Tuttle, Merlin D. 1991. "Saving North America's Beleaguered Bats." *National Geographic.* 188(2): 36-57.

Discover Bat Populations on the Internet!

www.batcon.org "BATS *Magazine Archive"*

Clawson, Richard L. 1987. "Indiana Bats: Down for the Count." *BATS.* 5(2): 3-5.

McCracken, Dr. Gary F. 1986. "Why Are We Losing Our Mexican Free-tailed Bats?" *BATS.* 3(3): 1-2.

Tuttle, Merlin D. 1994. "Saving Our Free-tailed Bats." *BATS.* 12(3): 12.

Visit BCI's website and search through 15 years of BATS *magazines.*

Overview

Students learn how to estimate numbers of animals in situations where it is impossible to directly count individuals.

Skills

Estimating population sizes, drawing conclusions about trends, mathematics (addition/subtraction, multiplication/division, fractions)

Video Connection

Part One: *Discover Bats!* How They Live, 12 minutes

Time

Two activity periods

Note: This activity must be done during lunch and at a time when students normally leave or enter the building. Teacher should decide in advance from which building exits students can safely observe other students.

Activity 1

1

Class views Part One of the *Discover Bats!* video, considering the difficulties of counting large colonies.

2

Teacher hands out "Read About Bats" background information for students to read aloud or independently.

3

Teacher hands out one copy of 16-A: Calculate This! and explains that the class is going to estimate how many students are in their school, using the same technique bat researchers use to count colonies of bats as they emerge from their roosts in the evening. Teacher needs to pick a time when all the students normally leave or enter a building.

4

Teacher determines how many exits the students should watch, then divides the students into that many groups. (Groups should have at least three (3) students each.) Teacher hands out two stopwatches and a tally meter or hand counter *(optional)* to each group.

Materials

1

Video, Part One

2

"Read About Bats" background information
(one copy for each student)

3

16-A: Calculate This!
(one copy for each group)

4

Stopwatches
(two for each group)

Tally meter
(optional, one for each group)

Activity 1

Materials

5

Each group of students quietly reads the 16-A: Calculate This! sheet together. Teacher helps groups to assign roles and class discusses any questions about the instructions.

6

Teacher sends each student group to a different exit, instructing them to gather the data and return to discuss it at a specific time or date. (Students may return during the next class period to discuss their findings.)

7

When class reconvenes, teacher hands out 16-B: Calculate This! and leads a discussion about their population estimates which might include the following questions:

7

16-B: Calculate This!
(one copy for each group)

✓ How closely did the class's estimate of total student population come to the number of students known to be at school?

✓ What possible biases are there to this method of estimation? Can the students think of ways to increase the accuracy?

✓ When is the best time to take the four samples?
—Is four enough?
—Does it make a difference if students tend to exit in groups or alone or at different speeds?

✓ What are the advantages and disadvantages of using this technique to count bats?
—Would you use this method if you needed to count bats exiting from a hole in the side of a building where you could not see inside?

✓ When very large numbers of bats emerge, would counting the numbers leaving per minute be accurate? Might it be similar to trying to count accurately if all the students in your school suddenly tried to rush out at once?

If time permits, adjust the data-gathering process according to the students' suggestions, and try again at another time to see if their accuracy improves. Challenge students to think of ways to estimate total student numbers without counting students, for example, counting desks or lockers.

Activity 2

1

Teacher explains to the class that they are going to estimate the number of students in their lunch room, pretending that the students are bats in a cave. The technique to be used is similar to the one scientists use to count the number of bats using a roost in a cave.

2

Teacher divides the students into two groups: "Estimators" and "Counters." Teacher hands out one copy of 16-C: Calculate This! to each group.

3

Teacher explains the responsibilities for each group, as indicated on 16-C: Calculate This! Teacher helps Estimators devise a way to choose random tables for their calculations.

4

Teacher sends groups to lunchroom, telling students to gather their data, then return at a specific time to discuss it using the questions at the bottom of 16-C: Calculate This!

5

When class reconvenes, teacher points out that this activity gives an example of how scientists estimate bat numbers. They first calculate the number of bats in an average square foot and then multiply that number times the number of square feet covered by bats in a roost (as shown by ceiling stains or guano on the floor). Teacher then leads a discussion about the estimates including:

✓ Was this technique for estimating numbers more or less accurate than counting emerging students?

✓ Pretend that each table represents an area of stained bat-roosting surface in a cave. If half of the tables were empty, would you conclude that this population was declining?

✓ How about if the tables were so crowded that some of the students didn't have space to sit down? (This would be equivalent to guano covering a larger area than roost stains.)

✓ Could you use this technique to count bats in a cave containing thousands of endangered bats that you could not disturb without causing harm?

✓ Which kind of count would best enable you to estimate both past and present numbers of bats to determine whether or not the bats were declining, remaining the same, or growing in numbers?

If time permits, adjust the data-gathering process according to the students' suggestions, and try again at another time to see if their accuracy improves.

E

Extension

Challenge the students to develop methods for estimating other large aggregations of plants or animals. For example, how would they go about measuring the number of (1) corn plants or ears of corn in an average field, (2) trees in a forest, (3) ducks on a pond, (4) pigeons in a park, or (5) blades of grass on the playground? Have students justify each step in the estimation process.

2

16-C: Calculate This!
(two copies, one for each group)

E

Student "Field Journals"

Instructions:

■ From your group elect a "Tracker" a "Timer" and a "Counter"

■ The Tracker uses a stopwatch to measure the entire length of time it takes for the majority of the students to pass through the exit, ignoring stragglers. The Tracker writes his result in the "Tracker Result" space below.

■ The Timer uses a separate stopwatch to measure four (4) one-minute sampling intervals, saying "start" and "stop" to indicate the beginning and end of each interval. The samples should be spread out through most of the entry or exit period.

■ The Counter begins counting students passing through the exit when the Timer says "start" and stops counting students when the Timer says "stop." The Counter records the number of students, using tally marks in the appropriate boxes below, then adds up the four interval counts and divides by four to calculate the average number leaving per minute.

	Interval 1	Interval 2	Interval 3	Interval 4	TOTAL
Number of Students Counted					

Interval #1   +   Interval #2   +   Interval #3   +   Interval #4 =   TOTAL

Counter's Calculation Here: Average Number
⟶ Leaving/Minute   = _____

Tracker's Result Here: ⟶ Total Time Taken for
Students to Emerge = _____

Now, estimate the total number of students exiting through this location with the following formula:

(Average Number leaving per Minute) X (Total Time Taken for Students to Emerge) =

_____

Instructions: Using completed copies of 16-A: Calculate This! from each group, answer the following questions.

Reconvene with all other groups and add your totals from each location together.

Total from All Groups = _____

1. How close does your number come to the total number of students known to be at your

school? _____

2. What might account for errors? _____   _____

_____

3. What are some other applications for this technique? _____

_____

_____

■ Divide into two groups: "Counters" and "Estimators."

■ Counters split into two additional groups. One group counts the total number of Students in the lunchroom. The other group counts the total number of Tables in the lunchroom. Each member of the Counters should make their own count. Then average all the counts together.

Total Number of Tables counted in lunchroom: _____

Total Number of Students counted in lunchroom: _____

■ Estimators randomly choose four lunch tables in the lunchroom then count and record how many Students are sitting at each of the four tables. Then add the number of Students recorded at each table together and divide by the number of tables chosen (4) to get an average number of Students per Table.

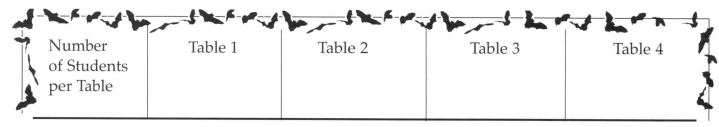

Number of Students per Table	Table 1	Table 2	Table 3	Table 4

Average Number
of Students per Table = (_____ + _____ + _____ + _____) ÷ 4 = _____

To estimate the number of Students in the lunchroom, multiply the Average Number of Students per Table times the Total Number of Tables in the lunchroom.

Average # of Students Per Table	X	Total Number of Tables in the lunchroom	=	Estimated Number of Students in lunchroom
_____		_____		_____

1. How closely do the Counters and Estimators agree?

2. If the Counters and Estimators came to different conclusions, why?

3. Which method of estimating the population size was more accurate? Which was easier? Why?

17 Calculating the Value of Bats

READ ABOUT BATS

One of the best ways to convince people that they should protect bats is to explain how many insects bats eat. Scientists have discovered that many small bats can catch up to 1,000 or more small insects in a single hour. A nursing mother bat eats the most—sometimes catching more than 4,000 insects in a night.

Little Brown Myotis eat a wide variety of insects, including pests such as mosquitoes, moths, and beetles. If each Little Brown Myotis in your neighborhood had 500 mosquitoes in its evening meal, how many would a **colony** of 100 eat? By multiplying the average number eaten (500) times the number of bats in the colony (100), we can see that this colony would eat 50,000 mosquitoes in an evening! (500 x 100 = 50,000).

Using a calculator and multiplying 50,000 mosquitoes times 30 days, the average amount of days in a month, you see that these same bats could eat one and a half million mosquitoes in a month (50,000 x 30 = 1,500,000), not to mention the many other insects they would catch!

While birds and other animals eat countless millions of insects by day, bats do the same by night.

DO BATS REALLY EAT BILLIONS OF BUGS?

Bracken Cave, just north of San Antonio, Texas, is home to about 20 million Mexican Free-tailed Bats. How many insects do you think 20 million bats can eat in a night or a month? We know that one mother free-tailed bat can eat approximately 10 grams of insects in a night (equal to the weight of two nickels). That doesn't sound like much, but for the whole colony it actually adds up to 220 tons of insects—the approximate weight of 55 elephants!

WHY DO WE NEED BATS AND OTHER ANIMALS TO EAT INSECTS?

Most insects are highly beneficial. Less than one in 100 species is a pest that attacks crops or bites people. Nevertheless, the few species that become pests are normally those that reproduce the most rapidly. Without **predators**, they would soon cause great damage to whole **ecosystems** and threaten our own survival. Bats, birds, and other predators help keep insect populations in balance. When these animals do their jobs, we get to benefit from the helpful insects without being harmed too much by those that become pests.

Insect pests that attack farmers' crops can lay hundreds of eggs in just a few hours or days. This means that if a bat eats a female before she lays eggs, the bat is actually protecting local farmers from hundreds of this insect's **larva**—the grubs and caterpillars that eat crops and gardens.

If a mosquito can lay 200 eggs that take a week to hatch and become new adults, and half (100) of those new adults are females, within just one month that one mosquito's eggs, along with those of her daughters and their daughters, could result in 100,000,000 (100 x 100 x 100 x 100) new female mosquitoes (adults die soon after laying eggs). Imagine, if none of those mosquitoes were eaten by predators like bats, how many there would be in two months or a year!

Now you see why we need to be kind to the helper-animals that keep pest insects in check. These helpers include bats, birds, frogs, toads, lizards, shrews, spiders, fish, and predatory insects such as ladybird beetles, wasps, and praying mantises. All these animals tend to feed on different kinds of insects at different times, keeping their numbers in check. While birds and other animals eat countless millions of insects by day, bats do the same by night.

Discover More About the Value of Bats!

Bash, Barbara. 1993. *Shadows of the Night: The Hidden World of the Little Brown Bat*. Sierra Club Books for Children, San Francisco, 30 pages.

Tuttle, Merlin D. 1997. *America's Neighborhood Bats*. (Rev. Ed.) University of Texas Press, Austin, 98 pages.

Discover the Value of Bats on the Internet!

www.batcon.org "BATS *Magazine Archive.*"

Murphy, Mari. 1993. "Bats: A Farmer's Best Friend." *BATS.* 11(1): 21-23.

McCracken, Gary F. 1996. "Bats Aloft: A Study of High-Altitude Feeding." *BATS.* 14(3): 7-10.

Rydel, Jens. 1990. "The Northern Bat of Sweden: Taking Advantage of a Human Environment." *BATS.* 8(2): 8-11.

Tuttle, Merlin D. 1994. "The Lives of Mexican Free-tailed Bats." *BATS.* 12(3): 6-14.

Visit BCI's website and search through 25 years of BATS *magazines.*

Overview

Students use math skills to learn about the ecological and economic impact of bats. Students practice their oral and/or written communication skills to convince others about the benefits of bats.

Skills

Addition, subtraction, multiplication, division, fractions, scientific notation, persuasive speaking and/or writing

Video Connection

Part Two: *Discover Bats! Where They Live and What They Do,* 14 minutes

Time

One activity period

Activity

1 Class views Part Two of the *Discover Bats!* video, watching for examples of the economic and ecological impacts of bats.

2 Teacher hands out "Read About Bats" background information for students to read aloud or independently.

3 Teacher hands out 17-A: Calculate This! Students calculate answers to problems. Calculators will be very helpful. Teacher hands out 17-B: Calculate This! to be completed by students in the classroom following 17-A: or as a homework assignment to reinforce skills learned in 17-A.

Note: Many small calculators will not handle the largest numbers included in this activity. Teacher may have to review mathematical principles for dealing with large numbers (e.g., scientific notation, or how to drop zeros at the beginning of the calculation and add them back at the end).

4 Teacher has students exchange papers and grade 17-A: Calculate This! Teacher can work the problems in front of the class on the board or have student volunteers pick problems to present and explain.

Materials

1 Video, Part Two

2 "Read About Bats" background information *(one copy for each student)*

3 17-A: and 17-B: Calculate This! *(one copy for each student)*

calculators *(optional)*

4 Appendix A for answers to 17-A: and 17-B: Calculate This!

5

Teacher leads further discussion of the implications of bat insect consumption, which might include the following topics:

✓ Noting the numbers of insects bats eat and the numbers of eggs those insects would lay if uneaten is a good introduction to a discussion on the importance of predators in maintaining the balance of nature. You can also relate these numbers to the total number of people living in your town or city. Further, the answers to the problems provide a good opportunity to discuss unusually large numbers; for example, students might enjoy discussing what it would mean to be a millionaire or billionaire, etc.

✓ Without a wide variety of predators, including minnows, larger insects, spiders, and bats, insects such as mosquitoes could multiply at astonishing rates and cause far more serious problems. Would it be easier to control them using just bats or just minnows, or might we be more successful by helping as many natural predators as possible? When we spray pesticides for mosquitoes, do we only kill mosquitoes? The answer is no. The poisons we use to kill mosquitoes, also kill their predators, such as bats. Because mosquitoes' natural enemies reproduce far more slowly (typically one young per year for bats), in the long run, the mosquitoes benefit, and we have to use stronger and stronger poisons at greater and greater risk to people and our environment.

E   **E**

Extension   Poster board,
Challenge students to come up with clever or creative ways to convey the   markers, craft
importance of the quantities of insects a bat can eat in a single night, month, or   supplies, etc.
whole summer season. For example, they could create interesting "bat facts"
similar to the "55 elephants" statistic stated in the background information. Or
they might choose to figure out more physical demonstrations.

The Mexican Free-tailed Bats that **roost** in Bracken Cave in Texas eat huge numbers of insects during the seven months they live there. These insects include crop pests, such as the corn earworm moth and the cucumber beetle, that cost American farmers billions of dollars each year. A mother Mexican Free-tailed Bat eats up to 10 grams of insects in a night, and one of her favorite foods is a moth that weighs one-quarter of a gram each, meaning that it takes four moths to make one gram.

1. How many of these moths does one mother Mexican Free-tailed Bat have to catch to make 10 grams?

2. If half of the moths eaten are females, and each female can lay 500 eggs, how many eggs could the 20 female moths lay?

3. If 20 female moths in an acre of crops can cause a farmer to spray **pesticides** to kill them, and the spraying costs $13 an acre, how much does each female moth cost the farmer?

4. At the above rate, what would a mother Mexican Free-tailed Bat feeding on moth pests over a farmer's crops be worth each night, assuming that half of the moths caught were females?

5. Large colonies of Mexican Free-tailed Bats eat many thousands of pounds of insects nightly. How many moths would it take to make one pound if it took four moths to weigh one gram, and 454 grams to make one pound?

6. The Mexican Free-tailed Bats at Bracken Cave eat approximately 400,000 pounds of insects nightly. How many moths that weigh one-quarter of a gram each would these bats have to catch to weigh 400,000 pounds?

Answer the following bonus questions on a separate piece of paper:

1. There are approximately 100 million Mexican Free-tailed Bats in Central Texas. If the 20 million bats from Bracken Cave eat 400,000 pounds of insects in a night, how many pounds would the 100 million free-tailed bats from all of Central Texas eat in a night?

2. Large numbers of moths are not always available, forcing the bats to switch to other varieties of smaller insects. On a night when they feed mostly on insects that weigh just one tenth of a gram each, it takes 4,540 of the smaller insects to make one pound. How many of these insects would the 100 million Mexican Free-tailed Bats of Central Texas eat in a night?

Little Brown Myotis are among the most common bats in America and often live near people. They eat many kinds of insects, including pests such as mosquitoes, moths, and beetles. Just one Little Brown Myotis can easily catch 1,000 mosquito-sized insects in a single hour, and a nursing mother eats approximately 4,500 such insects nightly.

1. If a young Little Brown Myotis catches 15 insects in a minute, how many is it catching in an hour if it continues to succeed at that rate (given that 60 minutes = one hour)?

2. If a **bat house** in your neighborhood attracts 20 Little Brown Myotis, and they each catch 1,000 mosquitoes in an hour, how many could all 20 catch in an hour?

3. If on one evening, instead of eating mosquitoes, your 20 bats ate a kind of moth that weighs one-tenth of a gram (it takes 10 to make one gram), and each bat ate 10 grams of food, how many moths would they eat?

Answer the following bonus questions on a separate piece of paper:

1. If you build a bat house that attracts 200 Little Brown Myotis mothers, and each eats approximately 4,500 insects nightly, how many insects would these bats eat in a night? In a week?

2. Assume that one-quarter of the insects caught by this colony in a single night are mosquitoes and that half of those are females that each could have laid 200 eggs if it had not been caught. How many mosquitoes would this colony catch in a night, and how many eggs could they have laid?

18 Working Together to Save Bats

READ ABOUT BATS

Many people know about Batman™ *, the comic book super-hero who helps people in danger. But did you know that there is a real-life Batman who helps bats in danger? Dr. Merlin Tuttle, founder of Bat Conservation International, has done so much work for bats that he is often called "The Real Batman." He has traveled all over the world to help people solve problems with bats in their areas. By combining his knowledge of bats with concern for the people involved, he helps communities find ways to live in harmony with bats in their natural **environments**.

"Once people understand how they can benefit from protecting bats, most are happy to help," says Dr. Tuttle. "Conservation crises usually result from ignorance, not because anyone has intentionally done something harmful."

You are going to help find a solution to a bat conservation problem. As your group works together, you can use the same techniques that Dr. Tuttle and other conservationists use to solve conservation problems. To do this, you will need to remember that most people have different needs and opinions, and these differences do not make one person good and another bad. People also have much in common. Everyone wants to be safe, to be appreciated by other people, to have nice homes and jobs, and to live in a healthy environment. Most people also enjoy nature and wildlife. The more we try to understand and respect each person's unique needs and fears, the more likely we are to avoid fights about the few things we disagree on. We may even become friends and help each other.

Always look for solutions that help everyone as much as possible. It is far better to save even half of the plants and animals we want to save than it is to fight so hard about how to do it that we lose them all!

To begin solving a bat conservation problem, Dr. Tuttle recommends that you just remember the "BATSSS," or BATS[3], Rules:

(B)e a Good Listener

Listen carefully to each person's opinions. Don't talk

> *"Once people understand how they can benefit from protecting bats, most are happy to help."*
> —Dr. Merlin Tuttle

while others are speaking. Repeat what has been said by others to show you understand.

(A)void Confrontation

Avoid quick reactions, raised voices, and interrupting. Ask people questions rather than assuming you know what they think.

(T)rack Common Needs

Figure out how each person can benefit from protecting habitat.

(S)trive for Fairness

Invite everyone involved in the problem to participate in finding a solution. Give everyone equal time and consideration for presenting their side.

(S)eek compromise

Help everyone agree on what the problem is. Encourage people to give and take.

(S)ay you can help

Discuss how you personally can help with a solution, then encourage others to do the same.

The BATSSS Rules can help people solve problems of all sizes and types. They work well for disagreements in the classroom, on the playground, or almost anywhere else. They can help with problems between just two people, between groups of people, or even between whole countries!

* Batman is a trademark of DC Comics, a division of Warner Bros.

Be a good listener

Avoid confrontation

Track common needs

Strive for fairness

Seek compromise

Say you can help

Read More About Saving Bats!

Ackerman, Diane. 1988. "A Reporter at Large (Bats)." *The New Yorker*, 64(2): 37- 62.

Pringle, Laurence. 1991. *Batman: Exploring the World of Bats*. Charles Scribner's Sons, New York, 48 pages.

Tuttle, Merlin D. 1995. "Saving North America's Beleaguered Bats." *National Geographic*. 188(2): 36-57.

Discover Saving Bats on the Internet!
www.batcon.org "BATS *Magazine Archive.*"

Tuttle, Merlin D. 1985. "Joint Effort Saves Vital Bat Cave." *BATS*. 2(4): 3-4.

Tuttle, Merlin D. 1986. "Endangered Gray Bat Benefits from Protection." *BATS*. 4 (4): 1-3.

Tuttle, Merlin D. 1990. "Return to Thailand." *BATS*. 8(3): 6-11.

Visit BCI's website and search through 25 years of BATS *magazines.*

Overview
Students participate in a simulation of an actual bat conservation problem. Four case studies from around the world are presented for four groups of students to use. Students role-play by adopting the identities of the various people and groups involved. They use a problem-solving process as they work together to find a solution. They present their problem and solution to the class. Then, the real-life situations are later shown in Part Three of the *Discover Bats!* video, accompanied by a Solution Summary for teacher-led discussion of each case study.

Skills
Problem solving, communication, negotiation, compromise, conflict resolution

Video Connection
Part Three: *Discover Bats!* How They Can Be Helped, 13 minutes

Time
Three activity periods

Activity 1

Materials

1 Teacher explains that students are going to learn skills they can use to resolve conflicts and achieve positive outcomes. Teacher asks students what kind of skills they use to get something they want from their parents or guardians. Teacher writes down student responses on board.

2 Teacher hands out "Read About Bats" background information for students to read aloud or independently.

2 "Read About Bats" background information *(one copy for each student)*

3 Teacher writes the rules for successful negotiation (BATS³) on the board and asks students to provide examples of these rules.
- **B**e a Good Listener
- **A**void Confrontation
- **T**rack Common Needs
- **S**trive for Fairness
- **S**eek Compromise
- **S**ay You Can Help

4 Teacher then challenges students to use these skills when trying to solve real-world conservation problems in this activity. To begin the activity, the teacher divides the class into four groups of at least four students each. There are four case studies, each with three to four roles. In some cases, more than one student may share a single role.

5

Teacher hands each group one copy of 18-A: Investigate This! and one of the four Discuss This! case-study sheets (18-B, 18-C, 18-D, and 18-E).

Note: Depending upon class size, not all case-study sheets (Discuss This! 18-B through E) need to be used.

6

Each group chooses or draws roles for each member of their group, according to the case. (If the number of roles does not match the number of students in the group, two or more students can work together on a single role.) Groups complete 18-A: Investigate This! sheet.

7

Students prepare to present their case study to the class for Activity 2.

5

18-A: Investigate This!
(One copy for each group)

18-B: Discuss This!
(One copy for group 1)

18-C: Discuss This!
(One copy for group 2)

18-D: Discuss This!
(One copy for group 3)

18-E: Discuss This!
(One copy for group 4)

Activity 2

Materials

1 Each group presents their case to the class. First, one person gives a general description of the case, then each member of the group explains his or her role and viewpoint. Finally, one person presents the group's solution.

2 For each problem, the class discusses the problem with the group, reviews the recommended solution, and decides to accept the solution or propose a better one. The solutions are written on the board for reference.

3 After all groups have presented their case studies, teacher leads a discussion to identify what the problems and solutions had in common and how they were different, which might include the following topics:

✓ People respond better when we carefully listen to them and care about their needs, even when their needs and viewpoints might conflict with ours.

✓ Fighting is costly and rarely results in lasting solutions to problems.

✓ Good negotiators always look for solutions that help everyone involved.

✓ Many conservation problems come from simply not understanding the value of animals or plants.

✓ Conservation projects are most successful when they help both wildlife and people.

1 Completed copies of 18-A: Investigate This! *(from Activity 1)*

Activity 3

1 Class views Part Three of the *Discover Bats!* video.

2 Teacher leads discussion after viewing the video, asking students to compare their case studies to the real-life situations. (See Appendix A for the Solution Summaries for each case study.) Questions for discussion might include:

✓ Were the real-life solutions similar to the students' solutions?

✓ Were there any solutions the students had not thought of?

✓ What was the most surprising solution?

E Extension
Challenge students to investigate a local, national, or global conflict receiving current media attention. This conflict can be environmental, political, or social. Have students collect newspaper and/or magazine clippings on the event or issue. Students should list the different "players" involved in the conflict and try to summarize their viewpoints. Then encourage students to propose a solution for the problem that will best benefit everyone. Solutions can be presented in poster format, or oral or written report formats.

1 Video, Part Three

2 Appendix A for solution summaries to 18-B:, 18-C:, 18-D:, and 18-E: Discuss This!

E Source articles from current newspapers or newsmagazines

18-A: Investigate This!　　　Scientist: _____

Case Study: _____

Instructions: Choose or draw roles for each member of your group out of those listed at the top of your "Talk About This!" case study sheet.

■ List each member of your group and which role he or she is representing:

Role   Member Name(s)

1. _____   _____

2. _____   _____

3. _____   _____

4. _____   _____

■ Read the background information for the case. Get all group members to agree on the problem and write a summary of the problem below:

■ Take turns allowing each member of your group to present his or her side of the problem, according to the roles you are playing. Each member should answer the question: What is *causing* the problem and how am I *affected*?

1. _____

2. _____

3. _____

4. _____

■ How are bats important to each member of your group?

1. _____

2. _____

3. _____

4. _____

■ Can your group come up with a solution that will please everyone? If so, what is your solution? If not, who disagrees and why, and what are the next best solutions?

18 Working Together to Save Bats/Discover Bats!

The BAT Files

THE CASE OF THE THAI BAT CAVE
HELPING A VILLAGE BY PROTECTING THEIR BAT CAVE

Case-study Roles

Monks   Hunters

Guano Miners   Conservationists

Understanding the Problem

The Khao Chon Pran Cave is found high on a hill in Thailand. Fruit bats, **nectar** bats, and insect-eating bats all make this cave their home. These bats and their seed-dispersing, **pollinating**, and insect-eating activities are important to the local economy. The droppings from the insect-eating bats, called **guano** (GWA-noh), make a rich **fertilizer** for the crops grown by local farmers. The fruit- and nectar-eating bats are a popular food in Thailand, and many people eat bats at the local restaurants. Unfortunately, the bats in Khao Chon Pran Cave are declining in number. Not long ago, more than six million bats of several different **species** would stream out of the cave each night. Now less than one million are left.

Monks

The Monks from a nearby Buddhist monastery own the cave and pay local villagers to enter and collect bat guano. They sell the guano for fertilizer to support the monastery. Fewer bats mean less income.

Guano Miners

The Guano Miners are paid by the Monks to go into Khao Chon Pran Cave each week to collect guano. With fewer bats there is less guano and they earn less money. If they did not mine during the two months when mothers were rearing young fewer bats would die.

Hunters

The Hunters catch fruit bats to sell for food. They catch them in nets at night when most people are asleep. They put nets over the cave entrance to catch lots of bats quickly. But they accidentally catch and kill thousands of tiny insect-eating bats that they can't sell. This hurts the miners needlessly. Hunters are running out of fruit bats to sell. If the fruit bats could recover to their original numbers, the Hunters could net then at fruit trees instead of at the cave, leaving the guano producing bats unharmed.

Conservationists

The Conservationists know that the insect-eating bats at Khao Chon Pran Cave are capable of eating over 100,000 pounds of insects nightly, including pests that attack farmer's crops. They also know that the fruit- and nectar-eating bats pollinate flowers of the **Durian** tree. Its fruit is worth $120 million a year to Asian markets. The fruit bats also disperse seeds of important timber trees needed by local villagers for lumber and firewood.

Conservationists realize that if bats are disturbed at their **roosts** in the season when they have babies, many of the babies will die. In fact, all the bats in the cave are in danger when they leave the cave each night because the hunters and their nets are waiting right at the entrance.

How can the Conservationists protect the bats while also helping the Monks, Guano Miners, and Hunters as much as possible?

Planning a Solution

As your group discusses the problem and plans a solution, it will be useful to keep the following questions in mind:

1. Must all hunting or guano mining be stopped entirely, or could Hunters and Guano Miners still work if they were simply careful not to kill bats needlessly?

2. If all guano mining or hunting were outlawed to protect the bats, how would everybody respond? What would happen?

3. Does the time of year when guano is collected affect the bats?

4. Could changes in hunting practices help the bats?

5. Can the government help?

6. How could the Conservationists most effectively approach the Hunters to discuss this problem?

THE CASE OF THE VAMPIRE BATS
SAVING BATS WHILE PROTECTING RANCHERS FROM PROBLEM VAMPIRES

Case-Study Roles
Cattle Ranchers
Government Officials
Conservationists

Understanding the Problem

Vampire Bats live only in Mexico and Central and South America. They are very social animals that groom each other, share food, and even adopt orphans. They must drink blood in order to survive. In **tropical** forests, they feed on wild animals such as **tapir** (TAY-per), wild pigs, or deer. However, in the last century people have cut most of the forests and replaced them with pastures in order to raise livestock, mostly cattle. The Vampire population has grown rapidly because of the new food supply.

Cattle Ranchers

The wounds that Vampire Bats leave behind on livestock can become infected with **parasites** that make the animals sick or die. Also, like all **mammals**, bats can transmit **rabies**. In fact, Vampire Bats can make a rabies outbreak spread rapidly among livestock. Many cattle die as a result, and whenever cattle die it costs ranchers lots of money. Ranchers try to kill the Vampire Bats by burning or sealing off caves where the largest bat colonies **roost**.

Government Officials

Under pressure from Cattle Ranchers, Government Officials support bat eradication programs. They do not understand that not all bats are Vampire Bats or that the majority of bat **species** are highly beneficial. The Government Officials simply try to help solve the problems Cattle Ranchers face from Vampires.

Conservationists

Because of the Vampire Bats, most people in **Latin America** want to kill all bats. This makes it very difficult to save bats. Conservationists realize that often the largest and most obvious colonies of bats are targeted for destruction, even though these bats are usually the beneficial fruit-, **nectar-**, and insect-eating species, and often do not even include Vampire Bats. As a result, millions of highly beneficial bats are killed, and the problem-causing Vampire Bats escape. After careful study, a method for killing only the problem-causing Vampire Bats has been developed. A few Vampires are caught in **mist-nets** set around sleeping cattle. Then a poisonous paste is spread on the backs of the bats, and they are released. The Vampires fly back to their **colony**. In the roost, all the bats help groom each other (similar to how cats groom), which means that other members of the Vampire Bat colony will contact the poison, and the whole group will die. Though it is sad to kill any animal, this method at least saves the many beneficial species from being killed. In fact, it doesn't even kill other Vampire Bats that live far away from the cattle ranches where they do not cause problems.

Unfortunately, the Cattle Ranchers, Government Officials, and Conservationists have a long history of not getting along. They are suspicious of each other's actions and are not likely to want to sit down together to solve this problem. How can the slaughter of beneficial bats be stopped?

Planning a Solution

As your group discusses the problem and plans a solution, it will be useful to keep the following questions in mind:

1. Should bat Conservationists help kill the hundreds of Vampire Bats that bite cattle if that would save millions of beneficial bats?

2. If the Conservationists help the Ranchers and Government Officials solve their problems with Vampire Bats, will the Conservationists be more likely to gain their help in saving beneficial bats?

3. Would Ranchers and Government Officials intentionally kill beneficial bats if they understood how valuable bats are? Why or why not?

4. There are only a few Conservationists. How can they best educate thousands of Ranchers and Government Officials in the many countries of Latin America where Vampire Bats are causing problems?

THE CASE OF THE BRIDGE BATS
PROTECTING MEXICAN FREE-TAILED BATS IN A BRIDGE

Case-Study Roles

Citizens of Austin	City Government
Public Health Officials	Conservationists

Understanding the Problem
The area around Austin, Texas, is the summer home of millions of Mexican Free-tailed Bats. Because of the city's rapid growth, however, many of the bats have lost the caves that used to be their homes. After the Congress Avenue bridge in downtown Austin was expanded, bats began to move into crevices between its new concrete beams. Now, hundreds of thousands of bats are living under the bridge and people are afraid of them.

Citizens of Austin
The Citizens of Austin have been warned by Public Health Officials that the bats might attack and give people **rabies**. In addition, the Austin newspaper has run threatening headlines such as "Bat Colonies Sink Teeth into City." The Citizens of Austin have begun signing petitions to have the bats removed or killed.

Public Health Officials
Austin's Public Health Officials want to protect people from dangerous encounters with wildlife. Rabies is a disease that is always fatal if untreated, and the best way to prevent transmission is not to allow people to come into contact with possibly sick animals. Having thousands of wild animals in the middle of a city seemed risky.

City Government
The City Government doesn't want Austin to get a bad reputation as an undesirable place to visit or live. In response to comments from the Citizens of Austin and the Public Health Officials, the City Government is beginning to look for ways to get rid of the bats.

Conservationists
The Conservationists know that the Public Health Officials and the newspapers don't understand the whole truth about bats—that bats rarely attack humans, even when sick, and that the Mexican Free-tailed Bats that live under the Congress Avenue bridge are among the world's most gentle animals. Bats are harmless to anyone who does not attempt to catch and handle them. The Conservationists don't want to see anyone get hurt, but they believe no one will be hurt as long as people leave the bats alone. If someone were bitten by a sick bat, the Conservationists know that it would increase everyone's worst fears.

The Conservationists realize that the people of Austin could enjoy watching the bats and also enjoy the benefits of having fewer insect pests in their city. These bats can eat 15 to 30 thousand pounds of insects each summer night, and many of the insects they catch are very harmful pests.

How can the Conservationists educate the Citizens of Austin to value rather than fear the bats so City Government will let the bats stay in their new roost?

Planning a Solution
As your group discusses the problem and plans a solution, it will be useful to keep the following questions in mind:

1. Why do the Citizens of Austin fear the bats?

2. How can you provide the Public Health Officials with information about the benefits of bats and the true risk of rabies without sounding like you do not appreciate their goals of keeping people safe?

3. If you offered to help educate people not to handle bats, do you think Public Health Officials might cooperate with your efforts?

4. What is the best way to convince all the people involved that bats are much more beneficial than they are dangerous?

5. How can the bats at the bridge help draw tourists to Austin instead of drive them away? What groups can help do this?

The BAT Files

THE CASE OF THE HIBERNATING BATS
CAVE EXPLORERS HELP SAVE A CAVE FOR ENDANGERED BATS

Case-Study Roles
Cave Explorers
Conservationists
Tennessee National Guard

Understanding the Problem
Hubbard's Cave in Tennessee is one of the world's most important **hibernation** sites for bats. It is home to eight **species** of bats, and hundreds of thousands of bats used to spend the winter there. The bats are all insect-eating species that help keep insect populations in balance over a five-state area. Unfortunately, the bats in this cave are declining because people who explore the cave during the winter are disturbing their **roosts**. (This forces bats to wake up and waste their stored fat, and many may starve before their hibernation ends in the spring.) The Tennessee National Guard wants to buy the land around the cave. They don't know about the bats or the Cave Explorers' interests.

Cave Explorers
Cave Explorers like to explore Hubbard's cave because it is large and of historic interest. Many are careful not to disturb formations or any of the creatures living in the cave, but others are careless, and some visitors even intentionally kill bats and harm the cave. Responsible Cave Explorers share the Conservationists concern for protecting bats from disturbance in winter, though they also fear being excluded from further exploration.

Tennessee National Guard
The Tennessee National Guard needs a new place for military practice. The land around Hubbard's Cave is perfect because it is in a remote area and their activities would be unlikely to disturb or threaten people.

Conservationists
Two of the bat species living in Hubbard's Cave are **endangered**, and if they continue to be disturbed, they may become **extinct**. The only sure way to protect the bats at this point is to build a huge gate at the entrance of the cave that will allow the bats to fly in and out but will prevent unauthorized people from entering. The gate must also be very strong so people can't break into the cave. The Conservationists have convinced the Tennessee Nature Conservancy (a conservation organization) to buy the cave, but the Tennessee National Guard is powerful and is already making plans for the area.

Even if everyone agreed to protect the cave, it would be extremely difficult and expensive to build a protective gate that would let bats in but keep people out. The cave entrance is huge and located high on a mountain top. How can the Conservationists convince people to work together to save this habitat for bats?

Planning a Solution

As your group discusses the problem and plans a solution, it will be useful to keep the following questions in mind:

1. Because the bats in Hubbard's Cave are endangered, the government could simply force everyone to stay out of the cave to protect the bats. How do you think people would react to this?

2. If the problem were explained to the Tennessee National Guard in a friendly manner, do you think it could be convinced to cooperate?

3. Would the cave have to be closed for the entire year?

4. How could Conservationists cooperate with responsible Cave Explorers to protect the cave and its bats from careless visitors?

5. Of all the people involved in this problem, who might be the most able to carry heavy materials up a mountain? How could they benefit by offering their assistance?

6. What can or should be done about the irresponsible cave visitors?

19 Building a Home for Bats

READ ABOUT BATS

Would you like to study real live bats or become a bat scientist? You don't have to wait until you go to college or until you get a job. You can start right now by building a **bat house**. With a little luck, you can observe bats right in your own neighborhood or backyard.

Many bats are looking for new homes. Often they have lost their original homes when **roost** trees were cut down or caves were disturbed. They want a home near food and water and one that is safe, dry, and warm—just like we do. By building a bat house that gives bats this kind of protection, you can help them survive. It's also a fun way to begin conducting your own research.

HOW DO YOU ATTRACT BATS?

Before you begin building a bat house, you must check to see if your area has a good place for bats to live. Some **habitats** are better for bats than others. It is best to find a place within a quarter mile of a lake, pond, river, or stream where the bats can drink and also find plenty of extra food for their **pups**.

Bats also like warm homes, so heat from the sun is very important. Even if you live in a hot southern climate, you need to find a site where your bat house will be warmed by the sun for at least six hours every day. In cooler climates, bats may need sun all day in order to stay as warm as they like (80°-100° F or 27°-38° C).

Painting bat houses also helps them to absorb heat from the sun. Generally, the farther north you live, the darker you should paint your house.

You need to find a good location for your bat house: in your own yard, at a park or nature center, or on the land of someone you know. Remember, you need to get permission to put up the bat house. Keep in mind that small children sometimes disturb bats or try to pick up an occasional sick bat. *This could be dangerous to both the bats and the child, so be careful not to place your house where this could be a problem.*

Your bat house should be mounted on a pole or on the side of a building, about 12 to 15 feet (11-13.5 m) above ground. This will allow the bat house to get

> *If you follow instructions carefully, there is a good chance that you will succeed in attracting your own bat colony.*

enough sun and also will help protect the bats from **predators** such as cats, snakes, and owls. Bats don't like bat houses mounted on trees, nor do they want any tree branches close to their house. The branches block fly-ways and provide perches for hungry owls.

If you follow instructions carefully, there is a good chance that you will succeed in attracting your own bat **colony**. With a good location, you may attract bats within just a few weeks, especially if you put your house up before spring, when bats return from **hibernating** or **migrating**. Be patient, however. It often takes a year or two for bats to find a new house and settle there.

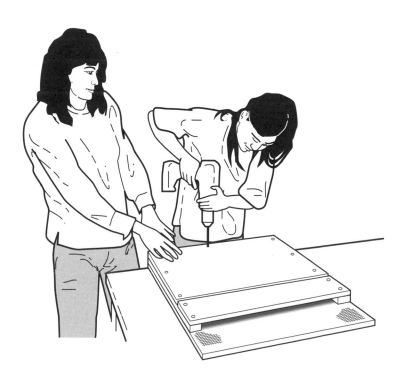

Read More About Bat Houses!

Tuttle, Merlin D., Mark and Selena Kiser. 2004. *The Bat House Builder's Handbook.* (Rev. Ed.) Bat Conservation International, Austin, 35 pages.

Discover Bat Houses on the Internet!
www.batcon.org "BATS Magazine Archive"

Kiser, Mark. 2002. "North American Bat House Research Project." *BATS.* 20(2): 19-21.

Kiser, Mark and Selena Kiser. 2002. "Cultivatig Bats." *BATS.* 20(1): 7-9.

Acker, Elaine. 1999. "Backyard Bats." *BATS.* 17(4): 3-9.

Visit BCI's website and search through 25 years of BATS magazines.

Overview

Students become personally involved in understanding and building artificial habitat for bats. Students learn to make careful observations of habitat and daily sun cycles.

Skills

Problem solving, habitat evaluation, woodworking, experimentation, use of a compass

Video Connection

Part Four, *Discover Bats!* Valuable Neighbors, 8 minutes

Time

Four activity periods: two in class and two field trips

Advanced Preparation for Teachers

1. *Review all information about bat houses and determine how many houses the class will make for this activity. Then purchase all needed materials found in the "Teacher's Instructions" beginning on page 161.*
   Note: This would be an excellent activity to do in a shop class.
2. *Pre-cut all wood for bat houses using a table saw. Holes for screws may also be pre-drilled when working with young children.*
3. *Pre-build one bat house.*
4. *Prepare for field trips. This lesson includes two field trips to the location where your class's bat houses will be mounted. Ideally, this would be a location near the school to which the class can walk, requiring only minimal adult supervision. Nature centers and organic gardeners may welcome use of their premises if other locations are difficult to find.*

Activity 1

1

Teacher tells the class that they are going to learn about artificial roosts for bats by building and installing one or more bat houses. Class views Part Four of the *Discover Bats!* video.

2

Teacher hands out "Read About Bats" background information for students to read aloud or independently.

Materials

1

Video, Part Four

2

"Read About Bats" background information
(one copy for each student)

Activity 1

Materials

3

Teacher shows students a completed bat house, so they understand how everything fits together. Teacher points out the different boards and the furring strips that are used as spacers.

3

One completed bat house for demonstration

4

Teacher breaks class into groups, giving each group the necessary materials to build one house.

4

Bat house pieces to be assembled, plus all tools required *(one complete set for each group of students. Refer to the materials list found in the "Teacher's Instructions" on page 161.)*

5

Teacher hands out 19-A: Bat House Assembly. Students follow instructions on sheet to put together their houses.

5

19-A: Bat House Assembly *(one copy for each group)*

6

After all houses are assembled, teacher discusses recommendations for painting the bat houses and solicits suggestions from students for the appropriate bat house color. Class paints houses with the first of three coats of exterior latex paint. A minimum of 30 minutes should be allowed for paint to dry between coats. That means the class cannot apply the second and third coats until the next class period (Activity 2).

6

Brushes and exterior latex paint in a color recommended for your climate. *(Refer to the "Guidelines for Painting" in the Teacher's Instructions on page 163.)*

Field Trip 1

Materials

1

Teacher hands out 19-B: Criteria for Successful Bat Houses and reviews bat house placement with groups using information from Teacher Instructions.

1

19-B: Criteria for Successful Bat Houses *(one copy for each group)*

19 Building a Home for Bats/Discover Bats!

Field Trip 1

2

Teacher hands out 19-C: Investigate This! and prepares students for a field trip to investigate possible bat house locations. Teacher may have to review compass use and directions for determining orientation. Students bring 19-C: Investigate This! on the field trip with them and begin writing answers to the questions while they are "in the field."

3

In the field, students can split up into groups to describe more than one possible bat house site on 19-C: Investigate This!

Materials

2

19-C: Investigate This!
(one copy for each student)

3

Chaperones and transportation as needed for field trip

pencils, clipboards or something to write on

tape measure, compass

Activity 2

1

Class applies the second coat of paint at the beginning of this period (and the third coat at the end).

2

While waiting for the second coat of paint to dry, class discusses 19-C: Investigate This! to be sure the bat house sites the groups have chosen are appropriate. Class discusses the pros and cons of different choices, and perhaps votes on which site is most likely to attract the first bats based on its location and what they have learned about bats' needs.

3

Class applies third coat of paint.

Materials

1

Exterior latex paint and brushes
(from Activity 1)

2

19-B: Criteria for Successful Bat Houses
(from Field Trip 1)

Completed copies of 19-C: Investigate This!
(from Field Trip 1)

3

Exterior latex paint
(from Activity 1)

1

Class returns to location(s) where houses are to be mounted. Students advise on exact placement by using their compasses and tape measures and by consulting their findings and discussions about 19-C: Investigate This!

1

Chaperones and transportation as needed to take field trip

19-C: Investigate This!

tape measure, compass

2

Students mount their houses with adult assistance.

Note: Plan ahead to be sure holes and concrete mix are ready at an appropriate time for pole-mounted houses.

2

Completed bat houses

Tools (and possibly poles) required for mounting.
(Refer to the mounting instructions found in the "Teacher's Instructions" on page 162.)

E

Extension
Challenge students to monitor their bat houses for a season, semester, or full year. They should make notes about occupancy (when the bats first come, when they leave) and fluctuations in colony size (the number of bats in the house). If the bat houses remain unoccupied, have students suggest modifications that can be made to increase chances of future occupancy. Findings can be summarized in an oral or written report or as a science fair project.

E

Student "Field Journals"

Teacher's Instructions

Beginning Advice

The following instructions include the advice needed to build and mount a simple bat house. However, for more detailed information, you may wish to purchase *The Bat House Builder's Handbook*. It is available from Bat Conservation International's online catalog at www.batcatalog.com. You can also find more information on bat houses at BCI's website: www.batcon.org.

Some teachers might opt to buy ready-to-hang bat houses for this lesson and concentrate solely on selecting a good site for mounting the house. Although garden stores and other retail shops sell bat houses, many are poorly designed and constructed. There are several critical features you should look for before purchasing a bat house. Make sure that it is at least two feet tall and has $3/4$-inch entry and roosting spaces, a landing area that is at least four inches long, and roughened roosting and landing surfaces. Also, before using any bat house, be sure it is tightly constructed, caulked, and painted an appropriate color. Superior quality bat houses are available through Bat Conservation International's catalog (www.batcatalog.com). To build and mount your own bat houses, review all the information below prior to presenting this lesson. Pay special attention to the "Key Criteria for Successful Bat Houses" on page 163.

Materials and Instructions for One Bat House

(multiply materials for each additional house)

Cutting wood pieces for houses:

✓ Table saw or circular saw

✓ $1/4$ sheet (2' x 4') cdx (outdoor grade) plywood
(Plywood only comes in $1/2$ or full sheets, however, a single bat house only requires $1/4$ sheet.)

Measure and cut plywood into three pieces, and label with a marker as follows:

26.5" x 24"	BACK BOARD
16.5" x 24"	FRONT TOP
5" x 24"	FRONT BOTTOM

> *Note: You can refer to 19-A: Bat House Assembly for a diagram of the different pieces.*

✓ One piece 1" x 2" (0.75" x 1.75" finished) x 8' pine or cedar furring strip
Measure and cut into three pieces and label with a pencil or marker as follows:

24"	TOP
20.25"	SIDE
20.25"	SIDE

✓ Power drill with 3/32" or smaller drill bit for pre-drilling screw holes *(optional)*

1. Pre-drill 11 screw-holes on the Back Board, four on each side and three across the top.

2. Pre-drill nine screw-holes on the front Top Board, three on each side and and three across the top.

3. Pre-drill four screw holes on the front Bottom Board, two on each side.

4. Be careful to place your holes so that screws from the front of the house do not hit screws from the back of the house.

Adding texture to roosting surfaces:

Bats need to have texture on their interior roosting surfaces and the landing area so they can climb and hang on easily. You will need to add texture to the inside of each Back Board before giving the pieces to the students to assemble. You can choose from two different ways to add texture (roughness):

1) Prepare a small block of wood with six screws in it. Each screw should protrude about $1/4$" out from the block, all on one side like a brush. Space them $1/4$" to $1/2$" apart. Applying pressure, drag the block repeatedly across the Back Board.
   You will need:

✓ 1" x 4" (0.75" x 3.75" finished) block of wood and six 1" screws

This scoring technique could also be done with a utility knife, but that may be time-consuming if multiple houses are built.

2) Purchase plastic netting and staple it securely to the Back Board with a staple gun.

You will need:

✓ ¹/₈" or ¹/₄" mesh plastic netting, 20" x 22.5"
[such as Internet, Inc., product # XV-1670. Call 1-800-328-8456.]

✓ Staple gun with ⁵/₁₆" staples

Putting houses together:

✓ #2 Phillips screwdriver

✓ 20 to 30 multipurpose (drywall) screws, 1"

✓ 1 tube latex (paintable) caulk

✓ 2" or 3" paint brush

✓ 1 pint exterior quality latex paint (light, medium, or dark brown or black, depending on location. See "Guidelines for Painting.")

Mounting houses on wooden poles:

✓ One wooden pole, preferably 16' tall or more (2' to 3' of the pole will be buried in the ground). Pressure-treated 4" by 4" wooden posts are highly recommended.

✓ Power drill and #2 Phillips screwdriver bit to drill holes into pole for screws

✓ Four to six 2 ¹/₂" or 3" galvanized wood screws

✓ Post-hole digger or shovel to dig hole for pole

✓ Concrete for filling in hole

✓ 25-foot tape measure

✓ Compass

If mounting the house on a pole, please be aware that you will need to dig a hole for the pole and then fill the hole with concrete to make it stable. The house will attach to the pole with screws, as shown in Figure 19.1. Two houses can be mounted back-to-back on one pole. This is especially recommended in hot climates.

Mounting houses on wooden buildings:

✓ Power drill and #2 Phillips screwdriver bit to drill holes for screws

✓ Four to six 2 ¹/₂" or 3" wood screws

✓ Two pieces 1" x 2" (0.75" x 1.75" finished) x 30" pine or cedar furring strips

✓ 25-foot tape measure

✓ Compass

If mounting the house on a wood building, we recommend adding two long furring strips to either side of the back of the house before attaching it to the building, as shown in Figure 19.2. Then you can simply attach the strips to the building using wood screws.

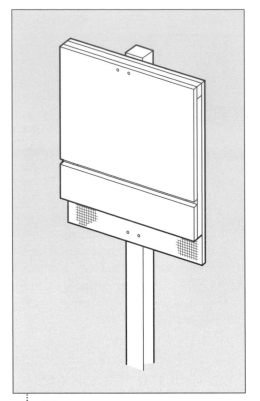

Figure 19.1

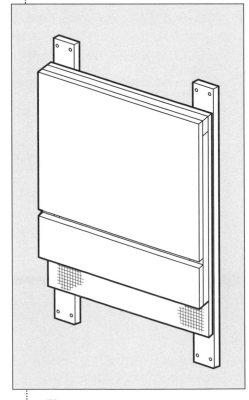

Figure 19.2

162

19 *Building a Home for Bats/Discover Bats!*

Key Criteria for Successful Bat Houses

Guidelines for painting:

In the northern half of the United States, you should paint your houses black or dark brown so they will absorb more heat from the sun. In most of the southern half, use a medium brown. In Canada and the coldest mountain areas of the U.S., stick with black, and in the hottest desert areas, use light brown.

If you decide to mount several houses together, you might try furthering your bat house experiment by painting some houses darker and others lighter. The color differences will offer the bats more temperature options, and give your class more information as to what the bats prefer. In the northern half of the North America, try black versus dark brown, and in most of the southern half, try dark brown versus medium or light brown. In Canada and the coldest mountain areas of the United States, stick with black, and in the hottest desert areas try white versus light brown.

Guidelines for mounting:

Bat houses mounted on wood or brick buildings or on poles are far more likely to attract bats than houses mounted on tree trunks, which tend to be too shaded and vulnerable to predators.

Use a compass to mount bat houses so they are facing east, south, or west where they will receive at least six, and up to 10 or more hours of daily sun.

If you have a good place to mount a bat house on the side of a building, you can place it below the eaves but not directly above windows or doors. In cool climates, bats will like medium- to dark-colored buildings. They will prefer light-colored buildings in very hot climates. Four or more bat houses can be mounted side by side within a few feet of each other if necessary. This may actually make them more attractive to bats. By moving among houses, bats can avoid parasites or choose warmer or cooler houses under different weather conditions.

Guidelines for monitoring bat house success:

If a class records bat house locations and keeps track of the houses over time, future students may have the opportunity to visit a successful bat house site to see for themselves how past students have helped bats. By adding houses at already successful sites, students will have more opportunities to experiment in subsequent school years, and they will be far more likely to succeed quickly in attracting new bats. A successful bat house site also provides special opportunities for publicity with the news media, with students providing interviews at the site. Have the students note the many values of sharing our neighborhoods with bats, but also have them warn people never to handle bats.

Color Recommendations for Painting Bat Houses

Average High Temperatures for July

Area 1: Less than 85° F – Black or dark shades of paint.
Area 2: 85°-95° F – Dark or medium shades.
Area 3: 95°-100° F – Medium or light shades.
Area 4: 100° F or more – White or light shades.

Years of research have shown that bat houses are more successful at attracting bats if they are painted or stained. The appropriate color depends on geographic location and the amount of sun exposure. At least six hours of direct sun daily are recommended for all bat houses where high temperatures in July average less than 100° F. Where July high temperatures average 80° F or less, houses should receive as much sunlight as possible. Adjust to darker colors for less sun. Use exterior-quality, water-based stain or latex paint, and choose flat paint rather than gloss or semi-gloss for best solar absorption.

Instructions: Follow the diagram and steps below to assemble your bat house.

■ 1. Attach the 1" x 2" top and side **furring strips** to the BACK BOARD (roughened side turned in) as follows:

First, put a $1/4$"-wide line of caulk along the top of the BACK BOARD, about one-half inch down from the edge. Then, lay the "TOP" furring strip on top of the caulk. Screw the furring strip to the BACK BOARD, with the screws entering from the back of the board (not from the furring strip side).

Put similar lines of caulk along the sides of the BACK BOARD, about one-half inch away from the edge. Lay the remaining two "SIDE" furring strips on top of the caulk. Then screw the strips and BACK BOARD together, again with the screws entering from the back of the board, not from the strips.

■ 2. Attach the front of the house, as follows:
Put a line of caulk on top of the furring strips. First, put the FRONT TOP on top of the caulk, aligned with the top of the BACK BOARD. Then place the FRONT BOTTOM on top of the caulk, leaving a $1/2$" space between the FRONT TOP and FRONT BOTTOM as a vent to allow air through. Finally, attach the FRONT TOP and FRONT BOTTOM to the furring strips with screws.

■ 3. Caulk around the outside joints to ensure the roosting chamber is sealed tight. Wipe up any extra globs of caulk with damp rags.

■ 4. Now you are ready to paint your bat house.

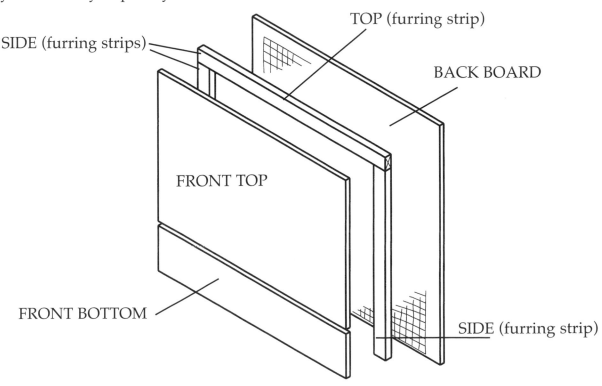

The Importance of Placement

When installing your bat house, don't forget these important guidelines:

Choosing a Location

You must be able to get permission to put up the bat house in your chosen location.

The bat house should be in a place where small children will not go near it.

Identifying Good Bat Habitat:

Look for a lake, pond, river, or stream within a quarter of a mile   the closer the better.

Bats like diverse habitats that include as many types of vegetation (shrubs, trees, etc.) as possible.

Considering Solar Exposure:

In colder climates, nothing should shade the area from the sun more than briefly. In moderate climates, all-day sun is best and morning sun is important. In hot deserts, morning sun and afternoon shade will keep your bat house warm but not too hot.

In the hottest desert areas, your bat house should face east. In moderate climates, it can face east, south or southeast.

In especially cool areas, your bat house should face south or southeast to receive the maximum amount of sun.

Providing Protection from Disturbance:

The house should be mounted on a pole or building 12-15 feet (11-13.5 m) above ground.

There should be an open flight path to the bat house with no branches or other obstructions within 20 feet (18 m).

As you go out to search for a location for your bat house, you will need to take a tape measure and a compass so you can measure distances and tell directions.

Bat House Habitat Report

1. Address where your bat house will be located _____

_____

2. Compass direction your bat house will face _____

3. Distance to nearest tree branches _____

4. Distance to the nearest lake, pond, river, or stream _____

5. Type of water source (lake, pond, river, or stream) _____

6. Surrounding habitat (forest, pastures, crop lands, fruit orchards, neighborhood housing, marshes or swamps, prairie, desert, or a mixture of these)

_____

7. What is the habitat like in your own words?_____

_____

8. If your mounting site is on a building, what color is the side of the building? _____

9. How high above ground will you be able to mount your bat house at this location? *(Measure from the ground to where the bottom of the bat house will be.)*_____

10. How many hours will your bat house be in full summer sun? _____ in shade? _____

11. What color is your bat house?_____

12. What are the advantages of the site where you are placing the bat house? Are there any

    disadvantages?_____

_____

13. Have any bats ever been seen near where you plan to put your house? _____

14. Draw a rough map of your bat house location on the back side of this sheet or a separate piece of paper. Be sure to note exactly where your house will be mounted and which direction is north. Include all buildings or trees that could cast shadows on your house at any time of day. Add notes about the habitat, such as type and location of nearby water, vegetation, and landscape.

20 Making Scientific Discoveries

READ ABOUT BATS

Have you ever wondered how scientists make new discoveries? If you are a very curious person, you might enjoy being a scientist. The first thing a scientist must do to make a discovery is to wonder about something. What makes an animal behave a certain way? For example, why is it that most **microbats** can "see" in total darkness while most **megabats** cannot?

A hundred years ago, scientists were extremely curious about this question. Could bats find their way in the total darkness of caves without using their eyes, or did they have some entirely new way of seeing? Did they need their ears? What if they lost the use of either their eyes or ears? Curious scientists blindfolded bats and found that it had no effect. Then they plugged bats' ears and the bats refused to fly in the dark. A few scientists guessed that bats might be listening to sounds too high for humans to hear, but most thought that was a ridiculous idea.

Many years later, **ultrasonic** microphones were invented, allowing people to actually hear the **high-frequency** sounds bats could hear. Using such a microphone, a scientist named Dr. Donald Griffin tested the **hypothesis** (high-POTH-eh-sis) that bats first send out high-frequency sounds and then listen for returning echoes. It was a very exciting discovery when he first heard such sounds through his microphones. Then he demonstrated that bats cannot **navigate** in complete darkness without making sounds and using their ears to hear them. This opened up a whole new field of research that has helped submarines to navigate at sea and blind people to "see" with sound. Dr. Griffin will always be famous for this big discovery.

Do You Have to Be a Scientist to Make Discoveries?

Dr. Merlin Tuttle, the founder of Bat Conservation International, made his first scientific discovery when he was just 16. That year his family moved to a new home in Tennessee, just a couple of miles away from a bat cave. Young Merlin observed that bats visited the cave only in spring and fall. This suggested to him that the cave was a resting place for bats while they were **migrating**. However, he had identified the animals as Gray Myotis, and all his books about **mammals** said this **species** of

Most of the more than 1,100 bat species in the world have not been studied beyond their original identification as new species. Countless new discoveries are just waiting to be made by curious people.

bat did not migrate. He continued to observe the Gray Myotis and became more convinced that they migrated somewhere each spring and fall.

In his senior year of high school in 1958, Merlin persuaded his parents to take him to meet bat experts at the Smithsonian Institution in Washington, D.C. "I brought my notes on three years of observations suggesting that the Gray Myotis were migrating," he says. "They gave me several thousand bands to put on the bats and said, 'Well, here's your chance to prove it.'"

"My whole family became involved, and my father, who was a biology teacher, spent hundreds of hours helping me capture and band bats. Just a few months after we began banding the Gray Myotis, some neighbors told us about a cave where bats **hibernate**. Because the cave they mentioned was about a hundred miles north of our home, we doubted whether it would be important to our bats. We assumed our bats would go south for the winter. Even so, curiosity got the best of us, and by an extreme stroke of luck, we found our banded bats in that cave! They had not only migrated, they had also gone north instead of south!"

ARE THERE NEW THINGS TO DISCOVER ABOUT BATS?

Scientists are continually making valuable new discoveries. Many of these discoveries are made while studying plants and animals that most people would assume are unimportant or even bad.

Most of the more than 1,100 bat species in the world have not been studied beyond their original identification as new species. Countless new discoveries are just waiting to be made by curious people.

In their work, scientists rely on what we call the "scientific method." Using the scientific method, researchers make an hypothesis. An hypothesis is a statement based on what is already known and which makes a prediction that can be tested. Scientists then use experiments to test the hypothesis to see if the results support it or disprove it. A disproved hypothesis can be rejected and then a new hypothesis can be formed for future experiments. You can begin learning this method right now by testing important hypotheses about **bat houses**.

Read More About Bat Research!

Johnson, Sylvia A. 1985. *Bats*. Lerner Publications Co., Minneapolis, 48 pages.

Pringle, Laurence. 1982. *Vampire Bats*. William Morrow & Co., New York, 62 pages.

Discover Bat Research on the Internet!

www.batcon.org "BATS *Magazine Archive.*"
Anon. 1995. "The Incredible Milk-Producing Male Bat." *BATS*. 13(1): 17.
Pettigrew, Dr. John D. 1986. "Are Flying Foxes Really Primates?" *BATS*. 3(2): 1-2.

Visit BCI's website and search through 25 years of BATS *magazines.*

Overview

Working with bat houses, students learn to conduct their own research — testing hypotheses and using the scientific method of discovery. In doing this, they develop thinking skills while improving knowledge of bat habitat requirements, compass orientation, and how the sun affects living things. They also learn to graph, compare, and interpret field data.

Skills

Research, problem solving, data collection and interpretation, hypothesis testing, working in a team, cooperation

Video Connection

Part Four: *Discover Bats!* Valuable Neighbors, 8 minutes *(optional)*

Time

Two class periods with a field trip to the school yard, plus three additional short field trips to the school yard, each trip lasting about 5-10 minutes

---

Note: Teacher needs four (4) identical bat houses. Students can make houses in Lesson 19: Building a Home for Bats, *or teacher can have ready-made houses that students can paint or cover with colored paper or "mock" bat houses made out of heavy cardboard or empty ¹/₂-gallon milk cartons All four bat houses should be painted and ready to place prior to beginning this activity.*

For younger students, teacher may want to teach just the basics of hypothesis testing and how scientists gather and interpret data. Older students could learn the more technical details about hypothesis testing:

1) null hypothesis — states that a variable makes no difference; for example, the sun does not affect bat house temperature
2) controlled variables — those that stay the same in each experiment; in this case, shape and design of bat house tested
3) independent variables — those that the experimenter changes to see if they make a difference; in this case, bat house color and sun exposure
4) controls — the part of an experiment in which the independent variable is controlled and does not change; in this case, a black bat house is placed in the shade while another identical black bat house is tested in the sun to measure the sun's effect on internal temperature relative to ambient temperature
5) sample size and statistics — important factors in determining confidence levels without personal biases

---

Activity 1

1

Teacher hands out "Read About Bats" background information for students to read aloud or independently and tells students that they will be using the scientific method to set up a bat house temperature monitoring experiment. They will be questioning whether the color of a bat house and its exposure to the sun will make a difference in its internal temperature. (Teacher could at this time review the different steps of the scientific method.) In this experiment, students will be using "null hypotheses." Teacher can either give the students these hypotheses or if the students grasp what a null hypothesis is, they can try to write the null hypotheses themselves.

✓ The color of a bat house has no effect on its internal temperature.

✓ Sunlight shining on a bat house has no effect on its internal temperature.

Note: By the end of the experiment, the students will have to reject both null hypotheses, since their results will show that bat house color and solar exposure both change internal temperatures.

Materials

1

"Read About Bats" background information
(one copy for each student)

Four bat houses or mock bat houses: two black, one brown, and one white

2

Teacher divides students into five groups telling each group that they are responsible for identifying and monitoring temperatures in one of the following locations:

✓ Ambient Temperature (shady location)
✓ Shaded Black Bat House
✓ Sunny Black Bat House
✓ Sunny Brown Bat House
✓ Sunny White Bat House

3

Groups assemble their respective materials and prepare to go out in the school yard to pick an appropriate location to set up the monitoring experiment.

Field Trip

1

Once outside, teacher explains that all bat houses should be mounted in a vertical position to trap similar amounts of heat and should all be facing the same direction to receive identical amounts of sun. For the purpose of this experiment, they do not have to be hung as high as they would be if they were actually supposed to attract bats. Class should look for an area where bat houses can be hung on a fence or wall or placed on short poles. This area should be near a shaded spot (under a tree or in full shade of a building) where the ambient temperature measuring device and one of the black bat houses can be easily placed. All bat houses should be placed at the same height off the ground.

Note: All bat houses must be of tight construction without air leaks except for the entrance and vents (if present).

1

Five thermometers *(one for each group)*

Four bat houses — two black, one brown, and one white

Masking tape *(one roll per group)*

Five 2' to 4' lengths of wooden doweling *(one for each group, length determined by height of bat houses)*

Five watches with second hands or stopwatches *(one for each group)*

Five clipboards or student "Field Journals" for recording methods and data *(one for each group)*

One compass

Misc. poles, hooks, brackets, etc., for mounting bat houses

2

Class agrees on location for monitoring experiment and uses compass to determine the orientation of the bat houses. All bat houses must face the same direction. Students record the compass direction on their clipboards or in "field journals." Teacher helps students to mount bat houses.

3

Once bat houses are mounted, teacher discusses where and how to take temperature readings. Teacher emphasizes that for scientific accuracy, students must all take the temperature readings in exactly the same way. Teacher leads a discussion about measuring protocol which might include the following:

✓ Will it make a difference if one thermometer is higher than another in the bat house or if it touches the top, front, or back of a house while recording?

✓ Will the heat, which comes from the sun, make the top or one side of the bat house hotter than the bottom and other sides? Why?

✓ Based on answers to these questions, which location inside the bat house represents the best place to monitor the temperature in order to learn about internal temperature?

(If students are unclear on any of these points, or if they disagree, teacher can encourage them to test a new hypothesis that will resolve their argument.)

4

Students agree on a protocol to ensure that all temperature readings are taken in the same way and without bias. Students then construct their temperature measuring devices and protocols to assure consistency by following the instructions below:

Tape each thermometer to one end of each wooden dowel so that the bulb of the thermometer extends half an inch from the end of the dowel. Then tape three wooden popsicle sticks so one is attached to the opposite side of the dowel and extends one-quarter of an inch beyond the thermometer bulb. The other two are attached to extend an equal distance to either side. (This will prevent the thermometer from coming into contact with any surface of the bat house when it is inserted.) All thermometers should be exactly the same.

Place one of the temperature measuring devices up into a bat house so that the thermometer-end rests against the roof to demonstrate the measuring technique. Have students repeat this for each house in the test. The Ambient Temperature monitoring group should hold their thermometer in the same fashion at the shaded location so that it is approximately the same height off the ground as those thermometers used to measure temperatures of the bat houses.

✓ Have the groups agree on how long it takes to get an accurate reading (at least two minutes is suggested), then be sure each group accurately times each reading to avoid additional biases.

✓ Make sure students do not inadvertently shade the bat houses with their bodies while taking a temperature reading.

Careful notes on exact monitoring protocols agreed upon should be recorded by teacher and students before returning to the classroom.

4

Wooden popsicle sticks

1

Back in class, teacher discusses other possible sources of bias in the data:

Thermometer calibration: Students should compare the readings on each of their thermometers after they have been placed in a well-stirred bowl of ice for at least two minutes. They should all read within a quarter of a degree of 32° F (0° C). If not, students will need to enter a calibration figure for their thermometer so readings for each group will be accurate. The deviation from 32° F (0° C) should be labeled on any iced thermometer that is not reading properly. This deviation will be added or subtracted from whatever measured figure the student takes with that thermometer during the course of experiments.

Time of measurement: Students should agree on exact times for taking morning, noon, and afternoon temperature readings. These times should work with everyone's schedule so each group makes a reading at exactly the same time under the same weather conditions.

Changing weather conditions: Students should try to conduct their monitoring on a sunny day so solar heating can most easily be observed. Any cloud cover or specific weather conditions should be indicated in the space provided on 20-A: Investigate This!

1

Bowl of ice water for calibrating thermometers *(optional)*

2

Teacher hands out copies of 20-A: Investigate This! to each group of students. Students should identify where their group will record their data and then work together to divide up the temperature monitoring responsibilities throughout the day and at each interval. Responsibilities might include:
✓ Holding the temperature probe
✓ Timing the temperature period (suggest at least two minutes)
✓ Reading the thermometer
✓ Recording the data
Each task must be repeated three times during the day as agreed upon in step 4 of the field trip, allowing students to trade responsibilities. The first temperature reading should not be taken until the bat houses have been in place for at least one hour.

2

20-A: Investigate This! *(five copies, one for each group)*

3

After all groups have collected their data, the class reconvenes to compile the results. Teacher hands out copies of 20-B: Calculate This! to each group or to all students and tells them to make a graph of the class results using different colors for each temperature monitoring station. Teacher should decide on the range of temperatures for the vertical axis of the graph and fill in these temperatures at five-degree intervals along the axis. Teacher can make a transparency copy of 20-B: Investigate This! and use an overhead projector to present the information as a group activity.

3

20-B: Calculate This! *(one copy for each student or group)*

Five different colors of markers, pens, pencils, or crayons

4

Teacher leads a discussion to compare the different temperature profiles from the monitoring project which might include the following questions:
✓ Did bat house color make a difference to the interior temperature? How did the temperature inside the shaded black house compare with that in the sunny black house?

4

Transparency copy of 20-B: Calculate This! *(optional)*

✓ What if the house in the shade had been white? Would it have affected the interior temperature?

✓ How did the time of day affect the interior temperatures between houses of different colors or sunny versus shaded houses of the same color?

✓ What would you expect the interior temperatures to be if all the houses were in the shade?

✓ What do the results say about the null hypotheses? Should they be accepted or rejected?

Teacher explains how exposure to the sun is one of the most important criteria identified for determining if bats will use a bat house. Nursery colonies like warm houses, ideally where temperature gradients cover at least a 10° to 15° F (9°-12° C) range, predominantly between 80° and 100° F (27°-38° C). This means that their roosts need solar heating in all but the hottest climates. Ask the students if any of the bat houses in the monitoring experiment were warm enough to attract bats. If so, which ones?

Teacher asks students to write a conclusion for the experiment in the space provided on 20-B: Calculate This! Teacher should stress that a scientific conclusion should include whether the null hypotheses were accepted or rejected and an explanation about what the results showed about solar exposure and the color of the bat houses.

E

Extension

Challenge students to design and carry out their own bat house research or other bat research project at home (with their parents' permission). Encourage students to design their own data-report forms to record all the necessary data and to form their own hypotheses and conclusions. Ideas for experimentation can be obtained from *The Bat House Builder's Handbook* or on the BCI website at www.batcon.org. Possible research topics might include:

✓ Do vent slots in bat houses change internal temperatures either above or below the vent location? Test with the vent open versus taped closed. The null hypothesis would be that the vent makes no difference to bat house temperatures.

✓ Do outside (ambient) temperatures affect internal bat house temperatures? The null hypothesis would be that ambient temperature has no effect.

✓ Does outside temperature at sundown affect the number of bats that visit a known drinking site before dark or the number that are seen feeding at a known feeding site before dark? The null hypothesis would be that the temperature has no effect.

✓ Do bright lights that attract insects affect where bats feed? Are there more bats feeding within less than 40 feet of lights than there are more than 40 feet away? The null hypothesis would be that lights have no effect on where bats feed.

Note: Mercury vapor lights seldom attract insects and thus should have no effect.

Research projects could be written up as reports, poster presentations, or science fair topics.

E

Bat houses, thermometers, masking or duct tape

Student "Field Journals"

Date:

_____

Weather Conditions:
(Check all that apply.)
❏ Sunny
❏ Partly Cloudy
❏ Overcast
❏ Rainy
❏ Windy

	Early A.M. _____	Midday _____	Late P.M. _____
Exact Time:			
Temperature Records			
Ambient (in shade) Recorder(s): _____			
Shaded Black House Recorder(s): _____			
Sunny Black House Recorder(s): _____			
Sunny Brown House Recorder(s): _____			
Sunny White House Recorder(s): _____			

Bat House Temperature Profiles

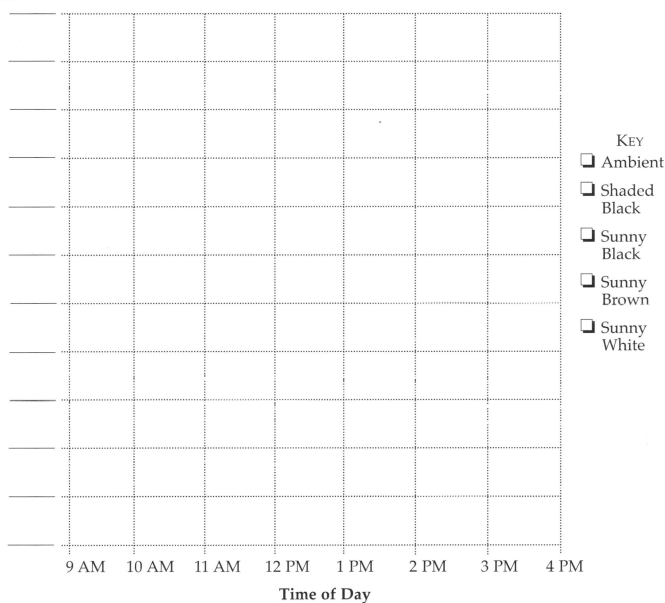

Temperature (°C/°F)

Time of Day

9 AM   10 AM   11 AM   12 PM   1 PM   2 PM   3 PM   4 PM

KEY
❑ Ambient
❑ Shaded Black
❑ Sunny Black
❑ Sunny Brown
❑ Sunny White

Hypotheses:
1. The color of a bat house has no effect on its internal temperature.
2. Sunlight shining on a bat house has no effect on its internal temperature.

Conclusions: _____

_____

_____

21 Planning a Bat Conservation Project

READ ABOUT BATS

Anyone of almost any age can help conserve bats. To become a bat conservationist, just tell others about bats or begin working on your own bat conservation project. For example, you can make a poster to put up at your school, recreation center, or library; you can give lectures, write letters to conservation agencies, newspapers, or community leaders; or you can write an article or try to get an interview with a local newspaper (especially at Halloween time, when people are thinking about bats). Whether through a class project or on your own, you can take pride in becoming part of the solution to conservation problems.

CAN YOUNG PEOPLE BE CONSERVATIONISTS?

When he was just nine years old, Bert Grantges, of Arlington, Texas, purchased his own slides of bats from Bat Conservation International (BCI) to show to other people. He overcame his fear of speaking by giving practice speeches, with his bat slides, to friends and family and then to other classrooms at his school. Soon he became such a popular speaker that he was invited to other schools and to some adult groups as well. By the time he was 12, he was traveling to other states and speaking before audiences of over 1,000 people. He even appeared on "The Tonight Show with Johnny Carson," one of the most popular TV shows of all time! In the ten minutes he spent on TV, he reached millions of people and taught them that bats should be appreciated. By the time Bert was 18 years old, he already had a career as a bat researcher; while he was still in college, he was hired to lead a U.S. Forest Service research project to study bat **roosting** needs in forests.

Colin Kapelovitz was only 12 years old when he got his home state of North Dakota to ban the use of Rozol, a poison used to kill bats. Colin had been interested in bats for many years and was a member of Bat Conservation International. When he read a report from BCI about the dangers of Rozol, he wrote to his State Senator, Jerry Waldera, to tell him about it. About a week later, Senator Waldera called and visited Colin at his home to discuss his concerns. The Senator was so impressed with Colin's knowledge that he introduced a bill to make the use of Rozol on bats illegal. Colin was even going to testify in person at the Senate hearing; but just before the hearing, Senator Waldera called Colin to tell him that the state legislature had already decided to ban Rozol based on the information that Colin had gathered.

How Do You Know What to Do?

Although Bert and Colin had completely different types of conservation projects, they were both successful for the same reason—because they chose to work on something that was important to them. Their friends and other people listened to Bert and Colin because they were so enthusiastic about their projects.

To begin any conservation project, you must decide what is important to you, what your talents are, and what you would like to accomplish. If you create your own project and work on it with enthusiasm, people will want to know more about it and about you.

Read More About Conservation Projects!

Churchman, Deborah. 1989. "The Boy Who Became Batman." *Ranger Rick*. 23(10): 18-21.

Pringle, Laurence. 1991. *Batman: Exploring the World of Bats*. Charles Scribner's Sons, New York, 48 pages.

Discover Conservation Projects on the Internet!

www.batcon.org "BATS Magazine Archive."

Anon. "For the Love of Bats." *BATS*. 7(3): 12-13.

Anon. "Rozol Use Against Bats Banned in North Dakota." *BATS*. 5(1): 6.

Murphy, Mari. 1994. "On the Track of Forest Bats." *BATS*. 12(2): 4-9.

Visit BCI's website and search through 25 years of BATS magazines.

Overview
Students work independently to design a bat conservation project or educational initiative that benefits bats.

Skills
Self-discovery, library research, communication, independent study

Video Connection
All four sections of the *Discover Bats!* video (47 minutes) are relevant, but none are necessary for this lesson.

Time
One activity period plus homework (This could also be a long-term project.)

Activity

1 Teacher hands out "Read About Bats" background information for students to read aloud or independently.

2 Teacher hands out 21-A: Investigate This! (four pages). Students pick a conservation project, using the information on 21-A: Investigate This! for ideas. Students can work individually or in groups.

E Extension
Challenge students to participate in local events that benefit or promote bat conservation or other conservation issues. Have students summarize the extent and outcomes of their participation.

Materials

1 "Read About Bats" background information *(one copy for each student)*

2 21-A: Investigate This! *(one copy for each student)*

E Student "Field Journals"

Ideas for Bat Conservation Projects

Instructions: Read the ideas below and decide what you would like to do for your project.

1. BE CLEVER AND ORIGINAL!

Are you good with words? Would you like to be a poet, songwriter, author, or advertising copywriter? Have you ever tried thinking like a bat? Perhaps you should create something original to teach your friends about bats.

- You could write a poem, a children's story, or a song about bats (you can just put new words to a tune you already know unless you are a musician too!).

- You could create a comic book that has a story about bats, or you could dream up an advertising campaign with a catchy slogan, for example, "Bats need friends too." Then you could make posters using your slogan.

- You could even create a board game about bats. For example, you could have people move their game pieces up or back based on messages such as this one: "Careless cave explorers disturb your **hibernation** roost. Go back three spaces."

Can you think of anything else you could create to share what you know about bats?

All of these projects are easy to share with people because they are entertaining. You can sing your song to friends or to your class, read your book to a younger relative or a friend, or display your ads at school or at the office of a parent or adult friend.

2. THROW A PARTY!

Do you like to eat? cook? plan or organize? Then maybe you should throw a lunch or dinner party to teach your friends about bats.

- You could invite a local restaurant chef or other good cook to work with you and your class to develop a special bat menu. A "bat menu" is one that includes products from fruits that rely on bats to **pollinate** their flowers or carry their seeds in the wild. Some of the fruits you might use are: mangoes, dates, figs, cashews, peaches, bananas, plantain, papayas, avocados, and guavas. Many special sauces for meat dishes use mangoes, papayas, and guavas. Cashews and avocados work well in salads, peaches are good in drinks, and all the fruits are delicious in desserts or fruit salads.

- Your whole class may want to help prepare special bat decorations and informative posters for the evening. If you get a restaurant to throw the party for you, you could ask the local paper to write a story that will give publicity to the restaurant and would also teach many people to appreciate bats. You could also ask the restaurant to donate a portion of their evening's sales to your favorite bat conservation project.

3. SPEAK OUT!

Would you like to be a leader, speaking in front of friends or even strangers without fear? There is no better way to start than by sharing your new knowledge about bats. If you already know that bats are not bad or frightening, you know more about bats than most people on earth—even more than most adults. That means that you have something to teach. Use your knowledge to put together a bat education program.

It might make your bat talk even more interesting if you have pictures of bats to show your audience. There are several ways to get pictures:

- You can draw or paint them yourself, using books from the library as reference.

- You can cut pictures out of magazines that have bat articles. (Ask permission first before cutting pictures out of magazines or books that do not belong to you.)

- You may be able to check out color slides or presentations showing bats chasing insects, pollinating flowers, spreading seeds, and much more from your school library. If not, you can purchase your own from Bat Conservation International.

4. WRITE ABOUT IT!

Write to local conservation organizations, and ask what they are doing to help bats. Some organizations still don't know how important bats are. They may not yet include bats in their work to help save animals and their **habitats**. Write those organizations or government agencies responsible for animals in your area to let them know why bats are important.

- If a conservation issue arises in your area that could hurt or help bats, write to your elected community leaders, wildlife officials, businesses, or whichever individuals or groups are most likely to be able to help. Let them know how their actions could affect bats. Also, remember that you are most likely to get their help if you are kind and courteous to them.

5. PUT ON A SHOW!

Ever thought about becoming an actor or actress? How about a director, playwright, or screenwriter?

- You could start your career right now by putting on a play about bats. Write a script for a play in which you and your classmates participate as bats, or some as bats and some as other animals or people.

- You can put on a puppet show or create a "game show," like those on TV, about bats.

- You could be the host of the game show and have guests try to answer questions about bats that you have written. Can you make your performance fun and interesting for an audience while still teaching them important things about bats?

6. GET SOME ATTENTION!

Are you a good writer? You might want to write an article for a local newspaper. When newspapers print frightening stories about how dangerous bats are, people become afraid and kill bats.

- You can help by writing a letter to the editor. Imagine seeing your name in the local newspaper! It is true that bats are wild animals and you could die of **rabies** from a bat bite, so don't argue about that. Simply point out that even sick bats rarely bite people. Bats typically bite only in self-defense, if a person handles them. If someone makes such a mistake, they should have the bat tested for rabies and be vaccinated if necessary. Nevertheless, bats are no more dangerous than other animals. Although we consider dogs, "man's best friend," they attack and kill more people in the United States in a single year than bats do in 10 years. In fact, car accidents with deer kill many more people each year than do rabid bats, but people rarely complain that deer are dangerous. Any animal, even dogs and deer, can be dangerous if we do not learn to live safely with them. If we simply do not attempt to handle bats, we have little to fear and much to gain from sharing our neighborhoods with them. Of course, in your letter you will also want to explain why bats are valuable friends.

- You may also want to invite the news media, especially newspaper and television reporters, to your classroom for an interview at Halloween time. They are often happy to interview students about the interesting facts they have learned about bats, and they may want to feature your bat art or special projects. They will be especially interested in an unusual interview site, like a classroom "bat cave" or a place where you have put up a bat house. In this way, you can reach thousands of people at once with your "Bats are good guys" message.

7. CREATE A WORK OF ART!

Do you like to draw? You can teach people about bats with a drawing, painting, or art done on a computer. You may want to borrow a bat book from the library and use the pictures for reference.

- You could also create a poster or a comic strip to show why bats are good guys.

- Your school is a perfect place to display your work, or you and your classmates might even cooperate on a project for display at a friendly local business. Some businesses enjoy showing off student art, especially when there is a conservation message.

8. GET INVOLVED IN YOUR COMMUNITY!

Would you like to be part of a team and contribute to a good cause? There are many important conservation projects that need people like you. You can contact a local wildlife agency or nature center to find out what bats need in your area. Often the best thing you can do is help raise money for your choice project.

- For example, you could hold a bake sale, a car wash, or collect aluminum cans. Then you could use the money you make to help in many ways. You could buy bat books, videos, and other educational materials for a classroom that cannot afford them, or to improve the collection at your own school or city library.

- You could help save a bat cave, sponsor a research project, or "adopt" a species of bat that is in danger. Bat Conservation International and other organizations are already working on many projects like these, and you can be an important part of them with your support. Don't think that you have to raise a lot of money to be helpful. If you can raise even $15, you can "adopt" a bat, which means that you will get a letter, picture, and description of your bat (though you don't get an actual live bat—sorry!), and your donation will help Bat Conservation International work even harder to protect bats.

Appendices and Index

Discover Bats!

Appendix A—Teacher's Answers

Answers to 1-A: Investigate This!

What I Know About Bats
True and False Test

1. False: Bats are not blind, they can see quite well.

2. False: Bats are not birds.

3. True: Vampire Bats feed entirely on the blood of other animals, often domestic chickens and cattle.

4. False: Bats "see with sound" and avoid flying into obstacles so they never get caught in people's hair.

5. False: There more than 10 different kinds of bats; there are more than a thousand different kinds.

6. True: Fishing bats from the Costa Rican rain forest scoop up small fish with their razor-sharp claws.

7. True: Bats that eat fruit carry seeds to new locations where they are more likely to grow.

8. False: Very few bats have rabies; but bats we can catch are more likely to be sick.

9. True: A little Myotis bat can catch a thousand or more mosquito-sized insects in one hour.

10. True: Mother bats have breasts like other mammals and nurse their babies.

Answers to 2-A: Investigate This!

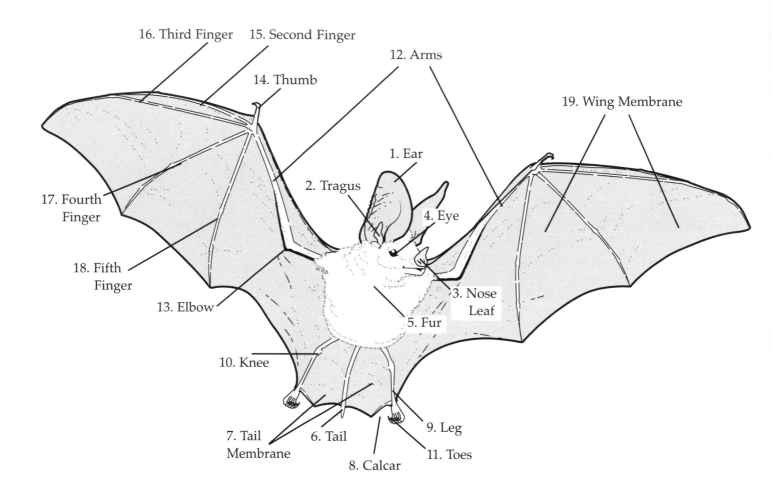

16. Third Finger   15. Second Finger

14. Thumb

12. Arms

19. Wing Membrane

1. Ear

2. Tragus

17. Fourth
Finger

4. Eye

18. Fifth
Finger

3. Nose
Leaf

13. Elbow

5. Fur

10. Knee

7. Tail
Membrane

6. Tail

9. Leg

8. Calcar

11. Toes

Answers to 3-A: Investigate This!

Roosts:
1. Cave
2. Cliff crevices
3. Abandoned mine
4. Hollow tree (could include beneath bark or holes in trees)
5. Under bridge
6. Attic
7. Building cracks (shutters, by chimney, etc.)
8. Bat House
9. Tree Foliage

Food:
1. Street lamps
2. Trees
3. Crops
4. River
5. Pond

Water:
1. River
2. Pond

Answers to Lesson 3 Extension

✔ Generally speaking, more habitats occur where there is the most topographic relief, as where mountains and lowlands meet. The greatest range of habitats in the United States occurs in southeastern Arizona where different mountain ranges, two deserts, and temperate and subtropical areas meet. In this area, nearly 20 species of bats can be seen in a single evening.

✔ The most bat species normally occur where there are the most habitats.

✔ Check 13-A: Range Maps for common North American Bat Species.

✔ Keep in mind that bats must live where their roost types and habitats are found. (See 13-B: Investigate This!)

Answers to 6-A: Investigate This!

Eating habits of bats shown in Part One *Discover Bats!* video:

> fishing bat fishing
> fruit-eating bat grabbing piper fruit
> flying fox grabbing a fig
> nectar bat eating saguaro cactus flower nectar
> nectar bat eating matisia vine flower nectar
> nectar bat eating markia vine flower nectar
> flying fox eating pollen from a liana vine
> flying fox feeding on durian flower nectar
> flying fox feeding on banana flower nectar
> insect-eating bat catching cricket
> insect-eating bats catching insects from pond
> carnivorous bat eating lizard
> Vampire Bat feeding on chicken blood

1. Answers will be subjective and differ among students.

2. Small bats are in greater danger of being caught by predators. Large flying foxes are too large for most predators to catch.

3. There are many adaptations, but those most likely to be noticed in the video are:
    Long, narrow wings—fast flight in the open (insect-eating, free-tailed bats)
    Short, broad wings—helicopter-like flight (insect- and meat-eating bats, California Leaf-nosed Bat and *Chrotoperus* bat)
    Large tail membranes—quick turns for chasing prey (insect- and meat-eating bats, California Leaf-nosed Bat and *Chropterus* bat)
    Narrow tail membranes—when quick pursuit of prey is not needed (fruit- and nectar-eating bats, long-nosed bats, flying foxes, vampires, etc;)
    Large ears—listening for faint prey sounds (insect- and meat-eating bats, California Leaf-nosed Bat, *Chrotoperus* bat, big-eared bat)
    Large feet— snagging prey from water (Fishing Bats)

4. By eating different foods, more kinds of animals can share a single habitat without competing with each other.

5. *Advantages*—When animals specialize on eating certain foods, they can adapt to be far more efficient at finding or catching them, at chewing them, or at digesting them. A highly adapted animal can beat other species in finding and eating that kind of food.

    Disadvantages—By becoming highly adapted to specialize on certain foods, an animal runs the risk of starving if its special food type ever becomes scarce. For this reason, highly specialized bats live in the most stable and predictable tropical habitats. Bats living in cold, temperate climates cannot afford to specialize. They eat a wide variety of insects, tending to catch whatever kind is available at a certain time, while tropical bats may specialize on certain kinds.

Folding Guide to 7-A: Bat Glider Instructions

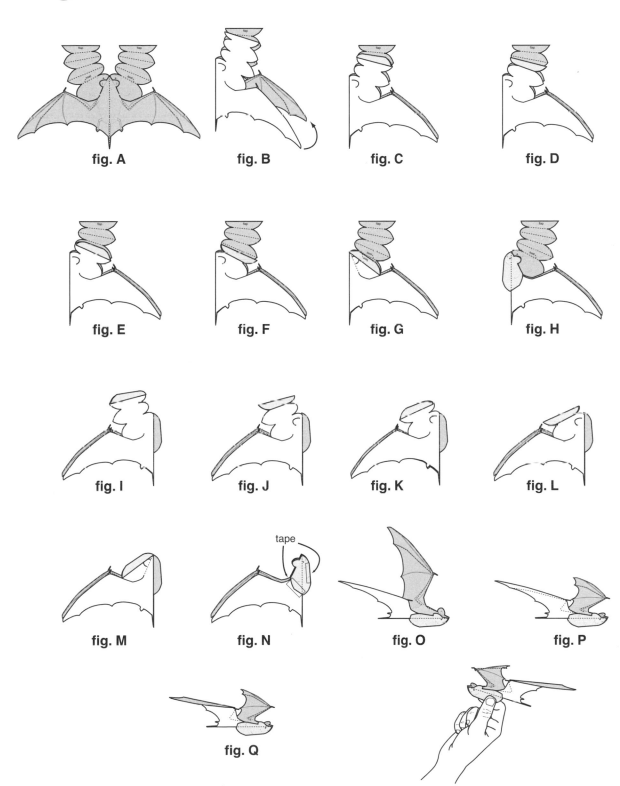

fig. A

fig. B

fig. C

fig. D

fig. E

fig. F

fig. G

fig. H

fig. I

fig. J

fig. K

fig. L

fig. M

tape

fig. N

fig. O

fig. P

fig. Q

Answers to 9-A: Investigate This!

Tri-colored bat		Purple Martin		Red Squirrel	
Advantage	Disadvantage	Advantage	Disadvantage	Advantage	Disadvantage
B&C	A	A&D	B&D	A&D	C&D

Answers to 9-C: Investigate This!

Instructions: Use the information from the "Sharing a Hibernation Cave" illustration to answer the following questions. Be sure to explain your answers.

1. No, they are not likely to compete for food. Their main arrival and departure times are different.

2. No, they are not likely to compete for roosting space. They are adapted to roost in such different temperature and humidity conditions that they couldn't use the same places in a cave.

3. Big Brown and Indiana Myotis wake up the most, but the cost is far higher for Big Brown Bats, because they have to warm up in colder temperatures and usually cannot share the heating cost with a cluster of others. Big Brown Bats must therefore use the most fat each time they wake up.

4. The Tri-colored Bat can sleep the longest. It hibernates where the temperature seldom changes, and it becomes coated in moisture droplets so it doesn't often have to wake up to adjust its temperature or drink.

5. The Big Brown Bat uses the least amount of fat while asleep because its metabolism is lower at the low roosting temperatures it chooses.

6. The Big Brown Bat uses more fat to wake up because it has to spend more energy warming itself from the lowest body temperature.

7. Big Brown Bats use the most fat. However, because they are extra tolerant of cold weather, they can feed later in fall and sooner in spring, so that their fat doesn't have to last as long.

8. Tri-colored Bats burn fat at the highest rates, because they hibernate at the highest temperatures. However, they also roost where they wake up the least. Since waking up just once can cost as much stored fat as remaining asleep for two months, it still uses the least fat and can hibernate the longest.

Answers to 10-A: Investigate This!

Food Pyramid

for the _____ Costa Rican Rain Forest _____ Habitat

Note: This is just one example of a food pyramid.
Answers will vary depending on who eats who.

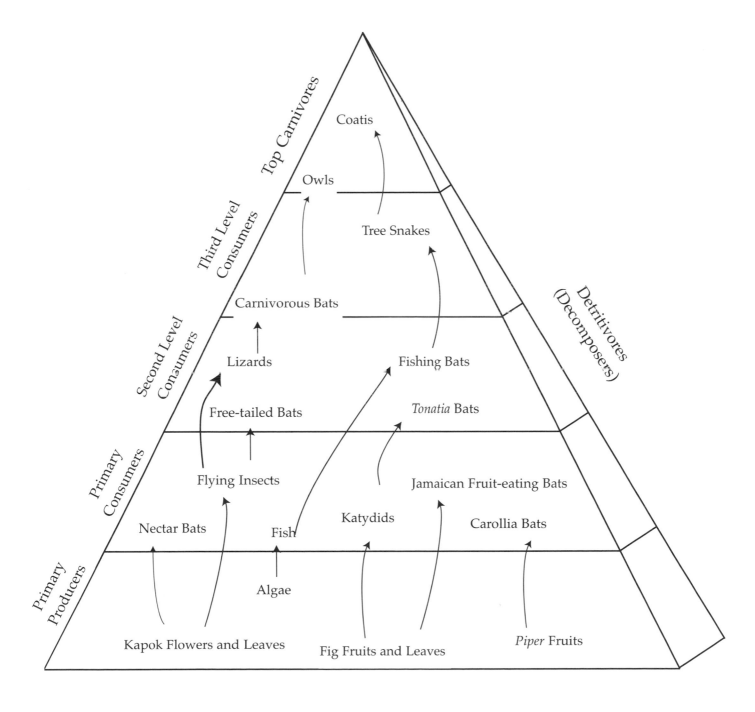

Answers to 11-B: Investigate This!

# Plant/Animal Pair	Effect of Plant on Animal	Effect of Animal on Plant
1. Organ Pipe Flowers/Bats	very positive effect (nectar feeds lots of bats)	very positive effect (bats pollinate plant)
2. Organ Pipe Flowers/Moths	little positive effect (few moths feed at flowers)	little positive effect (few moths pollinate plant)
3. Organ Pipe Flowers/ Hummingbirds	little positive effect (few birds feed at flowers)	little positive effect (few birds pollinate plant)
4. Saguaro Flowers/Birds	very positive effect (nectar feeds lots of birds)	very positive effect (birds pollinate plant)
5. Saguaro Flowers/Bees	very positive effect (pollen and nectar feeds bees)	very positive effect (bees pollinate plant)
6. Saguaro Fruit/Bats	very positive effect (fruit feeds bats)	very positive effect (bats disperse seeds)
7. Saguaro Plants/Hawk Nests	very positive effect (hawks receive safe shelter)	no effect (plant isn't harmed by nests)
8. Old Man's Flowers/Bats	no effect (bats don't eat nectar)	no effect (plant doesn't need bats)
9. Old Man's Flowers/Moths	very positive effect (nectar feeds lots of moths)	very positive effect (moths pollinate plant)
10. Nurse Plant Flowers/Bees	very positive effect (pollen and nectar feeds lots of bees)	very positive effect (bees pollinate plant)
11. Nurse Plant Flowers/Bats	no effect (bats don't eat nectar)	no effect (plant doesn't need bats)
12. Agave Flowers/Bees	very positive effect (pollen and nectar feeds lots of bees)	little positive effect (few bees pollinate plant)
13. Agave Flowers/Deer	very positive effect (agave stalks feed lots of deer)	negative effect (plant can't produce flowers)
14. Agave Flowers/Bats	very positive effect (nectar feeds lots of bats)	very positive effect (bats pollinate flowers)
15. Agave Flowers/ Hummingbirds	very positive effect (nectar feeds lots of hummingbirds)	little positive effect (few hummingbirds pollinate plant)

Answers to 12-A: Investigate This!

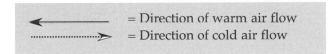

= Direction of warm air flow
= Direction of cold air flow

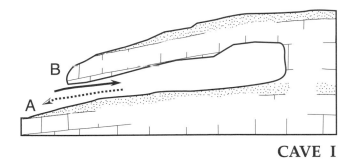

CAVE I

1. Most air flow (in and out) occurs in *summer*.

2. Cave will trap air that is *warmer* than the ground temperature.

3. Bats could use this cave for *rearing young*.

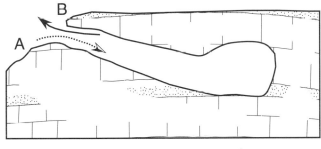

CAVE II

1. Most air flow (in and out) occurs in *winter*.

2. Cave will trap air that is *cooler*.

3. Bats could use this cave for *hibernation*.

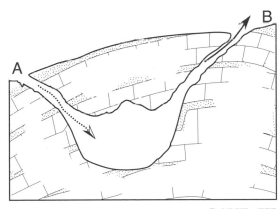

CAVE III

1. Most air flow (in and out) occurs in *winter*.

2. Cave will trap air that is *cooler*.

3. Bats could use this cave for *hibernation*.

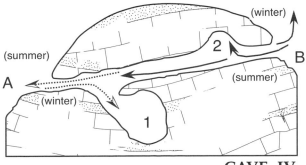

CAVE IV

1. Most air flow (in and out) occurs on the *hottest and coolest days* year round.

2. Cave will trap air that is *both cooler and warmer* than the ground temperature.

3. Bats could use this cave for *both rearing young and hibernation*.

Answers to 12-B: Investigate This!

All caves that are not geothermally heated (rare and not discussed here) are "warmer" than the outside air on cold winter days and "cooler" than outside air on hot summer days. A summary of airflow patterns in Caves I through IV follows:

In CAVE I, there would be airflow only in summer, cool air exiting along the floor at A, and warmer air entering along the ceiling at B. In winter, the relatively warmer air would be trapped inside, and there would be no airflow at A or B.

In CAVE II, there would be airflow only in winter, cool air flowing in along the floor at A and warmer air exiting along the ceiling at B. In summer, the relatively cooler, heavier air would be trapped inside and there would be no airflow at A or B.

CAVE III, also would exhibit airflow only in winter with air flowing in a rapid "chimney effect," which would be greatest on the coldest days. At that time, cool air would enter at entrance A, and relatively warmer air would exit at entrance B. In summer, the relatively cooler, heavier air would be trapped inside and there would be no airflow at A or B.

CAVE IV, would also exhibit strong "chimney effect" airflow, but in both the winter and summer. In winter, relatively warm air exits from entrance B. This creates a vacuum that sucks heavier winter air into the cave, far enough to trap it in location 1. In the summer, the relatively cool air will flow out from entrance A, creating a vacuum that sucks warmer outside air in through entrance B. Lighter, warmer air becomes trapped in location 2.

1. Caves II, III, and IV will be suitable for hibernation, because they all trap cool air.

2. Caves I and IV will be suitable for rearing young, because they both trap warm air.

3. In Cave IV, in the winter, location 1 will trap the coolest air and be the best location for a hibernating colony of bats.

4. In Cave IV, in the summer, location 2 will trap the warmest air and be the best location for a colony to rear young.

5. Cave IV is by far the best cave for Gray Myotis because it can be used for both hibernation and rearing young. It provides a cool air trap in location 1 during the winter and a warm air trap in location 2 during the summer; thus it can meet the bats' needs year round. The cost of spring and fall migrations would therefore be virtually eliminated since a colony would only have to switch locations in a cave instead of traveling between two caves that are sometimes hundreds of miles apart. (If Cave IV were *not* located near an appropriate feeding habitat, the fact that it provides a warm roost suitable for rearing young would be meaningless. Mothers would have to waste too much energy traveling to distant feeding sites.)

6. Even in a cold air trap (see Caves II and III), if the ceiling is dome-shaped, the area inside the dome will never freeze. The dome traps air that is warmed by the cave's walls in that chamber and thus remains above freezing, though the air flowing into the cave may be well below freezing.

Answer to Bonus Question

If entrance B were bulldozed shut, there would no longer be any airflow at entrance A during the winter. (Cave IV would be very similar to Cave I now with just a single entrance and a gradual up-slope.) Because there would be no airflow in the winter, the temperature in location 1 would not be much different from the average ground temperature of the area, and this area would now be too warm for hibernating bats. As you can see, any disturbance of the airflow or entrance size and shape can greatly affect the interior temperatures of caves and severely impact bats.

Answers to 14-A: Investigate This!

Key

1. Kapok Tree
2. Fig Tree
3. Palm Trees
4. (a) Bromeliads
   (b) Orchids
5. Harpy Eagle
6. Toucan
7. Parrot
8. Flycatcher
9. Owl
10. Jaguar
11. Monkey
12. Agouti
13. Coati
14. Nectar-feeding Bats
15. Fruit-eating Bat
16. Free-tailed Bats
17. Round-eared Bat
18. Gecko
19. Tree Snake
20. Termite Nest
21. Bees
22. Fig Wasps

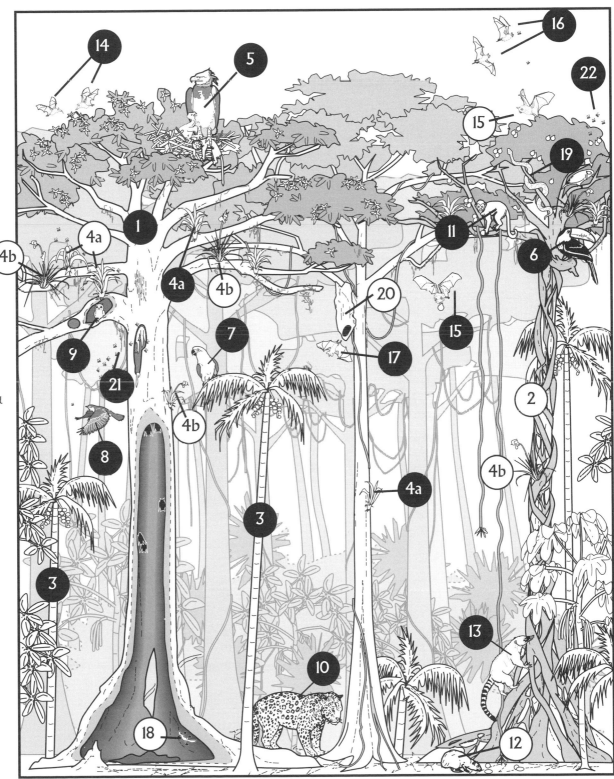

Answers to 14-C: Discuss This!

1. All the plants and animals could be harmed, and many might die. Giant kapok trees provide shade and support for other trees, growing platforms for thousands of epiphyte plants, and homes and food for many animals.

2. Without fig wasps, no more figs would be produced. Bats, agoutis, toucans, monkeys, and parrots all eat figs. Without figs, they could starve to death.

3. Harpy eagles, tree snakes, owsl, and jaguars do not eat figs, but do need to eat other animals that eat figs.

4. Predators help fig and other fruit trees by forcing fruit bats to carry fruit away to eat, thus spreading more seeds. However, too many predators would harm trees by not leaving enough bats. This is a good example of the need for balance in nature.

5. If all bats died, birds would only feed on insects that fly by day. If all birds died, bats would only feed on insects that fly at night. Losing either bats or birds would leave a large proportion of insects un-eaten, and the whole forest could be seriously harmed.

6. No. If all the rain forests were cut down, there would be no more homes for the animals. Without homes, the animals would die and even if new trees were planted, there would be no animals to keep them healthy. Rain forest plants and animals are extremely dependent on each other and cannot survive apart. Some animals pollinate the flowers of rain forest plants. Without pollination, plants cannot produce fruit. Other animals eat the fruit and disperse the seeds of these plants. Without seed-dispersal, plants cannot colonize new areas or produce young plants to take the place of aging parent plants.

7. Worldwide, we rely on rain forests for oxygen, many medicines, and other valuable products. We need their effects on weather and rainfall to ensure successful crops that feed us.

Bonus Question:

60,000 divided by 2 = 30,000 seeds each night

30,000 divided by 100 = 300 seedlings will be planted each night

300 x 365 = 109,500 planted each year by one bat

109,500 x 100 = 10,950,000 seedlings planted in a year by a colony of 100 short-tailed fruit bats

Answers to 15-A: Investigate This!

1. The smaller a cleared area is, and the more surrounded by remaining forest, the quicker it will be reseeded by animals crossing. When tree cutting just keeps spreading from the forest edge, as it often does, animals simply retreat farther into the remaining forest. They have no incentive to cross the cleared area, so do not drop seeds that could help new forest to grow.

2. A wildlife sanctuary in a rain forest serves like Noah's ark. If it is large enough, critical species survive, ensuring the option of expanding these forests in the future when we better learn their value and how to use them. Many wild rain forest plants contain genes that are extremely valuable for improving disease resistance in agricultural crops, such as bananas and avocados. Sanctuaries also are invaluable laboratories for scientific discoveries or for simple human enjoyment.

3. Losing a large cave-dwelling population of fruit or nectar bats could be a disaster for the forest, since many of its largest trees and most important plants would lose essential seed dispersers or pollinators.

4. Less cutting now means less short-term income from sale of timber and livestock, but it also can assure steady income for future generations. Once too large an area of rain forest is cut, it cannot regrow, and soil nutrients may rapidly disappear, leaving the land far less valuable in a few years. A patchwork of partial cutting gives the forest a chance to regrow and essential wildlife a chance to survive. Game management that ensures healthy wildlife populations is essential to long-term forest use. Economically, historic rain forest lands are far more productive as forests than when converted to crop and cattle areas.

5. This is the kind of difficult choice that modern conservationists must increasingly face. People are most likely to protect wildlife if it pays for itself through tourism, limited hunting, or regular harvest. We may hate to kill any of the animals we protect, but if animals have high enough populations and reproductive rates to sustain some deaths, the income they bring may convince people to protect them instead of replacing them with cattle or other livestock. We must always consider all the options and which might work best in each case.

Answers to 17-A: Calculate This!

Mexican Free-tailed Bats
1. 4 X 10 = 40 moths
2. 20 X 500 = 10,000 eggs
3. 13 divided by 20 = $0.65
4. 20 X $0.65 = $13
5. 4 X 454 = 1,816 moths
6. 1,816 X 400,000 = 726,400,000 moths (or 7.264×10^8 moths)

Bonus Questions:
1. 5 X 400,000 = 2,000,000 pounds (or 2×10^6 pounds)
2. 4,540 X 2,000,000 = 9,080,000,000 insects (or 9.08×10^9 insects)

Answers to 17-B: Calculate This!

Little Brown Myotis
1. 15 X 60 = 900 insects
2. 20 X 1,000 = 20,000 mosquitos (or 2×10^4 mosquitos)
3. 10 X 10 X 20 = 2,000 moths (or 2×10^3 moths)

Bonus Questions:
1. 200 X 4,500 = 900,000 and 900,000 X 7 = 6,300,000 insects per week (or 6.3×10^6 insects per week)
2. 900,000 ÷ 4 = 225,000 mosquitos (or 2.2×10^5 mosquitos)
   and
   225,000 mosquitoes in a night ÷ 2 = 112,500 female mosquitos X 200 = 22,500,000 eggs! (or 2.25×10^7 eggs!)

Solution Summary to 18-B: Discuss This!

THE CASE OF THE THAI BAT CAVE
HELPING A VILLAGE BY PROTECTING THEIR BAT CAVE

<u>How the Problem Was Solved</u>
The Conservationists made friends with the Hunters and Guano Miners and asked their assistance to study the problem, explaining that if the bats declined much more, none would be left to hunt. They learned from the Hunters that many times more bats were being killed than necessary, because nets were set over the cave entrance instead of near fruiting trees that attracted only the fruit bats that people liked to eat. They also learned that Guano Miners were disturbing roosts in the cave more often than necessary, including during the two months in spring when mother bats were trying to rear young.

The Conservationists recommended that no bat netting be allowed at the cave entrance in order to protect insect-eating species that were valuable to farmers and Guano Miners. This also gave the fruit bats a chance to escape until numbers built up enough for them to be easily caught at fruit trees. Conservationists also recommended that the guano mining not be done when mothers were rearing young.

The Monks and Conservationists contacted the Thai government and explained that the income from guano mining for fertilizer could be approximately $100,000 U.S. dollars annually. A game warden would cost only about $4,000 a year. Thus, the government could collect more than enough taxes to pay for a game warden. Even the Hunters would benefit, because the warden would make sure there were always enough bats left for future hunting. The Monks and villagers would benefit from not disturbing mother bats with young, because the colony would grow and produce more guano.

The government hired the requested game warden.

<u>Long-Term Effects</u>
Ten years later, the income from bat guano mining had risen from $12,000 to close to $100,000 U.S. each year. Everyone was pleased. The Hunters were still hunting, but with their nets set away from the cave. Because the community now understands they should appreciate their bats, many Hunters' children do not aspire to become bat hunters. Hunting will likely end with the next generation.

It is important to note, however, that this was not a case of good guys versus bad guys. Both the Hunters and the game warden are good men who are working hard to care for their families. There was just a serious conservation problem that needed solving. If the Conservationists had failed, both the Hunters and the Guano Miners would have lost their jobs and had a hard time supporting their families. Good conservation is also good for people, and it is far more likely to succeed when everyone concerned understands and helps.

Solution Summary to 18-C: Discuss This!

THE CASE OF THE VAMPIRE BATS
SAVING BENEFICIAL BATS WHILE PROTECTING RANCHERS FROM VAMPIRE BATS

<u>How the Problem Was Solved</u>
The Conservationists met with Government Officials responsible for controlling Vampire Bats to discuss what could be done to help both sides solve their problems. Both groups agreed that Vampire Bats must be killed to control the spread of disease and parasites, but that control efforts should be more efficient and that beneficial bat species should be protected. Both sides also agreed that broad education was the only real solution.

The Conservationists raised funds to produce an educational video on how to control Vampire Bats. They invited the local experts in Vampire control to serve as scientific advisors and appear in the video. The Government Officials in Vampire control agreed to participate.

Long-Term Effects

Government Officials throughout Latin America now use this Vampire control video to train other Officials and Ranchers. The video is shown to large groups in community centers, which leads to discussion and cooperation between neighboring Ranchers. Now, when Vampire Bats cause a rabies outbreak in cattle, Ranchers can quickly learn how to solve their problem. They also learn how important the other bats are. Revenue from the sale of the video pays for future copies, ensuring a permanent supply.

Former enemies have become allies as a result of this approach. Many Ranchers and Government Officials that formerly killed all bats now cooperate with Conservationists to save beneficial species. Because this solution is innovative and successful, it has received a fair amount of publicity from newspapers and other media. This has helped to spread the message even further and gain the participation and support of more key officials, scientific leaders, and educators. Local citizens throughout Latin America have begun to learn that not all bats are Vampires and that bat conservation is important.

Solution Summary to 18-D: Discuss This!

THE CASE OF THE BRIDGE BATS
PROTECTING MEXICAN FREE-TAILED BATS IN A BRIDGE

How the Problem Was Solved

Conservationists met privately with leading Public Health Officials in Austin and pointed out that they shared the Health Officials' concern for protecting people. They explained that these bats do not bite unless handled and offered to help educate people to appreciate but not handle the bats. Of course, they also explained the great benefit of bats eating large quantities of insects.

The Public Health Officials saw the value of working with the Conservationists, and soon they were helping. Together, Health Officials and Conservationists contacted city officials and convinced them to put up signs at the bridge that explained the value of bats, but also warned people not to handle the bats. This made bat-watching safer and more interesting for tourists.

Both Conservationists and Public Health Officials gave television and newspaper interviews to help people understand the bats and learn to live safely with them. The same newspapers and television stations that had formerly run frightening, incorrect stories began to help educate the people of Austin about the value of bats.

The Conservationists also produced educational materials for local schools, and student bat clubs were formed. Soon, school children were wearing buttons that said, "Ask me about bats." They helped their parents learn about bats and went to the bridge and helped tourists learn about bats. This helped a great deal.

Long-Term Effects

Ten years later, the Mexican Free-tailed Bat colony under the Congress Avenue bridge has grown to one-and-a-half million bats. No one has ever been attacked by one of these bats, and only a very few people have foolishly attempted to handle the bats. The people of Austin are now very proud of their bats.

Each summer, tens of thousands of tourists come to Austin from all over the world just to see its famous bats. Local businesses are delighted, because the tourists spend hundreds of thousands of dollars on hotels, food, souvenirs, and much more, greatly helping the economy.

The city's largest newspaper, the *Austin American-Statesman,* has built educational signs and a special bat-viewing area at the bridge. Waiters at nearby restaurants explain the bat flights to patrons as they dine. Local hotels and riverboat tour companies promote bat watching, and local businesses help Bat Conservation International to print 75,000 educational brochures each summer. They also provide a trained interpreter (guide) at the bridge on weekends to answer questions and help tourists better understand the bats.

This huge success probably would not have been possible if Conservationists had simply gotten mad and attacked Health Officials and the news media for the wrong things they had said. By making friends and offering to help, everyone involved became long-term winners.

Solution Summary to 18-E: Discuss This!

THE CASE OF THE HIBERNATING BATS
CAVE EXPLORERS HELP SAVE A CAVE FOR ENDANGERED BATS

<u>How the Problem Was Solved</u>
Conservationists met with the National Guard Commanders and explained the value of the bats in Hubbard's Cave. The commanders said there were plenty of other places for military practice and even offered to help the Conservationists. As a training exercise, they organized their huge cross-country vehicles and national guardsmen to haul the supplies needed to build a protective gate. They carried more than 50 tons of steel, concrete, and other materials up the rugged mountain to the cave entrance.

The Conservationists realized that not all Cave Explorers were bad. They respected the responsible Cave Explorers, and asked them to help design and build the world's largest cave gate. They also promised to allow them to continue exploring the cave in the seasons when bats were not present. As a result, Cave Explorers from the National Speleological Society and the American Cave Conservation Association worked extremely hard and volunteered their equipment every weekend for a month to build the huge gate. They were very proud of their work in the end.

<u>Long-Term Effects</u>
An extremely strong gate was built that has not been broken into by vandals in more than 10 years. Such a gate could not have been built without all the help from the National Guard and responsible Cave Explorers.

The bat population is now protected and recovering. Responsible Cave Explorers are better off, because they can still explore the cave, which is now protected from destruction by careless cave visitors and vandals. The cave is more fun to explore in the summer anyway.

The National Guard has taken great pride in helping make such important conservation progress possible. They received a special award for their assistance and much good publicity from the media.

Appendix B—Bibliography

Regional Bat Distribution and Identification References

<u>United States and Canada—General</u>

America's Neighborhood Bats. (Rev. Ed.) Merlin D. Tuttle. University of Texas Press, Austin, 98 pages. 1997.

Bats. M. Brock Fenton. Facts on File Inc., New York, 207 pages. 1992.

Bats of America. Roger W. Barbour and Wayne H. Davis. University Press of Kentucky, Lexington, 286 pages. 1969.

Mammals of North America, 4th Edition. Peterson Field Guides. F.A. Reid. Houghton Mifflin Company, Boston and New York, 599 pages. 2006.

National Audubon Society Field Guide to North American Mammals. (Rev. Ed.) John O. Whitaker, Jr. Alfred A. Knopf, Inc., New York, 942 pages. 1996.

The Bats of Europe and North America. W. Schober and E. Grimmberger. T.F.H. Publications, Neptune City, NJ, 239 pages. 1997.

<u>Southwest</u>

Bats of Carlsbad Caverns National Park. Kenneth N. Geluso, J. Scott Altenbach, and Ronal C. Kerbo, Carlsbad Caverns Natural History Association, Carlsbad, 32 pages. 1987.

The Bats of Texas. David J. Schmidley. Texas A&M University Press, College Station, 188 pages. 1991.

Mammals of Arizona. D.F. Hoffmeister. The University of Arizona Press, Tucson, 602 pages. 1986.

Mammals of New Mexico. J.S. Findley, A.H. Harris, D.E. Wilson, and C. Jones. University of New Mexico Press, Albuquerque, 360 pages. 1975.

Mammals of Oklahoma. W. Caire, J.D. Tyler, B.P. Glass, and M.A. Mares. University of Oklahoma Press, Oklahoma City, 582 pages. 1989.

The Mammals of Texas. William B. Davis and David J. Schmidley. Texas Parks and Wildlife Press, Austin, 519 pages. 2004. 6th Edition.

<u>Southeast</u>

Arkansas Mammals: Their Natural History, Classification, and Distribution. John A. Sealander and Gary A. Heidt. University of Arkansas Press, Fayetteville, 308 pages. 1991.

A Guide to Arkansas Mammals. J.A. Sealander. River Road Press, Conway, Arkansas, 313 pages. 1979.

A Guide to Mammals of the Southeastern United States. Larry N. Brown. University of Tennessee Press, Knoxville, 256 pages. 1997.

Bats of Florida. C.S. Marks and G.E. Marks. University Press of Florida, Gainesville, FL, 188 pages. 2006.

Handbook of Mammals of the South-Central States. Jerry R. Choate, J. Knox Jones, Jr., and Clyde Jones. Louisiana State University Press, Baton Rouge, 304 pages. 1994.

Mammals of Great Smoky Mountains National Park. Donald W. Linzey. McDonald and Woodward Publishing Co., Blacksburg, 140 pages. 1995.

The Mammals of Louisiana and Its Adjacent Waters. G.H. Lowery, Jr. Louisiana State University Press, Baton Rouge, 565 pages. 1974.

Northeast and Mid-Atlantic

Bats of the Eastern United States. Michael J. Harvey. Arkansas Game and Fish Commission, Little Rock, 46 pages. 1992.

Guide to the Mammals of Pennsylvania. Joseph F. Merritt. University of Pittsburgh Press, Pittsburg, 408 pages. 1987.

Mammals of the Adirondacks: A Field Guide. William Chapman and Dennis Aprill. North Country, Unity, 159 pages. 1990.

Mammals of the Carolinas, Virginia, and Maryland. William David Webster, James F. Parnell, and Walter C. Briggs, Jr. University of North Carolina Press, Chapel Hill, 267 pages. 1985.

Mammals of the Eastern United States, 3rd Edition. J.O. Whitaker Jr. and W.J. Hamilton Jr. Comstock Publishing Associates, Ithaca, NY, 583 pages. 1998.

Mammals of Virginia. Donald W. Linzey. McDonald and Woodward Publishing Co., Blacksburg, 450 pages. 1996.

Midwest

A Guide to the Bats of Iowa, Nongame Technical Series No. 2. C.M. Laubach, John Bowles, and R. Laubach. Iowa Department of Natural Resources, Des Moines, 32 pages. 1994.

A Guide to the Mammals of Ohio. Jack L. Gottschang. Ohio State University Press, Columbus, 176 pages. 1981.

Bats of Indiana. , J.O. Whitaker Jr., et al. Indiana State University Press, Terre Haute, IN, 59 pages. 2007.

Bats of Michigan. A. Kurta. Indiana State University Press, Terre Haute, IN, 72 pages. 2008.

Mammals of the Great Lakes Region. Allen Kurta. University of Michigan Press, Ann Arbor, 350 pages. 1995.

Mammals of Illinois. D.F. Hoffmeister. University of Illinois Press, Chicago, 348 pages. 1989.

Mammals of Indiana. Marcus Ward Lyon, Jr. Arno Press, New York, 384 pages. 1974.

Mammals of Kentucky. Roger W. Barbour and Wayne H. Davis. University Press of Kentucky, Lexington, 321 pages. 1974.

Mammals of Minnesota. Evan B. Hazard and N. Kane. University of Minnesota Press, Minneapolis, 286 pages. 1982.

Wild Mammals of Missouri. Charles W. Schwartz and Elizabeth R. Schwartz. University Press of Missouri, Columbia, 368 pages. 1981.

Mammals of Wisconsin. H.H.T. Jackson. University of Wisconsin Press, Madison, 504 pages. 1961.

Plains

Guide to Mammals of the Plains States. J.K. Jones, Jr., D.M. Armstrong, and J.R. Choate. University of Nebraska Press, Lincoln, 371 pages. 1985.

Handbook of Mammals of the North-Central States. J. Knox Jones, Jr., and Elmer C. Birney. University of Minnesota Press, Columbia, 346 pages. 1988.

Mammals in Kansas. James W. Bee, Gregory Glass, Robert Hoffman, and Robert R. Patterson. University of Kansas Press, Lawrence, 300 pages. 1981.

Rocky Mountains

Bats of Colorado—Shadows in the Night. David M. Armstrong, Rick A. Adams, Kirk W. Navo, Jerry Freeman, and Steven J. Bissell. Colorado Division of Wildlife, Denver, 30 pages. 1984.

Bats of the Rocky Mountain West. R. Adams. University Press of Colorado, Boulder, CO, 289 pages. 2003.

Mammals of Colorado. James P. Fitzgerald, Carron A. Meaney, and David M. Armstrong. University of Colorado Press, Boulder, 488 pages. 1994.

Mammals of Nevada. Raymond E. Hall. University of Nevada Press, Reno, 710 pages. 1995.

Mammals of the Northern Rockies. T. Ulrich. Mountain Press, Missoula, 160 pages. 1986.

Mammals of the Pacific Northwest. C. Maser. Oregon State University Press, Corvallis, OR, 406 pages. 1998.

Mammals in Wyoming. Tim W. Clark and M.S. Stromberg. University of Kansas Press, Lawrence, 314 pages. 1987.

Appendices

West

California Mammals. E.W. Jameson, Jr., and Hans Peeters. University of California Press, Berkeley, 403 pages. 1987.

Mammals in Hawai'i. Quentin P. Tomich. Bishop Museum Press, Honolulu, 374 pages. 1986.

Mammals of the Pacific States. Lloyd G. Ingles. Stanford University Press, Stanford, 506 pages. 1965.

Canada

Alberta Mammals. Hugh C. Smith. The Provincial Museum of Alberta, Edmonton, 239 pages. 1993.

Bats of British Columbia. D.W. Nagorsen and R.M. Brigham. University of British Columbia, Vancouver, 176 pages. 1993.

Handbook of Canadian Mammals: Volume 2, Bats. C.G. van Zyll de Jong. National Museum of Natural Sciences, Ottawa, 212 pages. 1985.

The Mammals of Eastern Canada. R.L. Peterson. Oxford University Press, Oxford, 465 pages. 1966.

Mammifères du Québec et de l'Est du Canada. J Prescott and P. Richard. Éditions Michel Quintin, Québec, 399 pages. 1996.

Latin America (Mexico, Central America, South America)

Costa Rica Bats. R. LaVal and B. Rodriguez-Herrera. Instituto Nacional de Biodiversidad, Santo Domingo de Heredia, Costa Rica, 320 pages. 2002.

A Field Guide to the Mammals of Central America and Southeast Mexico. F.A. Reid. Oxford University Press USA, 344 pages. 1997

Guide to the Mammals of Salta Province, Argentina. M.A. Mares, R.A. Ojeda, and R.M. Barquez. The University of Oklahoma Press, Norman, 303 pages. 1989.

Mammals of the Neotropics—The Northern Neotropics, Volume I: Panama, Columbia, Venezuela, Guyana, Suriname, French Guiana. J.F. Eisenberg. University of Chicago Press, Chicago, 449 pages. 1989.

Mammals of the Neotropics—The Southern Cone, Volume II: Chile, Argentina, Uruguay, Paraguay. K.H Redford and J.F. Eisenberg. University of Chicago Press, Chicago, 420 pages. 1992.

The Natural History of Vampire Bats. A.M. Greenhall and U. Schmidt. CRC Press, Boca Raton, 246 pages. 1988.

Neotropical Rainforest Mammals: A Field Guide. L.H. Emmons. University of Chicago Press, Chicago, 281 pages. 1990.

Neotropical Tent-Roosting Bats. B. Rodriguez-Herrera, R. Medellin and R.M. Timm. Instituto Nacional de Biodiversidad, Santo Domingo de Heredia, Costa Rica, 178 pages. 2007.

Europe

A Guide to Bats of Britain and Europe. W. Schober and E. Grimmberger. Hamlyn Publishing Group Limited, London, 224 pages. 1987.

The Handbook of British Mammals.(Second Ed.) G.B Corbet and H.N. Southern (eds.). Blackwell Scientific Publications, Oxford, 520 pages. 1977.

Africa

Bats of South Africa. P.I.Taylor. University of Natal Press, Scottsville, South Africa, 207 pages. 2000.

East African Mammals: Volume IIA, Insectivores and Bats. J. Kingdon. University of Chicago Press, Chicago, 341 pages. 1974.

Field Guide to the Mammals of Southern Africa. C. and T. Stuart. Struik Publishers, Cape Town, 272 pages. 1988.

The Bats of Egypt. M.B. Qumsiyeh. Texas Tech University Press, Lubbock, TX, 102 pages. 1985.

The Mammals of the Southern African Subregion. R.H.N. Smithers. University of Pretoria Press, Pretoria, 736 pages. 1983.

The Mammals of Arabia. (Second Ed.) D.L. Harrison and P.J. Bates. Harrison Zoological Museum Publication, Kent (England), 354 pages. 1991.

<u>Australia, New Guinea, and New Zealand</u>

Australian Bats. S. Churchill. New Holland Publishers, Sydney, Australia, 230 pages. 1998.

Bats of Papua New Guinea. F.J. Bonaccorso. Conservation International, 489 pages. 1998.

Complete Book of Australian Mammals. R. Strahan, Ed. Angus & Robertson Publishers, Sydney, 529 pages. 1983.

Flying Foxes: Fruit and Blossom Bats of Australia. L. Hall and G. Richards. University of South Wales Press and Krieger Publishing Company, Malabar, FL, 135 pages. 2000.

Mammals of Australia. R. Strahan, Ed. Smithsonian Institution Press, Washington D.C., 756 pages. 1995.

Mammals of New Guinea. T. Flannery. Robert Brown & Associates, Carina, Queensland (Australia), 568 pages. 1990.

Collins Guide to the Mammals of New Zealand. M. Daniel and A. Baker. William Collins Publishers Ltd., Auckland, 228 pages. 1986.

Mammals of the South-West Pacific and Moluccan Islands. T. Flannery. Reed Books, Chatswood (New South Wales), 464 pages. 1995.

<u>Asia</u>

Bats of the Indian Subcontinent. P. Bates and J.J. and D.L. Harrison. Harrison Zoogical Museum Publication, Kent, 258 pages. 1997.

Mammals of Thailand. B. Lekagul and J.A. McNeely. Sahakarnbhat Co., Bangkok, 758 pages. 1977.

A Field Guide to the Mammals of Borneo. J. Payne and C.M. Francis. The Sabah Society, World Wildlife Fund Malaysia, Kuala Lumpur, 332 pages. 1985.

Annotated Bibliography of Reference Resources About Bats

General Introductory Books about Bats
Perfect for beginning bat enthusiasts and introductory study of bats, these sources contain information on general bat biology, distribution, and basic bat conservation issues.

Allen, G.M. 1939. *Bats.* Harvard University Press, Cambridge (Reprint: 1962. Dover Publications Inc., New York), 369 pages.
  Written by a classic bat biologist whose primary interest included bats and how they lived. Contains information on distribution, habitats, diet, flight, and migration. Also includes chapters on bats and man, bats in art, and folklore.

Fenton, M.B. 1992. *Bats.* Facts on File Inc., New York, 207 pages.
  A well-illustrated introduction to the worldwide diversity of bats presented in a full-color format. Contains information about echolocation, migration, foraging strategies, roosting behavior, social organization, population dynamics, bats and public health, and conservation.

Graham, G.L. 1994. *Bats of the World: A Golden Guide.* Golden Press, New York, 160 pages.
  A pocket-sized introduction to the world of bats and their field characteristics. Includes information about distribution, taxonomy, natural history, and conservation.

Richarz, K. and A. Limbrunner. 1993. *The World of Bats.* Franck-Kosmos Verlags-GMBH & Co., Stuttgart, Germany (English translation by W. Charlton), THF Publications, 192 pages.
  An excellent, well-illustrated introduction to bats of the world. Includes information on feeding strategies, general natural history, etc. Includes a section on "Bats and Humankind," which covers the roles of bats in local economies and folklore.

Tuttle, Merlin D. 1997. *America's Neighborhood Bats* (Rev. Ed.). University of Texas Press, Austin, 98 pages.
   An excellent layman's introduction to American bats, covering a wide range of issues from public health and nuisance concerns to bat values and conservation needs. Common North American bats are featured with natural history information, color photographs, and a key to identification.

Tuttle, Merlin D., Mark and Selena Kiser. 2004. *The Bat House Builder's Handbook*. (Rev. Ed.) Bat Conservation International, Austin, 35 pages.
   A valuable "how to" manual on the design, installation, monitoring, and conservation impact of artificial bat roosts. Includes several easy-to-build plans and up-to-date research results on artificial roosting preferences of common North American bat species.

Wilson, D.E., 1997. *Bats in Question: The Smithsonian Answer Book*. Smithsonian Institution Press, Washington D.C., 168 pages. A user-friendly format introducing the world of bats through questions and answers highlighting the most commonly asked questions about bats, myths and misconceptions, and the need for bat conservation. This is the one resource for all introductory inquiries about bats.

Advanced Study and Research Information
For the serious student, these texts are comprehensive treatments of bat research and biology dealing with distribution and diversity, reproductive behavior, ecology, physiology, and systematics of bats.

Altringham, J.D. 1996. *Bats Biology and Behaviour*. Oxford University Press, Oxford, 262 pages.
   This book is aimed primarily at undergraduate and graduate students wishing to learn about bats, but also illustrates how a study of one group of animals can contribute to a wider understanding of the processes which shape the natural world. It includes comprehensive information on the evolution and diversity of bats, flight, echolocation, hibernation, reproduction and development, behavioral ecology, and conservation.

Buchmann, S.L. and G.P. Nabhan. 1996. *The Forgotten Pollinators*. Island Press, Tucson, 320 pages.
   Without interaction between animals and flowering plants, the seeds and fruits that make up nearly 80 percent of the human diet would not exist. Here, the authors explore the vital but little-appreciated relationship between plants and the animals they depend on—bats, bees, beetles, butterflies, hummingbirds, and countless other animals.

Hall, E.R. 1981. *The Mammals of North America, Volume II*. John Wiley and Sons, New York, 1,181 pages.
   Contains excellent coverage of North American bat species. Includes range maps, taxonomic characteristics, and a species identification key.

Kunz, T.H. (Ed.) 1982. *Ecology of Bats*. Plenum Press, New York and London, 425 pages.
   Contributions from the world's foremost bat biologists make this volume essential reading for all serious students of bat biology. Contents include chapters on roosting ecology, reproduction, growth and survival, physiology, morphology, feeding behavior, bat/plant interactions, and more.

————. 1988. *Ecological and Behavioral Methods for the Study of Bats*. Smithsonian Institution Press, Washington, 533 pages.
   An excellent resource for anyone interested in field research on bats. Topics covered include bat capture, care in captivity, marking and observational techniques, radiotelemetry, photography, age determination, reproductive assessment, allozyme techniques for kinship assessment, and much more. The detailed chapters are clearly written, well illustrated, and include extensive bibliographies. Addresses for equipment and supplies are included.

Macdonald, D. (Ed.) 1987. *The Encyclopedia of Mammals*. Facts on File Publications, New York, 895 pages.
   A comprehensive resource of world mammal species. Includes detailed species list index, color plates of each mammalian order, and descriptive family information including geographic distribution.

Appendices

Nowak, R.M. and J.L. Paradiso. 1983. *Walker's Mammals of the World*, Vol. 1, 4th edition. John Hopkins University Press, Baltimore, 568 pages.
  Designed to appeal to both professional and general readers. Includes accurate and well-documented descriptions of the lives and habits of the world's bat species. Includes information on habitat, population dynamics, reproduction, and longevity.

Nowak, R.M. 1994. *Walker's Bats of the World*. Johns Hopkins University Press, Baltimore, 287 pages.
  Adapted from *Walker's Mammals of the World*, this text provides an introduction to the 18 bat families and numerous representative species. It also includes a world distribution of bats, appendix, and copious literature citations. Browse the on-line edition at: *http://www.press.jhu.edu/books/walkers_mammals_of_the_world/chiroptera/chiroptera.html*

Wilson, D.E. and D.M. Reeder, (Eds.) 1993. *Mammal Species of the World*. Smithsonian Institution Press, Washington, 1,206 pages.
  Perhaps the definitive reference of world mammal species. Includes the detailed classification of all 925 species of bats developed by bat specialist Karl Koopman from the American Musuem of Natural History in New York.

Books for Young Readers
Over the years, creative authors and outstanding artists and photographers have combined forces to educate young readers about bats and their importance to our environment. These texts represent both non-fiction and fictional mainstays in BCI's educational initiatives for young conservationists.

Ackerman, Diane. 1997. *Bats: Shadows in the Night*. Crown Publishers, 31 pages.
  In this beautifully photographed book, acclaimed nature writer Diane Ackerman retells her adventures traveling across Texas with Merlin Tuttle in search of bats. For grades 4 and up.

Bash, B. 1993. *Shadows of the Night: The Hidden World of the Little Brown Bat*. Sierra Club Books for Children, San Francisco, 30 pages.
  With easy-to-read text and glowing water colors, the author paints a beautiful picture of a year in the life of a little brown bat, dispelling the mystery that surrounds these harmless and beneficial creatures of the night. For grades 2-5.

Cannon, Janell. 1993. *Stellaluna*. Harcourt, Brace, & Company, New York, 48 pages.
  1994 winner of the prestigious American Bookseller's Book of the Year (ABBY) Award; a beautifully illustrated story of friendship and discovery about a young fruit bat separated from her mother and raised by birds. For grades K-2.

Cherry, Lynne. 1990. *The Great Kapok Tree: A Tale of the Amazon Rain Forest*. Harcourt Brace, & Company, New York, 36 pages.
  This beautifully-illustrated book tells a simple story with vivid illustrations that capture the reality and lushness of the rain forest. As a man chops away at a great kapok tree, the heat and efforts of his work exhaust him so that he falls asleep. One by one, the creatures (not including bats) who live in the tree emerge and plead with him not to destroy their world. For grades 4 and up.

de Mauro, Lisa. 1990. *Explorer Books: Bats*. Bantam Doubleday Publishing Group, New York, 60 pages.
  A factual account of bat diversity throughout the world. Easy-to-read text is complemented with black-and-white photos by Merlin Tuttle. For grades 4-10.

Goodman, Billy. 1992. *The Rainforest: A Planet Earth Book*. Little Brown and Company, New York, 96 pages.
  Beautiful, full-color photos and a clear, easy-to-understand text, introduce young readers to the many forms of life (not including bats) found in this fascinating environment and explains the causes and effects of deforestation, as well as efforts to live in harmony with the forests while also providing for indigenous peoples. For grades 4-7.

Gray, Susan H. 1994. *Bats: A New True Book*. Children's Press, Chicago, 45 pages.
An easy-to-read introduction to the diversity of bats. Contains color photos, a glossary, and index. For grades 2-4.

Gunzi, Christiane. 1993. *Cave Life (Look Closer)*. Dorling-Kindersley, New York, 29 pages.
Presented in an eye-catching style, this introductory text discusses and describes in detail the unique adaptations of plants and animals that live in caves including bats, cave fish, peacock butterfly, crickets, and maidenhair ferns. For grades 4-7.

Halton, Cheryl M. 1991. *Those Amazing Bats*. Dillon Press Inc., Minneapolis, 96 pages.
Describes diversity, behavior, and benefits of bats. Features the work of Merlin Tuttle, bat house plans, appendix of endangered bats, and glossary. For grades 4-6.

Jarrell, Randall. 1964 (Re-issued 1996). *The Bat Poet*. Harper Collins Juvenile Books, 44 pages.
A classic and delightful book telling a fable about an eccentric little brown bat who writes poems for the other forest creatures and discovers his own nature in the process. Beautifully rendered black-and-white illustrations throughout. For grades 4 and up.

Johnson, Sylvia A. 1985. *Bats*. Lerner Publications Co., Minneapolis, 48 pages.
Winner of the New York Academy of Sciences Children's Science Book Award; an appealing introduction to the habits of bats and the many ways bats benefit humans. Color photographs throughout. For grades 4-8.

Julivert, Maria Angels. 1994. *The Fascinating World of Bats*. Barrons Juveniles, New York, 31 pages.
This superb nature book features scientifically accurate and vivid full-color art. Different species of bats are shown and described, and children learn how these flying mammals have adapted to different climates and environments. Bats are shown in their cave dwellings and in flight, and echolocation is described in detail. For grades 4-7.

Lollar, Amanda. 1992. *The Bat in My Pocket*. Capra Press, California, 86 pages.
Animal lovers of all ages will be fascinated by the details of bat behavior in this true story of the rapport between the author and an injured Mexican free-tailed bat she rescues. Includes bat house plans. For grades 5 and up.

Lovett, Sarah. 1991. *Extremely Weird Bats*. John Muir Publications, Santa Fe, 50 pages.
Easy-to-read text and colorful line drawings depict 21 of the world's most interesting and unusual bat species. Large color photos and colorful drawings. For grades 2-5.

Lundberg, K.T. 1996. *Bats for Kids*. NorthWord Press, Minocqua, Wisconsin, 48 pages.
This story joins a group of curious children as they learn about the fascinating lives of bats. Facts about natural history, hibernation, feeding, reproduction, echolocation, and more are woven into this tale of discovery. For grades 4-6.

Maestro, B. 1994. *Bats: Night Flyers*. Scholastic, New York, 32 pages.
In this book, husband and wife team Betsy and Giulio Maestro team up to present an excellent factual overview of the lives of bats all over the world. Bright watercolor illustrations on every page complement the text. For grades 2-5.

Navarro, L. 1997. *Marcelo el Murcielago (Marcelo the Bat)*, Bat Conservation International, Austin, 38 pages.
A bilingual story in elementary English and Spanish about a young Mexican free-tail bat learning the ways of the world as he discovers the facts about migration. For grades K-4, and foreign language students of all ages.

Oppel, Kenneth. 1997. *Silverwing*, Simon and Schuster, New York, 160 pages.
This is the story of "Shade," the runt of his Silverwing bat colony, determined to prove himself on a perilous migration to hibernate. During a fierce storm, he loses the others and soon faces the most incredible journey of his short life. This excellent fictional adventure contains many accurate bat facts about hibernation, migration, and natural history. For grades 6 and up.

Pringle, Laurence. 1982. *Vampire Bats*. William Morrow & Co., New York, 62 pages.
    A factual account of the natural history of vampire bats written in easy-to-read text. Ideal for student research or for anyone wanting to learn basic facts about these notorious bats. Illustrated with black-and-white photos. For all ages.

Pringle, Laurence. 1991. *Batman: Exploring the World of Bats*. Charles Scribner's Sons, New York, 48 pages.
    Traces Merlin Tuttle's fascination with bats from his youth to present. It tells how he became a nature photographer and founded Bat Conservation International. This account of an exceptional scientist at work is illustrated with 24 of Tuttle's outstanding color photographs of bats. Substantial information about bat biology and conservation needs is included. For grades 5-8.

Rink, Deane and Linda C. Wood. 1989. *Bats*. Zoobooks. Wildlife Education Ltd., San Diego, 17 pages.
    Full-color pages loaded with photographs and illustrations about bats. Includes myths about bats, anatomy, diet, ecological roles, and diversity, plus games and activities. For grades 1-4.

Stuart, Dee. 1994. *Bats: Mysterious Flyers of the Night*. Carolrhoda Books, Inc., Minneapolis, 45 pages.
    A thorough explanation of bats with striking color photographs on every page. Descriptions of feeding, migration, birth, and other subjects introduce younger readers to 19 new vocabulary words. For grades 2-4.

Appendix C—Bats of The United States and Canada

FAMILY MORMOOPIDAE
Mormoops — Ghost-faced Bats

Mormoops megalophylla — Peters's Ghost-faced Bat — Southern U.S.; Rio Grande Valley, TX and southern AZ

FAMILY PHYLLOSTOMADAE
Artibeus — Neotropical Fruit Bats

Artibeus jamaicensis — Jamaican Fruit Bat — Florida Keys

Choeronycteris — Long-tongued Bats

Choeronycteris mexicana — Mexican Long-tongued Bat — Southwestern U.S.; southern CA, AZ, NM, and south TX

Leptonycteris — Long-nosed Bats

Leptonycteris yerbabuenae — Lesser Long-nosed Bat — Southwestern U.S.; southeastern NM, southwestern NM

Leptonycteris nivalis — Mexican Long-nosed Bat — Southwestern U.S.; southern NM and Big Bend TX

Macrotus — Leaf-nosed Bats

Macrotus californicus — California Leaf-nosed Bat — Southwestern U.S., southern CA, Colorado River valley, Southern NV and AZ

FAMILY VESPERTILIONIDAE
Antrozous — Pallid Bats

Antrozous pallidus — Pallid Bat — Western North America; southern British Columbia, south to Mexico, through western U.S. north through TX, OK, KS and east through CO, WY, UT, and ID

Corynorhinus — New World Big-eared Bats

Corynorhinus rafinesquii — Rafinesque's Big-eared Bat — Southeastern U.S.; eastern TX to northern FL, north to VA, west to IN through AR.

Corynorhinus townsendii — Townsend's Big-eared Bat — Western North America; southern British Columbia, south to Mexico, east to TX, OK, CO, and WY with isolated endangered sub-species in Ozarks, east KY and the Virginias

Eptesicus — Serotines

Eptesicus fuscus — Big Brown Bat — North America; British Columbia east to Newfoundland, throughout the U.S., south to Mexico

Euderma — Spotted Bats

Euderma maculatum — Spotted Bat — Western North America.; southern British Columbia south to Mexico, east to west TX, CO, WY, and MT

Idionycteris — Big-eared Bats

Idionycteris phyllotis — Allen's Big-eared Bat — Western U.S.; AZ, southern UT, and southwestern NM

Lasionycteris — Silver-haired Bats

Lasionycteris noctivagans — Silver-haired Bat — Northern North America; south AK, east to Newfoundland and south to most of the continental U.S. (except FL) to Mexico and Gulf States in the east

Lasiurus — Hairy-tailed Bats

Lasiurus blossevillii	Western Red Bat	Western North America; southern British Columbia, south to Mexico, NV and UT and east to AZ, NM and west TX
Lasiurus borealis	Eastern Red Bat	Eastern North America; southern Alberta to Newfoundland and south to Mexico and Gulf States (except south FL), west to NM, TX, KS, NE, ND and SD
Lasiurus cinereus	Hoary Bat	North America; northern Alberta south to Mexico and Gulf States (except south FL) and Hawaii
Lasiurus ega	Southern Yellow Bat	Extreme Southern U.S., south TX to Mexico
Lasiurus intermedius	Northern Yellow Bat	Southern U.S. SC, to FL, Gulf Coast, and south TX to Mexico
Lasiurus seminolus	Seminole Bat	Southern U.S.; extreme south TX and Gulf States north along the coast to the Carolinas, west to southeast OK
Lasiurus xanthinus	Western Yellow Bat	Southwest U.S.; southeastern CA, southern AZ, NM and TX

Myotis — Little Brown Bats

Myotis auriculus	Southwestern Myotis	Southwestern U.S.; southeastern NM and southwestern AZ
Myotis austroriparius	Southeastern Myotis	Southeastern U.S.; east TX east to NC, north to IL and IN
Myotis californicus	California Myotis	Western North America; southern British Columbia to Mexico, south through the western U.S., north thru west TX to MT
Myotis ciliolabrum	Western Small-footed Myotis	Western North America; southern British Columbia and Alberta south through the western U.S. to Mexico, east to west TX, OK, KS, NE, and SD
Myotis evotis	Long-eared Myotis	Western North America; southwestern Canada, south to Central CA, NV, northern AZ and NM
Myotis grisescens	Gray Myotis	East Central U.S.; MO, TN, and KY, to north FL
Myotis keenii	Keen's Myotis	Northern Pacific Coast of North America; southeast AK south to coastal British Columbia and the Olympic Peninsula of WA
Myotis leibii	Eastern Small-footed Myotis	Northeastern North America; southern Ontario south to eastern OK, east to north GA, north to ME and southern Quebec
Myotis lucifugus	Little Brown Myotis	North America; central AK east throughout Canada, south to Mexico, except central TX, LA, and south FL
Myotis occultus	Arizona Myotis	Southwestern U.S.; southern CA to AZ, NM and CO
Myotis septentrionalis	Northern Myotis	Northeastern North America; southeastern British Columbia to Newfoundland, south to southern SD, NE, KS, OK, central AR, east through AL and southwestern GA, and north to VA
Myotis sodalis	Indiana Myotis	Eastern U.S.; eastern OK, north to southern WI and MI, east to NY, VT and NH, south to PA, WV, western NC, and AL
Myotis thysanodes	Fringed Myotis	Western North America; south-central British Columbia south through WA, OR, ID, CA, NV, UT, CO, CA, AZ and NM to Mexico and the Big Bend Region of TX
Myotis velifer	Cave Myotis	Southwestern U.S.; AZ, southern CA, and NM, west KS, OK and central to west TX

Myotis volans	Long-legged Myotis	Western North America; southeast AK to British Columbia, WA, OR, ID, MT, to Mexico and Big Bend TX
Myotis yumanensis	Yuma Myotis	Western North America; southern British Columbia south through WA, ID, MT, OR, CA, UT, AZ, NM to Mexico and the Big Bend, TX

Nycticeius — Evening Bats

Nycticeius humeralis	Evening Bat	Eastern U.S.; east TX north to south SD east to east PA and south along the Atlantic coast to south FL and Gulf States

Pipistrellus — Pipistrelles

Parastrellus subflavus	Canyon Bat	Western U.S.; southern WA south to Mexico, north though central TX to OK, northwest though CO to southern ID
Perimyotis subflavus	Tri-colored Bat	Eastern North America; southern Ontario east to Newfoundland, south along the Gulf Coast and southern FL

FAMILY MOLOSSIDAE

Eumops — Greater Mastiff Bats

Eumops floridanus	Florida Bonneted Bat	Extreme southern U.S.; south FL and the Florida Keys
Eumops perotis	Greater Bonneted Bat	Southwestern U.S.; central CA to Big Bend TX, south to Mexico
Eumops underwoodi	Underwood's Mastiff Bat	Extreme southwest U.S.; extreme south AZ to Mexico

Molossus — Mastiff Bats

Molossus molossus	Pallas's Mastiff Bat	Florida Keys

Nyctinomops — New World Free-tailed Bats

Nyctinomops femorosaccus	Pocketed Free-tailed Bat	Southwestern U.S.; southern CA east to Big Bend TX south to Mexico
Nyctinomops macrotis	Big Free-tailed Bat	Western U.S.; southern CA, NV, UT and CO east to southwest KS and northwestern OK, Big Bend TX to Mexico

Tadarida — Free-tailed Bats

Tadarida brasiliensis	Mexican Free-tailed Bat	Southern U.S.; all states to Mexico south of a line extending from southern OR east to southern NE

Appendix D—Bats and Public Health

Living Safely With Bats by Merlin D. Tuttle

Excerpted from BATS, 13(4): Winter, 1995, p. 14

The tragic death of a 13-year-old Connecticut girl from rabies in October 1995 triggered an avalanche of dire warnings about the supposed dangers of sharing our neighborhoods with bats. Some communities have recommended eviction of any bats living near humans, and others have even mandated removal of backyard bat houses. Are such actions justified? Let's examine the facts.

Two diseases have been transmitted from bats to humans in North America: histoplasmosis and rabies. Histoplasmosis is a respiratory disease caused by a fungus that grows in soil enriched by animal droppings, most frequently birds. Ninety percent of all reported cases come from the Ohio and Mississippi River valleys where warm, humid conditions favor fungal growth. The disease is rare or nonexistent in most of Canada and the far northern and western U.S. The majority of cases are asymptomatic or involve flu-like symptoms, though a few individuals become seriously ill, especially if exposed to large quantities of spore-laden dust. To be safe, simply avoid breathing dust in areas where there are animal droppings.

Rabies is a viral infection of the central nervous system and is easily prevented by vaccination. The modern rabies vaccine ranks among the safest and least painful of all vaccines and provides excellent protection. Anyone bitten or exposed to the saliva or nerve tissue of a rabies-suspect animal should immediately obtain post-exposure treatment. This treatment has been simplified and no longer requires a lengthy series of shots in the stomach as it did in the past.

Worldwide, more than 30,000 humans die from rabies each year, and 99 percent of these deaths are due to contact with rabid dogs. In modern countries, where most dogs and cats are now vaccinated against rabies, the disease is rare in humans. Only about one person per year contracts rabies in the U.S. Dog bites remain the most frequent cause for vaccination in North America, but fatalities more often result from contact with wildlife, which is less likely to be reported and treated.

Inexplicably, a strain believed to be associated with the silver-haired bat (*Lasionycteris noctivagans*) now accounts for the majority of all North American human rabies cases. How this rare transmission occurs remains a mystery, since silver-haired bats seldom contact people and do not form colonies in buildings or bat houses. Such cases typically cannot be traced to any known exposure.

The good news is that the North American bat species most frequently found in our homes or bat houses, big and little brown bats (*Eptesicus fuscus* and *Myotis lucifugus*), are not known to have caused a single case of human rabies in the past 15 years. In fact, only four cases are believed to have come from common house-dwelling species in American history. Furthermore, there is no evidence that bats living in buildings ever transmit rabies through parasites, the air, or fecal material.

Since 1980, 14 Americans have died of rabies contracted from bats. Eight of those cases were ascribed to silver-haired bats. Placed in perspective, we are hundreds of times more likely to die from riding a bicycle, falling down stairs, or hitting a deer while driving. Dog attacks kill as many Americans annually as have died in the past 15 years from contact with bats. Death from bat rabies grabs headlines only because it is so rare.

Children should be taught to appreciate but never handle bats or any other wild animals. Only experienced animal rehabilitators, researchers, or educators should attempt to keep bats in captivity. Such people must be protected by pre-exposure immunization. The virus can lie dormant in any mammal for many months before making it visibly sick or contagious. Rabies outbreaks in animals such as raccoons, skunks, and foxes are unaffected by, and independent of, the disease in bats. There is no evidence that outbreaks of rabies occur in bats, nor that the current incidence is any higher than in decades past. In bats, only about one-half of one percent contract rabies, and these typically remain non-aggressive, biting only in self-defense, if handled.

The odds of contracting rabies are virtually nonexistent for anyone who: 1) vaccinates family dogs and cats; 2) avoids handling wildlife; and 3) obtains prompt vaccination following any suspected exposure. There is no evidence to suggest that elimination of bats from buildings or bat houses would make any neighborhood measurably safer. In fact, loss of bats increases demand for pesticides that already threaten both human and environmental health. You can help by countering with facts when local media run needlessly scary stories.

Editor's note: For the most up-to-date information about bats and public health, see BCI's website: www.batcon.org

Appendix E—Glossary

A

adapt (uh-DAPT) — to change to meet new or special needs; a species alters or adjusts itself to better survive in its environment

adaptation (ah-dapt-TAY-shun) — an inherited change by which a species or individual improves its condition in relation to its environment

aerial insectivore (AIR-ee-al in-SECT-tih-vore) — any animal that chases or catches insect prey in flight (see also "foliage gleaner")

agave (ah-GAH-vay) — a low-growing tropical American plant, such as the century plant, related to the lily and having fleshy leaves and a tall stalk of flowers; some species are used for their valuable fibers (for example, sisal) or for their fermented pulp which is used to make tequila liquor

ambient (AM-bee-ent) — surrounding; ambient temperature is recorded in the open air of a shaded location

anticoagulant (ANN-tie-coh-AG-yoo-lant) — something that prevents the clotting or congealing of a substance, especially blood

aquatic (ah-KWA-tick) — living or active in or on water

asymptomatic (ay-sim-toe-MAT-tick) — showing no signs of a disease, disorder or other condition

B

bachelor (BATCH-el-or) — a young male animal that doesn't breed; in bats, bachelor colonies contain both non-breeding males and females

baobab (BAY-oh-bab) — a tree with a stout trunk up to 30 feet in diameter, with large, hanging flowers that are white and a hard-shelled fleshy fruit; found in tropical African savannas and provides food or shelter for many kinds of animals

bat detector (BAT dee-TECK-tor) — an electronic instrument used by bat researchers that translates the high-frequency echolocation calls of bats into sounds that can be heard by humans

bat house — a structure that is built to provide roosting habitat for bats; usually made from wood, having ³/₄-inch wide roosting spaces inside, and an open bottom

bromeliad (broh-MEE-lee-add) — a plant of the pineapple family, including Spanish moss and other "air plants," that benefits from growing on other plants, especially large trees

C

cacti (CACK-tie); singular: **cactus** (CACK-tus) — a large group of plants native to arid regions of the New World that have thick, fleshy, often prickly stems that function as leaves

calcar (CAL-car) — a projection of cartilage that extends from the ankle of a bat along the edge of the tail membrane towards the tail; provides support druing aerial turns

camouflage (CAM-oh-flaj) — concealment from predators by appearing to be a part of the natural surroundings

canine (CAY-nine) — the tallest, pointed tooth located between the front teeth (incisors) and the shorter and broader pre-molars

canopy (CAN-oh-pee) — high, interlocking branches of large trees, as in a rain forest

carnivore (CAR-nih-VORE) — an animal which eats meat

carnivorous (Car-NIH-ver-ess) — meat-eating

cartilage (CAR-tih-laj) — a tough, white tissue that attaches to the surfaces of bones where a bone connects with a tendon or where two bones meet

camp — the tree-top roosting place for a colony of flying foxes

chaparral (SHAP-ah-RAL) — a scrubland habitat of dense, spiny, evergreen shrubs; characterized by mild, rainy winters and long, hot, dry, summers.

Chiroptera (k'eye-ROP-ter-ah) — taxonomic order containing all bats, the only flying mammals; from the Latin: "Chiro-" meaning hand-like, and "-ptera" meaning wing

Chiropteran (k'eye-ROP-ter-en) — having to do with bats

coati (coh-AH-tee) — an omnivorous, racoon-like mammal that lives in tropical and sub-tropical habitats of the New World

colony (COL-oh-nee) — a group of the same kind of animals or plants living or growing together

community (cah-MEW-nit-tee) — all the organisms inhabiting a restricted area, such as a field, pond, or cave

coniferous (koh-NIF-er-us) — evergreen, cone-bearing trees, such as pine, spruce, hemlock, or fir

consumer (con-SOO-mer) — an organism that feeds on other organisms or organic matter

crepuscular (kree-PUS-queh-lar) — becoming active at twilight, near sunset or sunrise

D

deciduous (dee-SID-you-us) — a type of tree that loses its leaves annually, usually in the fall

decomposer (DEE-com-PO-zer) — an organism, especially bacteria or fungi, which breaks down non-living organic matter such as corpses, plant material, and the wastes of living organisms

desert (DEZ-zurt) — a dry, often barren or sandy region with little rainfall (less than 30 cm per year) that can naturally support little or no vegetation

Desmodontidae (DEZ-mow-DON-tid-day) — a family of bats comprised of all true vampires, those which feed on blood; characterized by having neither a nose-leaf nor a tail; found in Latin America only

detritivore (dee-TRIT-ih-vore) — a special class of consumers, such as bacteria and fungi, that derives energy from organic wastes and dead organisms

disperse (dis-PURSE) — to scatter in various directions as in scattering seeds away from a parent plant

diverse (DIE-verse) — varied; of many types or kinds

diversity (die-VERSE-ih-tee) — having a variety of different types; being distinct or unlike in kind, form, and/or function

durian (DUR-ee-en) — a tree found in southeastern Asia that bears fruit with a hard, prickly rind and soft, stinky yet pleasant-tasting pulp; also the name of the fruit

E

echidna (eh-KID-nah) — a burrowing, egg-laying mammal with a spiny coat, slender snout, and sticky tongue for catching insects; found in Australia, Tasmania, and New Guinea; also known as the spiny anteater

echolocate (ECK-coh-LOW-kate) — the ability of an animal (mostly bats, porpoises, or whales) to find its way by listening to the echoes of sounds it produces

echolocation (ECK-coh-low-CAY-shun) — the process by which an animal orients itself by listening to the echoes of the sounds that it has produced

ecologist (ee-CALL-oh-jist) — a person who studies the relationships between animals and plants and their environments

ecology (ee-COL-oh-jee) — the scientific study of the relationships between living organisms and their environments

ecosystem (EE-coh-SIS-tem) — all the interacting organisms of a community and their non-living surroundings regarded as a unit

ecotourism (ee-coh-TOOR-iz-um) — the business of providing trips, vacations, and/or sight-seeing excursions to view wildlife and nature

emerge (ee-MERJ) — for bats, to leave a cave or other roost, usually at dusk

emergence (ee-MER-jens) — for bats, the act of leaving a cave or other roost, usually at dusk

emu (EE-m'you) — a large, fast running flightless Australian bird related to the ostrich

endangered (en-DANE-jurd) — threatened with extinction

environment (en-VIE-ron-ment) — the resources such as air, water, minerals, and living communities that surround and affect an organism, especially those that contribute to its growth and survival

epiphyte (EP-ih-FIGHT) — plants that grown on other plants, relying upon them for support, but that are capable of producing their own nutrients by photosynthesis

epiphytic (EP-ih-FIT-ick) — being like a plant that benefits from being attached to another plant or animal but that does not provide a benefit in return

evolution (EV-oh-LOO-shun) — changes in the characteristics of a plant or animal species, over generations of time, that usually help them adapt to better survive the conditions where they live

exoskeleton (EX-oh-SKEL-eh-ton) — an external protective or supporting structure of many invertebrates, such as the hard, external skeleton of insects and crustaceans (like shrimp and lobsters)

extinct (ex-STINGKT) — no longer existing, as when the last individual of a plant or animal species dies

extinction (ex-STINGKT-shun) — the process of a species dying out to the point where no more are left

F

fertilize (FUR-till-eyez) — to provide soil with nutrients to aid the growth of plants

fertilizer (FUR-till-eyez-er) — something that provides soil with nutrients to aid the growth of plants

flying fox — a fruit-eating bat having a dog-like face and ears; of the genus Pteropus, or the taxonomic sub-order Megachiroptera; found mostly in tropical Africa, Asia, Australia, or the South Pacific

foliage (FOLE-ladj) — plant leaves as a whole; a cluster of leaves

foliage gleaner (FOLE-ladj GLEEN-er) — any animal that hunts in vegetation, especially birds or bats that catch insects from leaves or the ground (see also "aerial insectivore")

food chain — a series of organisms, each eating or decomposing the preceding one, as when an insect eats a plant and then is eaten by a bat

food pyramid — a network of many interconnected food chains and feeding relationships, starting with a broad base of plant producers and animal consumers and peaking with only a few top level carnivores

forearm (FOR-arm) — the part of a mammal's arm extending from the wrist to the elbow; in bats, measurements of its length are often used to identify one species from another

frequency (FREE-quen-see) — the amount of repetition of a cycle (such as a wave of sound) within a specified time period

frugivore (FROO-gah-VORE) — an animal which eats fruit

frugivorous (Froo-GIVE-ver-ess) — fruit-eating

fungus (FUN-gus); plural: fungi (FUN-guy) — a plant-like organism, lacking chlorophyll, which obtains nutrients and energy by secreting enzymes that break down organic matter in living or dead organisms (see also "detritivore")

fungal (FUN-gul) — pertaining to a fungus

furring strips (FUR-ring STRIPS) — narrow strips of material, often wood, used to make spaces, as between roosting partitions in a bat house

G

guano (GWA-noh) — animal dropping or excrement, usually composed of seabird or bat droppings harvested and sold as fertilizer from islands where large numbers of birds breed or from caves where large numbers of bats roost

H

habitat (HAB-ih-tat) — the environment in which an organism or population of plants or animals lives; the normal kind of location inhabited by a plant or animal

herbivore (ERB-ih-vore) — an organism that eats plants, such as a rabbit or a cow

herbivorous (Eer-BIVF-ver-ess) — plant-eating

hibernaculum (HIGH-bur-NACK-you-lum); plural: **hiburnacula** (HIGH-burr-NACK-you-lah) — a shelter for a hibernating animal, usually a cave or mine where bats hibernate in winter

hibernate (HIGH-bur-nate) — to pass the winter in a deep sleep in which the metabolism is extremely slow (see also "hibernation")

hibernation (High-bur-NAY-shun) — the act of passing the winter in a dormant state in which the metabolism is slowed to a tiny fraction of normal (see also "hibernate")

high frequency (HIGH FREE-quen-see) — a sound that is above the level of human hearing (see also "ultrasonic")

histoplasmosis (HIST-toh-plaz-MOH-sis) — a fungus that infects human lungs, causing respiratory illness; results from breathing spores of a certain fungus

homeothermic (ho-MEE-oh-THUR-mick) — maintaining a nearly constant and warm body temperature regardless of environmental temperature; warm-blooded

hypothesis (high-POTH-eh-sis) — a statement considered to be true for the purpose of investigation or argument, and must be stated in a manner that can be tested and that could be proven false

I

insectivore (in-SECK-tih-vore) — any animal that feeds mostly on insects

insectivorous (in-sect-TIV-or-us) — insect-eating

K

kapok (KAY-pock) — a silky fiber obtained from the seed pods of the silk-cotton tree; used for insulation and as padding in mattresses, pillows, and life preservers

karst — an area of rock made of limestone in which erosion has produced cracks, sinkholes, or underground cavities such as caves

keystone species (KEY-stone SPEE-seez) — a central or supporting element in a habitat or ecosystem; an organism upon which numerous other plants and/or animals rely for food, shelter, growth, development, and/or reproduction

kilohertz (KILL-oh-hurts) — a unit used to measure sounds; a thousand waves of sound (or echolocation calls) emitted in a second equals one kilohertz; while human sounds are mostly low (less than 1000 waves of sound per second, most bat sounds are high frequency (more than 2000 waves per second)

L

Latin America (LAT-tin ah-MARE-ih-cah) — all countries located south of the United States in the New World; includes Mexico and all countries in Central America and South America, with official languages mostly Spanish or Portuguese

latitude (LAT-ih-tood) — the distance north or south of the equator; indicated by horizontal lines on a map or globe and measured in degrees

larva (LAR-vuh); plural: **larvae** (LAR-vay) — the wingless, often worm-like, juvenile or sexually immature forms of insects which undergo metamorphosis to become adults (as when a caterpillar becomes a butterfly)

larynx (LARE-inks) — the upper part of the respiratory tract that includes the vocal chords that enable vocalizations

lichen (LIKE-en) — any of many plants made up of a fungus in close combination with certain species of green or blue-green algae, typically forming a crust-like, scaly, or branching growth on rocks or tree trunks

longitude (LAWN-jih-tood) — the distance east or west of the line described by a great circle of the earth passing through both the geographical poles and through Greenwich, England; indicated by vertical lines on a map or globe and measured in degrees

M

mammal (MAM-al) — a class of vertebrate animals that includes more than 4,000 species, distinguished by self-regulating body temperature, hair, and in the females, mammary glands (breasts) to nurse their young

maternity roost (mah-TURN-ih-tee ROOST) — a location where mother bats go to give birth and nurse and care for young

megabat (MEG-ah-bat) — see "Megachiroptera"

Megachiroptera (MEG-ah-k'eye-ROP-ter-ah) — a suborder of bats containing about 173 species that have claws on both their thumbs and second fingers, also distinguished by large eyes, fox- or dog-like faces, and simple rounded ears; found only in the Old World tropics; called "megabats" or "flying foxes" (see also "Microchiroptera")

membrane (MEM-brain) — a thin, flexible layer of tissue covering surfaces, or separating or connecting regions, structures, or organs of an animal or plant, including the two layers of skin from which bat wings are made

mesquite (mess-KEET) — any of a number of species of thorny trees or shrubs of the Mimosa family having small, feathery leaves and producing seeds in bean pods; found in the southwestern United States and Mexico

metabolism (meh-TAB-oh-LIZ-um) — the combination of chemical and physical processes required to maintain life, usually progressing most rapidly at higher body temperatures, as indicated by a rapid heart rate or fast breathing

metacarpal (met-ah-CAR-pull) — the five bones between the fingers and the wrist in the hand of a person, in the wing of a bat, or in the forelimb of an animal

microbat (MY-crow-BAT) — see "Microchiroptera"

Microchiroptera (MY-crow-k'eye-ROP-ter-ah) — a suborder of bats containing about 813 species that have claws only on their thumbs, also distingushed by often complex facial structures and ears with a large tragus; found worldwide, also called "microbats" (see also "Megachiroptera")

migrate (MY-grate) — to change location periodically, especially to move seasonally from one region to another

migration (My-GRAY-shun) — the act of changing location, especially seasonally

mist net — a very finely threaded net that is stretched between two poles to capture bats or birds

Molossidae (mow-LOSS-sid-day) — a family of bats known as "free-tailed bats" characterized by a tail which extends beyond the tail membrane for at least one third its length and ears which appear joined or nearly joined above the forehead; found throughout the world in tropical and sub-tropical habitats

Mormoopidae (more-MOO-pid-day) — a family of bats known as "ghost-faced bats" characterized by strange leaves and lappets above and below the mouth; found in tropical and sub-tropical habitats in the New World only

N

natural resources — natural products that have value, such as timber, fresh water, or minerals

navigate (NAV-vih-gate) — to make one's way across a defined area; to travel

nectar (NECK-tar) — a sweet liquid secreted by most flowers to attract animal pollinators

nectarivore (NECT-ter-ah-VORE) — an animal that eats nectar (liquid found in flowers)

nectarivorous (Nect-ter-IV-or-ess) — to be like an animal that eats nectar (liquid found in flowers)

New World — the western hemisphere; the region of the planet including North America, Central America, and South America, and nearby islands

Noctilionidae (NOCK-till-lee-ON-nid-day) — a family of bats known as "bulldog" or "fishing bats" characterized by heavy dog-like jowels, exceptionally long feet and toes, and a habit of snatching fish and aquatic insects out of still pools and streams; found in Latin America

nocturnal (nock-TURN-ahl) — active only at night or having flowers that open only at night

nose leaf — a triangular projection of flesh found on the noses of some Microchiropteran bat species, appears to function in directing echolocation signals emitted through the nose

nurse plant — usually a tree or bush which provides shade for another plant during the early stages of its growth into a mature, reproductive individual

nursery colony (NUR-sir-ee COL-oh-nee) — a group of animals that comes together to rear young

O

ocotillo (oh-coh-TEE-yo) — a cactus-like bush composed of thorny wooden branches with small tear-shaped green leaves, topped with scarlet tubular clusters of flowers; found in deserts of the southwestern U.S. and Mexico

Old World — the eastern hemisphere; the region of the planet including Europe, Asia, Africa, Australia and the Pacific and Indian Ocean islands

omniverous (OM-nih-ver-ess) — to be like an organism that eats both plants and meat, such as a bear or coati

omnivore (OM-nih-VORE) — an organism that eats both plants and meat, such as a bear or coati

P

paloverde (pal-oh-VER-dee) — any of several species of trees or shrubs with spiny branches, very tiny leaves, and bright yellow flowers; found in the southwestern United States and Mexico

parasite (PAIR-ih-site) — an organism that feeds on another organism while contributing nothing to the survival of its host; for example, fleas and ticks

pesticide (PES-tih-side) — a chemical used to kill animals, mostly insects, often harmful to humans as well

phalanges (fah-LAN-geez) — the long bones of the fingers or toes

Phyllostomidae (F'EYE-low-STOW-mid-day) — a large family of bats known as the "New World leaf-nosed bats" characterized by a triangular nose-leaf projecting above the nostrils; found in sub-tropical and tropical areas of the New World only

pioneer plants (P'EYE-oh-neer PLANTS) — the first plants to grow in a new area, often after the original trees or plants have been cleared; plants that can withstand extra hot or dry conditions and modify the soil and micro-climates to allow other plants to colonize the area

piper (PIE-per) — a plant of the pepper family that produces fruit on upright or hanging stalks

piscivore (PISK-kah-vore) — an animal which eats mainly fish

piscivorus (PISK-kiv-or-ess) — to be like an animal which eats mainly fish

plantain (plan-TAIN) — a large tropical plant resembling a banana and bearing similar edible fruit

platypus (PLAT-tah-puss) — a semi-aquatic, web-footed, egg-laying mammal having a broad, flat tail and a snout resembling a duck's bill; found in Australia and Tasmania

pollen (PAUL-en) — the fine powder-like material produced by the anthers of flowering plants that provides the source of the male elements (gametes) in fertilization

pollinate (PAUL-en-ate) — to carry pollen from male flowers to female flowers or to male and female parts of a single flower, either on the same plant or on different plants of the same species

pollinator (PAUL-en-ate-or) — an animal that pollinates plants

predator (PRED-ah-tore) — an animal that lives by catching and eating other animals

prey — a creature hunted or caught for food

primary consumer (PR'EYE-mare-ee con-soo-mer) — organisms that eat plants or algae, such as herbivores

primary producer (PR'EYE-mare-ee pro-DOO-sir) — any organism that is capable of manufacturing its own food from inorganic materials, usually accomplished by plants that create new energy from a combination of inorganic materials and sunlight in a process known as photosynthesis

Pteropodidae (TARE-oh-PO-did-day) — a family of bats comprised of all Megachiroptera and known as the "flying foxes" or "Old World fruit bats" characterized by a claw on both the thumb and the second finger and simple rounded ears; found in tropical habitats of the Old World only

pup — a baby or young bat

R

rabies (RAY-beez) — a disease caused by a virus; almost always fatal, usually transmitted by bites from mammals or through contact with infected saliva and/or nervous tissue; can be prevented by prompt vaccination

rain forest — a dense, usually tropical, evergreen forest which receives heavy rainfall, more than 255 cm (100 inches) per year; generally found near the equator

range map — a geographic illustration of where a species lives or can be found

riparian (r'eye-PAIR-ee-an) — on or near the bank of a natural stream, river, or lake; habitats that include mostly moisture-loving plants and the animals that rely upon them

roost — a place where a flying animal, usually a bird or bat, can sleep or rest, usually by perching or hanging

S

saguaro (sah-WAR-oh) — an extremely large cactus, three to 12 meters (10 to 40 feet) tall, of the southwestern United States and northern Mexico, with upward curving branches, white flowers, and red fruit

sanguivore (SAN-gua-VORE) — an animal which eats mainly blood

sanguivorous (SAN-guiv-vor-ess) — to be like an animal which eats mainly blood

savannah (suh-VAN-uh) — a grassland or prairie habitat with few trees, usually found in tropical or sub-tropical areas of Africa or South America

second-level consumer — in a food chain, the organism, a carnivore, which eats herbivores

seed dispersal (SEED dis-PER-sal) — the process of scattering seeds away from the parent plant, usually by an animal that eats the fruit and thus increases the probability that the seed will grow into a new plant

sonar (SO-nar) — a system by which transmitted sound waves and their echoes are used to locate unseen objects by animals that emit high frequency sounds from their mouths or noses; acronym for So(und) Na(vigation) R(anging)

species (SPEE-seez) — a group of related organisms that can mate and produce healthy offspring, typically similar in appearance

superstition (SOO-per-STISH-en) — a belief, practice or rite held in spite of evidence to the contrary; a belief resulting from ignorance of the laws of nature or from faith in magic or chance

superstitious (SOO-per-STISH-ess) — having beliefs in spite of evidence to the contrary; having beliefs based on ignorance of the laws of nature or from faith in magic or chance

T

tail membrane (TAIL MEM-brain) — the area of skin which joins the legs and/or tail of a bat

tapir (TAY-peer) — a large mammal of tropical America and southern Asia with split hooves, a heavy body, short legs, and a fleshy, pig-like nose; related to the rhinoceros and horse

taxonomy (tax-ON-ah-mee) — the science of classifying organisms into categories of related kinds

temperate (TEM-prit, or TEM-per-it) — neither extremely hot nor cold in climate, relatively mild; either of two middle-latitude zones of the earth lying between 23 1/2 and 66 1/2 degrees north and south of the equator

terrestrial (tair-REST-tree-al) — of the earth or its land-dwelling inhabitants, growing or living on land

third level consumer — in a food chain, a carnivore that eats another carnivore that ate a primary consumer

torpor (TOR-pur) — mental or physical inactivity or sluggishness, resulting from lowered body temperature at levels part way between normally active and hibernation

top level carnivore — in a food chain, a meat-eating organism that eats other meat-eaters that have eaten primary or second level or third level consumers

tragus (TRAY-gus) — a tiny finger-like projection of skin-covered cartilage in front of a bat's ear

trophic level (TROH-fick LEV-all) — a feeding level in a food chain or food pyramid characterized by organisms that occupy a similar functional position as producers or consumers in an ecosystem

tropical (TROP-ih-call) — occuring in places or relatively high temperature and humidity; usually located between the tropics of Capricorn and Cancer

tropics (TROP-icks) — regions of the earth's surface lying roughly between the latitudes of 24 degrees north and 24 degrees south of the equator, usually marked by hot and humid climates often receiving high amounts of rainfall

U

ultrasonic (UHL-trah-SAWN-ick) — sound frequencies above the range that human ears can hear, or above approximately 20,000 cycles per second (20 kilohertz)

V

Vespertilionidae (VESS-per-til-lee-ON-nid-day) — a family of bats known as the "vesper bats" or the "plain-nosed bats" characterized by having no facial flaps, leaves or projections, a tail completely enclosed in the tail membrane, and widely seperate ears; found throughout the world in temperate, sub-tropical and tropical habitats

BCI Memberships

Membership in Bat Conservation International is your introduction to a little-known world of more than 1,100 of the earth's most intriguing animal species. You will receive *BATS*, a quarterly magazine that provides continuing education about bats; the opportunity to visit Bracken Bat Cave near San Antonio, Texas, and witness the extraordinary nightly emergence of the world's largest bat colony; invitations to join exclusive international eco-tours in tropical locations; and opportunities to participate in workshops and field projects with leading bat biologists.

Join BCI at www.batcon.org

Index

Appendices